Teaching Adolescent Writers

Kelly Gallagher

Stenho
Portland

Stenhouse Publishers
www.stenhouse.com

Credits
Page 78: From the *Orange County Register,* July 15, 2005. Reprinted by permission of the *Orange County Register,* copyright 2006.
Page 84: From *Newsweek,* Dec. 23, 2002. Copyright 2002 Newsweek, Inc. All rights reserved. Reprinted by permission.
Page 120: From *The Huffington Post.* http://www.thehuffingtonpost.com/arianna-huffington/from-the-dept-of-contrit_b_15885.html. Used with permission of Arianna Huffington and HuffingtonPost.com.
Pages 120–121: From the *L.A. Times,* January 1, 2006. Copyright 2006 L.A. Times. All rights reserved. Reprinted by permission.

Library of Congress Cataloging-in-Publication Data
Gallagher, Kelly, 1958–
     Teaching adolescent writers / [by Kelly Gallagher].
     p. cm.
     Summary: "Describes strategies for teaching writing to adolescents, including teaching the reasons writing is important, meeting student needs in learning writing, modeling good writing by the teacher, using real-world models of writing, giving students choice, writing for authentic, real-world purposes, and assessing student writing"—Provided by publisher.
     ISBN-13: 978-1-57110-422-9 (acid-free paper)
     ISBN-10: 1-57110-422-4 (acid-free paper)
     1. English language—Composition and exercises—Study and teaching (Secondary) 2. English language—Composition and exercises—Study and teaching (Middle school) I. Title.
LB1631.G16 2006
808'.0420712—dc22   2006023578

Cover, interior design, and typesetting by Martha Drury
Manufactured in the United States of America on acid-free paper
12   9 8 7

For those teachers who, despite the numerous obstacles placed in their way, walk into their classrooms every day dedicated to improving their students' writing.

Contents

Acknowledgments

One does not write a book alone—especially while teaching full time. You would not be holding this book in your hands without the loving support of my family. I am indebted to my wife, Kristin, who not only keeps the ship afloat while I am adrift, but who also forgives me for using lame metaphors like the one found in this sentence. I also want to thank my beautiful daughters, Caitlin and Devin, for their patience and support. I am indeed fortunate to be their dad.

Special thanks to Bill Varner, my editor at Stenhouse. This is our third book together, and I could not ask for a better editor. Bill, I deeply appreciate your expertise and guidance. Much appreciation to Erin Whitehead for her keen copyediting eye and to Jay Kilburn for his help with the artwork. I would also like to thank Martha Drury for her wonderful design, Rick Wormeli for the cover photo, and Nate Butler for all the support he has given me from the Right Coast. Thank you to Philippa Stratton, Tom Seavey, and the staff at Stenhouse for your unflagging support.

Kudos to my English-teaching colleagues at Magnolia High School for their role in shaping my teaching: John Greenwald, Amie Howell, Melissa Hunnicutt, Virginia Kim, Sheri Krumins, Margaret Macchia, Katrina Mundy, Esther Noh, Lindsay Ruben, Robin Turner, Michelle Waxman, and Dana White. I would also like to thank my principal, Dr. Ken Fox, for his continued support.

Thanks to Señor Puente, Steve Gonzales, for all he does for the students of Magnolia High School. It is an honor to work with someone who, against the odds, keeps his eye on the ball.

I'd like to acknowledge those who have been particularly supportive from the offices of the Anaheim Union High School District, specifically Jane Davis, Mike Matsuda, and, of course, Judy Oceguera.

Sincere thanks to those teachers who have made me a better teacher of writing, specifically, Julie Lecesne-Switzer, Mike Switzer, Ellen Lafler, Richard Cornwell (who coined the revision acronym "STAR"), Joanna Exacoustos, Sandy Nevarez, Norelynn Pion-Goureau, Stephanie Sullivan, Jo Lack, Poppy Hill, Jan Strahl, and the many fellows of the South Basin Writing Project.

The following people were particularly influential in developing my thinking about the teaching of writing:

Mary K. Healy, an early leader in the Bay Area Writing Project, who years ago opened my eyes to the importance of a writing-centered classroom. I want to be Mary K. when I grow up.

Catharine Lucas, retired professor of writing at San Francisco State University, who was the first to prompt me to think deeply about writing. Before Catharine came along, I was unaware that I was unaware. Thanks to her, I am now frequently aware that I am unaware.

Ron Strahl, the director of the South Basin Writing Project and professor of English at California State University, Long Beach, who not only has taught me much about writing but also continues to challenge me to reflect on my teaching practices.

Nina Wooldridge, the co-director of the South Basin Writing Project, who has single-handedly made me a better writing teacher. Her work echoes throughout this book, and I thank her for teaching me how to grade an essay.

My students at MHS, who teach me something about writing every day.

And, of course, my first writing influences—my mother and father.

Running with the Literacy Stampede

L et's start with a scenario I ask my students at the beginning of the school year:

You're standing in a large field minding your own business when you hear rumbling sounds in the distance. The sounds begin to intensify, and at first you wonder if it is thunder you hear approaching. Because it's a beautiful, cloudless day you dismiss this notion. As the rumbling sound grows louder, you begin to see a dust cloud rising just over the ridge a few yards in front of you. Instantly, you become panicked because at that exact moment it dawns on you that the rumbling you're hearing is the sound of hundreds of wild bulls stampeding over the ridge. There are hordes of them and they are bearing down right on top of you. They are clearly faster than you and there is no time to escape. What should you do? Survival experts recommend only one of the following actions:

A) Lying down and curling up, covering your head with your arms

B) *Running directly at the bulls, screaming wildly and flailing your arms in an attempt to scare them in another direction*

C) *Turning and running like heck in the same direction the bulls are running (even though you know you can't outrun them)*

D) *Standing completely still; they will see you and run around you*

E) *Screaming bad words at your parent(s) for insisting on a back-to-nature vacation in Wyoming*

According to the *Worst Case Scenario Survival Handbook,* a favorite in my classroom library, the correct answer is C. When encountering a stampede of bulls, the handbook states, you should "not try to distract them. . . . If you cannot escape, your only option is to run alongside the stampede to avoid being trampled. Bulls are not like horses and will not avoid you if you lie down—so keep moving" (Piven and Borgenicht 1999, p. 49).

It's an important lesson that I want my students to consider carefully: If you don't want to be crushed by an oncoming stampede, you have to run with it.

Though few of my students have ever been to Wyoming, much less seen an actual stampede, all of them come to me in danger of being trampled. Not by actual bulls, mind you. My students are threatened by a different stampede—a literacy stampede. Consider the following:

- More information was produced in the last thirty years than in the previous 5,000 years *combined* (Wurman 1989).
- A weekday edition of *The New York Times* contains more information than the average person was likely to come across in a lifetime in seventeenth-century England (Wurman 1989).
- Information is doubling every four years (Wurman 1989).
- The blogosphere is now doubling in size every six months. It is sixty times larger than it was three years ago (Sifry 2006).
- The Internet is the fastest growing communications media in world history. It took the Web four years to reach 50 million users. Compare this to the number of years it took radio (38), personal computers (16), and television (13) to reach that many users (Warschauer 1999).
- Getting into college is more competitive than ever. A friend of mine was accepted to UCLA twenty-five years ago with an SAT score of 1,070. In 2005, the last year before the scoring range of the test changed, the average SAT score needed for admittance was 1,310. What's more, the new SAT has eliminated the analogy section and has replaced it with close readings and on-demand writing. Getting into good schools now requires a higher level of reading and writing than ever before. Last year UCLA turned down over 7,000 students who had a 4.0 GPA or higher (College Board 2006).
- The job market is rapidly changing. Unskilled jobs are disappearing. There are two reasons for this: (1) technology is replacing menial jobs,

and (2) unskilled jobs are increasingly outsourced. Today, "Eighty percent or more of the companies in the service and finance, insurance, and real estate sectors, the corporations with the greatest employment-growth potential, assess writing during hiring." In addition, half of all companies take writing into account when making promotion decisions. As one executive remarked, "You can't move up without the writing skills." (National Commission on Writing 2004a).

After I share this information in class, and with the stampede metaphor in mind, I pose a second scenario to my students:

> *You are growing up in the dawn of the Information Age. More than ever before in history, the ability to read and write will determine how far you will go in this world. For the most part, people who read and write well will compete and prosper; people who read and write poorly will be left behind. Simply put, there is a literacy stampede approaching, and it is bearing down right on top of you. What should you do?*
>
> *A) Go home, curl up on the sofa, watch a lot of MTV, and hope the demands of the literacy stampede go away.*
> *B) Stare the Information Age in the face, screaming wildly and flailing your arms, in an attempt to make it go away.*
> *C) Elevate your reading and writing abilities to the point that you can run with the literacy stampede.*
> *D) Stand completely still. Pray that the Information Age will avoid you.*
> *E) Scream bad words at your parent(s) for conceiving you in the shadow of a literacy stampede.*

I want my students to recognize the stark choice they face—either they work hard at elevating their literacy skills or they risk being trampled by today's literacy stampede.

Running with the Literacy Stampede

If students are going to have a fighting chance of running with the bulls, it is obvious that their ability to read and write effectively will play a pivotal role. In a previous book, *Deeper Reading,* I discuss at length the importance of helping students critically read difficult literature. I make the argument that teaching kids how to be critical readers in the classroom helps our students to become discerning readers outside of school. A student who critically reads *Hamlet* develops a lens useful for critically reading a politician, a commercial, or a ballot proposition.

In this book the focus shifts to sharpening the other element vital to our students' developing literacy: writing. Now, more than ever, writing plays a central role in our students' literacy. As stated in *Because Writing Matters,* a book by the National Writing Project and Carl Nagin, writing "is no longer a concern, as it was in Harvard in 1874, of an exclusively white, male elite; in today's increasingly diverse society, writing is a gateway for success in academia, the new workplace, and the global economy, as well as for our collective success as a participatory democracy" (2003, p. 2). In an increasingly demanding world of literacy, the importance of our students leaving our schools as effective writers has magnified. The ability to write well, once a luxury, has become a necessity. Today, writing is foundational for success.

Righting Writing Wrongs

I am now again a full-time high school teacher, but for three years I took time out of the classroom to serve both as the English Coordinator for a large urban secondary school district (eighteen schools, 37,000 students) and as a consultant to other school districts. One of the perks of the coordinator job (besides having more than twenty-two minutes to eat lunch) was that over a three-year period I had the opportunity to visit many English classrooms. During these visits I witnessed a lot of great teaching—particularly the teaching of writing. Let me preface what follows by first noting that outstanding writing instruction is taking place in many of our schools under some rather adverse conditions.

That said, I have growing concerns about writing instruction in our classrooms. In California, where I teach, these concerns emerge when tenth-grade students are required to write an on-demand essay as part of passing the High School Exit Exam. The essays are scored on a scale from one to four, with four being highest (a three is considered passing). Two readers read each essay, and the scores are averaged. Here are the results of the March 2002 test administration (the latest year in which the state released the figures broken down by each score level):

Score	Percent of Students Scoring
No score	6.5
1	15.5
1.5	13.7
2	27.4
2.5	15.3
3	12.2
3.5	5.9
4	3.5

(California Department of Education 2002)

A closer look at these results reveals some startling information:

- Over one-third of students scored at 1.5 or lower.

- Almost two-thirds scored at 2 or lower (and the "bar" for a score of 2 is not set very high; a "2" essay is what I would expect from a fifth- or sixth-grade student).
- Less than 10 percent of the students scored at 3.5 or higher.

I'd like to share with you figures for score breakdowns later than 2002, but the California Department of Education stopped releasing these figures to the public. I'm guessing that is a sign that things are not improving. Another sign is that the tenth-grade *average* essay score for the March 2005 test was 2.3 (California Department of Education 2005).

These poor results were also echoed in an informal study done in 2006 by the South Basin Writing Project at an urban southern California high school. After closely examining over 1,700 student papers, the project found the following:

- About 50 percent of the students did not demonstrate that they understood the basic essay form. These students wrote as if answering a test question—one chunk of writing that only engaged the prompt at the simplest level.
- Many students summarized the reading passage rather than interact with the passage. Many simply summarized in chronological order.
- Essays that contained clear thesis statements were few and far between.
- Students struggled with writing effective introductions. Many did not have introductions at all.
- Many demonstrated a lack of writing fluency, leading us to believe they are simply not writing enough on a daily basis.

Lest you think these low scores are a problem only found in California, there is evidence that secondary students are struggling across the country as well. In a national study conducted in 2002 by the National Assessment of Educational Progress (NAEP), the writing skills of adolescents were assessed to see if their skills were "advanced," "proficient," "basic," or "below basic." NAEP defines these terms as follows:

Writing Proficiency Level	NAEP Definition
Advanced	This level signifies superior performance.
Proficient	This level represents solid academic performance for each grade assessed. Students reaching this level have demonstrated competency over challenging subject matter, including subject matter knowledge, application of such knowledge to real-world situations, and analytical skills appropriate to the subject matter.
Basic	This level denotes partial mastery of prerequisite knowledge and skills that are fundamental for proficient work at each grade level.
Below Basic	(No definition is given, but one can infer that a student writing at "below basic" lacks mastery of basic skills.)

(NCES 2004)

When I look at these NAEP definitions of writing proficiency and juxtapose them with the rising demand of literacy skills my students will need in order to succeed in the dawn of the Information Age, I can't help but think that "proficient" is the minimum bar every one of our students needs to reach. At the proficient level, students can write at grade level, can apply their knowledge to real-world situations, and can demonstrate analytical thinking. These are baseline skills our students will need to succeed after leaving our schools.

Alarmingly, when you look at students' performance nationally, only 31 percent of eighth graders and 24 percent of twelfth graders performed at or above the proficient level of writing (NCES 2003). Put another way, more than two-thirds of middle school students and more than three-fourths of high school students lack proficient writing skills—those skills needed to run with the literacy stampede (Figures 1.1 and 1.2 show a state-by-state breakdown of the percentages of fourth- and eighth-grade students).

The NAEP study contained other interesting findings:

- Though students at grades four and eight raised their writing scores between 1998 and 2002, the scores of twelfth-grade students declined, with lowest performing students showing the greatest declines. Only seniors writing in the 75th percentile or higher showed any growth from 1998; *all other twelfth-grade percentiles declined* (my emphasis).
- Females outperformed males by twenty-one points at grade eight and by twenty-five points at grade twelve. The gap at the eighth-grade level was about the same as it was it 1998. The gap at the twelfth-grade widened.
- There are performance gaps as measured by race/ethnicity:

8th Grade		12th Grade	
Race/ethnicity	*Percentage "at or above" Proficiency*	*Race/ethnicity*	*Percentage "at or above" Proficiency*
Asian/Pacific Islander	41%	White	28%
White	38%	Asian/Pacific Islander	25%
Hispanic	16%	Hispanic	13%
Black	13%	Black	9%
			(NCES 2003)

The conclusion is inescapable. Though there certainly are examples of excellent teaching occurring in our schools, we have a long way to go overall to bring many of our students up to the levels of writing proficiency they will need to walk through those key gateways awaiting them: the gateway to academia; the gateway to an emerging workplace; the gateway to the global economy. Clearly, as teachers of writing, our work is cut out for us.

Defining the Problem

Why are our students struggling when it comes to writing? Certainly there are a number of factors out of our immediate control (e.g., poverty, lack of

Teaching Adolescent Writers

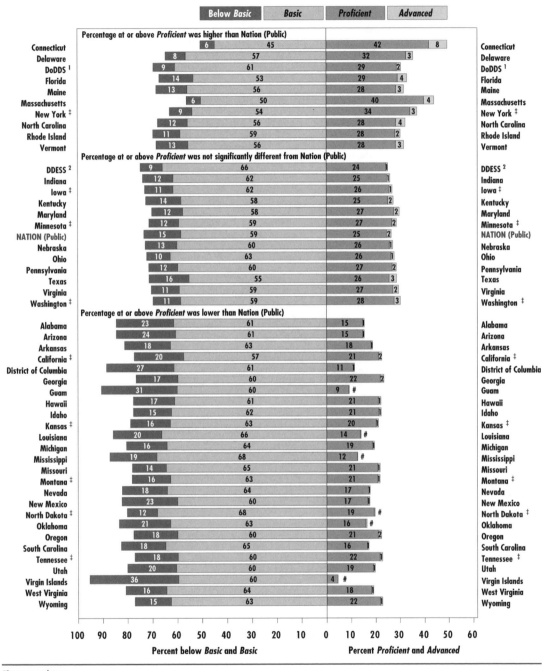

Percentage rounds to zero.
‡ Indicates that the jurisdiction did not meet one or more of the guidelines for school participation in 2002.
[1] Department of Defense Dependents Schools (Overseas).
[2] Department of Defense Domestic Dependent Elementary and Secondary Schools.
NOTE: Percentages may not add to 100 due to rounding.
SOURCE: U.S. Department of Education, Institute of Education Sciences, National Center for Education Statistics, National Assessment of Educational Progress (NAEP), 2002 Writing Assessment.

Figure 1.1 *State-by-state NAEP breakdown of "proficient" writers*

Chapter 1: Running with the Literacy Stampede

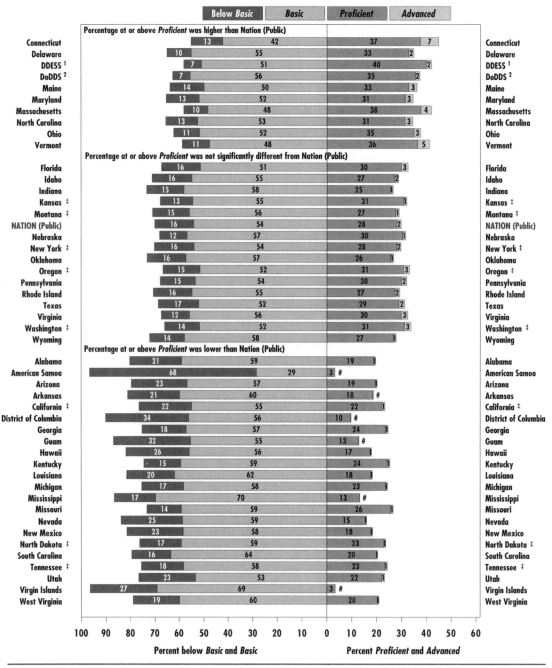

Grade 8

The bars below contain percentages of students in each NAEP writing achievement level range. Each population of students is aligned at the point where the *Proficient* category begins, so that they may be compared at *Proficient* and above. States are listed alphabetically within three groups: the percentage at or above *Proficient* was higher than, not found to be significantly different from, or lower than the nation.

Figure 1.2 *State-by-state NAEP breakdown of "proficient" writers*

parental involvement, second language issues). Dwelling on these issues, however, is counterproductive and a waste of time and energy. The premise of this book is that we are better served by focusing on what we can control—namely, our teaching. My experience in the South Basin Writing Project has taught me that well-trained teachers of writing produce students who write better, and that despite the obstacles we inherit, good teaching matters a great deal. Students with talented and dedicated teachers become better writers. See Appendix 1 for a list of books every teacher of writing should own.

So why are so many secondary students struggling with writing? From my observations of classrooms both within and outside of my state, a number of reasons emerge. With apologies to David Letterman, what follows are my top ten concerns about the teaching of writing in our secondary schools. Strategies to address each of the following concerns will be addressed in subsequent chapters.

Top Ten Writing Wrongs in Secondary Schools

1. Students are not doing enough writing

To become an expert swimmer, one must do a tremendous amount of swimming. One can't just wish to be an expert swimmer; becoming an expert swimmer takes practice and hard work. A lot of practice and a lot of hard work.

Writing, like swimming, is a skill, and as such, only improves with much (guided) practice. In talking with students, I am surprised how little writing is expected of them. This is particularly true in content areas other than language arts, but, unfortunately, remains true in many language arts classrooms as well. To significantly improve their writing skills, our students need to swim in the writing "pool" much more frequently.

2. Writing is sometimes assigned rather than taught

It's one thing to assign writing to students; it's another to *teach* them how to write. Students are being asked to write to elevated writing standards without the proper level of instructional support. Students in classrooms where writing is assigned often show improved fluency, but it has been my experience that without explicit writing instruction their skills stagnate. As a result, students may be writing frequently but not really showing the level of progression we expect. Improved fluency is a good start, but this fluency will not translate to better writing unless targeted instruction is involved.

3. Below-grade-level writers are asked to write less than others instead of more than others

With struggling adolescent writers, the tendency of some teachers is to slow down and assign less. Expectations are lowered. Students in the low track are more likely to do less writing and more worksheets. Unfortunately, these students, who need twice as much writing instruction, end up receiving half the writing instruction of others. In essence, this approach ensures that these students will never catch up. Though a cliché, the old adage is true: no one rises to low expectations.

4. English language learners are often shortchanged as well

Recently I visited a classroom in which ELLs spent forty-five minutes diagramming sentences. There was no hint of authentic reading or writing. There was no evidence of genuine fluency building. There was also no classroom library. This is not an isolated incident—I have seen similar evidence of low expectations in other ELL classrooms as well.

5. Grammar instruction is ineffective or ignored

There is a worksheet mentality out there, particularly with the teaching of correctness. (That is, if grammar is taught at all. In some classes I have visited, grammar instruction is all but ignored.) This worksheet approach alone does not work, and worse, it eats away valuable instructional time. Judith Langer, in *Effective Literacy Instruction* (2002), found in her research that the most effective grammar instruction is grounded in a balanced approach. According to Langer's research, students need (1) separated instruction—where the rules are taught separately; (2) simulated instruction—where students apply these skills in their own reading and writing; and (3) integrated instruction—where students apply the skills to real-world situations. Unfortunately, Langer found that 50 percent of teachers use the separated skills approach only—an approach she found to be ineffective. The balanced teaching of specific grammar skills advocated by Langer is missing in many of our classrooms.

6. Students are not given enough timed writing instruction or practice

Most state frameworks are very clear about what kind of discourses students will be required to write (e.g., autobiography, literary analysis, persuasion). What is not clear from reading many of the states' frameworks is that a student's ability to graduate from high school may hinge on his or her ability to write an essay *on demand.*

Many of the skills required to write well on demand differ from those needed to write a worthwhile multidraft process paper. Instead of having students continue to wrestle with those analogy questions, the new version of the SAT requires students to complete on-demand writing. Those who have had timed writing instruction and practice stand a far better chance at performing well when confronted with writing under pressure. Those students who sit down "cold" to an on-demand essay are at a distinct disadvantage.

Timed writing is not being given nearly the attention it deserves considering the importance it plays in helping students not only to pass state tests, but to score well on the SATs, to help get accepted into colleges, and to succeed in finding meaningful jobs.

7. Some teachers have little or no knowledge of district and state writing standards

When I work with teachers in content areas other than English, I notice quite often that they have very little understanding of their state's writing requirements. The writing requirements of high-stakes exams are often seen as an English teacher problem—a rather unfortunate attitude when you consider that much of the writing on these exams is not what I would call "English-y." Students on the SAT, for example, may be asked to write about a historical document or a scientific discovery, and those who sit down to that test with extensive writing experience in their history and science classes will be those who end up with the higher scores.

For an assessment as important as a district or state proficiency exam or the SAT, you would think that every content-area teacher would be aware and focused on the writing standards. Unfortunately, this is not always the case. (Try your own informal survey: approach teachers from different content areas and ask them if they can name the types of writing your students might face on your district or state assessment—remembering, of course, that students may be asked to write an essay after reading a passage from any content area.) Our students' chances of developing into effective writers will be maximized only if teachers in *all* content areas take ownership of their district and state writing standards. We must move content-area teachers beyond the idea that they are responsible for teaching their content only; all teachers share the responsibility of not only teaching their content but also promoting the literacy level of their students. What good is it if a student leaves a class able to tell you the causes of the Civil War, but unable to read and write well enough to get into a university or to get a good job? Too many teachers see themselves solely as teachers of their content; our students would be much better prepared for the literacy stampede if all teachers recognized that developing the writing skills of their students is as important as dispensing information. Facts and figures often have a short shelf life; learning to write well lasts a lifetime.

8. Writing topics are often mandated with little thought about the prior knowledge and interests of the students

If we want students to become lifelong writers, students must see writing as intrinsically important—not just another school assignment. Students must find writing assignments to be relevant and meaningful. Our standards must be high and challenging (to use Vygotsky's term [1978], we must guide our students through their zones of proximal development). Maxine Greene (1995) calls this "wide awake" teaching and learning—where students develop an understanding of what to write, why they're writing, and how they could be using writing in their lives.

Before reluctant writers can write well on state-mandated exams, they have to write well in our classes. Students produce excellent writing when they are writing for authentic purposes. Fostering student buy-in for writing comes from balancing teacher-mandated topics (which can be open-ended) with giving students choices of interesting writing assignments.

9. Teachers are doing too much of the work. Students are not doing enough work

I have spent many weekends poring over and commenting on my students' papers, only to have them casually glance at my comments upon return. After this happened one too many times, I realized that somewhere, sometime, the workload balance between teacher and student had tilted. I was doing too much of the work.

This realization was reinforced on the very first day of school this year. I stood outside my door before school greeting kids as they arrived at my class. I shook hands, made small talk with students I knew from previous years, and welcomed unfamiliar faces. Out of the corner of my eye I noticed one student slowly approaching. Perhaps "approaching" is not the correct word to describe his leisurely movement toward my door. He was doing the "senior stroll." (You know the "senior stroll"—it's that universal walk students adopt to send two clear messages: [1] they are above wanting to come to school, and [2] they would rather undergo extensive root canal while being forced to listen to a continuous looping of "It's a Small World" than attend your English class.) As this particular student strolled to my door, I noticed he wore a tee shirt with large lettering, and when he was close enough, I could make out the top half of his shirt: "They say hard work never killed anybody . . ." A wave of guilt swept over me as I realized I might have misjudged this student based on his appearance. This guilt soon evaporated, however, when I glanced down and read the second half of the quote on the bottom of his shirt: ". . . but why take a chance?" My first thought at that moment was that my summer vacation was officially over. My second thought was that, from the very first class meeting, I would have to start to break down the increasingly prevalent feeling amongst my students that "work" is a bad four-letter word.

Students need to learn that "work" is a good four-letter word, because with the class sizes we face and the number of writing standards that we must teach, we, as teachers, cannot do all the work. We need help. Our students must be shaken out of this learned helplessness they have acquired when it comes to writing. We must teach them that when they turn something in without effort, we will not accept it. We must teach them that just because they are finished with a first draft, they are not finished with the paper. We must teach them to respond meaningfully to each other's papers. It is important to note that I am not advocating peer editing. I think peer editing is a bad idea. I do believe, however, that students can be taught to help revise papers vis-à-vis read-around-groups, partner sharing, whole-class modeling, and discussion. Though many students do not have the skills to carefully edit (correct errors), they do have the ability to help one another revise (make the content of their papers better). Students who can assist one another with revising help lower the burden on the teacher. If the teacher works hard, the students must meet us halfway by working hard as well.

10. Teachers need help assessing student writing

When to assess, how to assess, and what to assess are issues that remain cloudy for many teachers, and these issues are the reasons why many cut back the amount of writing they demand from students. The possibility of drowning in a paper load has also discouraged many a teacher from giving students the frequent writing experiences they need. Teachers are often at a loss when it comes to getting a handle on three key elements:

1. How to design assessments that drive better teaching
2. How to provide meaningful feedback that helps students learn
3. How to handle the paper load

Until teachers have a handle on these three elements, they will remain reluctant to make writing a centerpiece in their classrooms.

Righting Writing Wrongs: The Pillars of Writing Success

With these ten writing wrongs in mind, this book will propose a model for building strong adolescent writers. The model is built on the premise that effective teenage writers emerge when the following six student needs are met:

1. Students need a lot more writing practice.
2. Students need teachers who model good writing.
3. Students need the opportunity to read and study other writers.
4. Students need choice when it comes to writing topics.
5. Students need to write for authentic purposes and for authentic audiences.
6. Students need meaningful feedback from both the teacher and their peers.

Perhaps it would be useful to consider each of these needs as a pillar that helps support a structure. Instead of building a house, the "structure" this model depicts is a strong adolescent writer (see Figure 1.3). Each of these pillars plays an integral role in building strong writers; take one pillar away and the structure might still stand, but it will be weakened. It is the combined strength of these pillars that serves to build a strong writing foundation.

Using these pillars as a model for building strong writers, this book will share those practices I have found helpful in giving my students the opportunity to develop their writing skills to a level where they can run with the literacy stampede. Each subsequent chapter will examine one of the six pillars

Figure 1.3 *Writing pillars*

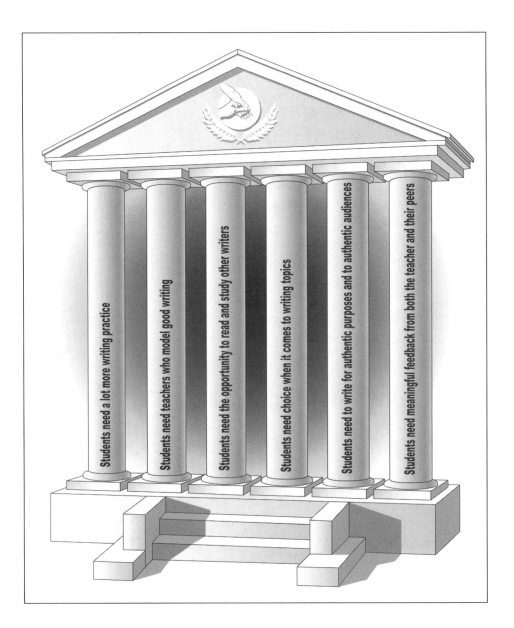

Students need a lot more writing practice

Students need teachers who model good writing

Students need the opportunity to read and study other writers

Students need choice when it comes to writing topics

Students need to write for authentic purposes and to authentic audiences

Students need meaningful feedback from both the teacher and their peers

in depth and will share strategies that have helped my students develop and sharpen essential writing skills. To address the Ten Writing Wrongs, the remaining chapters break down as follows:

Chapter 2 will begin by addressing the notion that our students simply are not writing enough in school or at home. This problem will be outlined and specific strategies to help students write more will be suggested. The strategies offered will help answer the following questions:

- How can I move students past a dislike of writing?
- How does setting up a writer's notebook prompt my students to write more?
- How can I help students perform better on timed (on-demand) writing tasks?

Teaching Adolescent Writers

- How do I move students beyond a "I wrote it once, I'm done" mentality and into multidraft writing?

In Chapter 3, the focus shifts to the important role that teacher modeling plays in the development of young writers. In this chapter I will examine why it is critical for teachers to write alongside their students and explain which modeling strategies are most effective in helping students to write better.

Not only is it vital that teachers model their own writing, it is also important that students have an opportunity to read and study other writers. In Chapter 4 I will explore how to bring models from other writers into the classroom in ways that positively impact our students' writing.

Chapter 5 will examine the importance of providing students choice when they write. First, this chapter will make the argument that choice creates a sense of ownership in young writers. Then, specific strategies to effectively implement choice (not an easy task when we are overwhelmed with vast numbers of standards to teach) will be shared.

In Chapter 6 I will explore the idea that students write better when their purpose for writing is clearly identified and when they are writing to authentic audiences. This chapter will share methods to help students recognize various purposes for writing and suggest strategies to motivate students by creating writing situations in which they are writing to audiences beyond the teacher.

If students should be writing much more than they are now, how does a teacher provide meaningful feedback to so many papers from so many students? Chapter 7 will address how to handle the paper load in a way that provides meaningful feedback to adolescent writers without driving the teacher to a lifelong residence in a rubber room.

Writing Reasons

Before we delve into those strategies that effectively address the Ten Writing Wrongs, we must not overlook one key element found in successful writing classrooms: motivation. I make this point in my first book, *Reading Reasons,* when I outline ten intrinsic reasons why adolescents should be readers. I tell my students they should read because . . .

. . . reading is rewarding.
. . . reading builds a mature vocabulary.
. . . reading makes you a better writer.
. . . reading is hard and "hard" is necessary.
. . . reading makes you smarter.
. . . reading prepares you for the world of work.
. . . reading well is financially rewarding.
. . . reading opens the door to college and beyond.
. . . reading arms you against oppression.

Yes, we can teach our students what good readers do, but if they don't care, if they don't intrinsically value developing their reading skills, if they see reading as just another school task, then teaching them to read effectively becomes extraordinarily difficult.

If motivation plays a critical role in developing young readers, it is certainly true that motivation plays a critical role in developing young writers as well. Writing is hard, and if students don't have intrinsic reasons to work hard at developing their writing skills, they won't diligently develop their writing skills. Simply assuming our students come to us with the desire to improve their writing is a recipe for failure.

Though subsequent chapters will focus on teaching students the pillars of good writing, let's first address the motivation issue. I have learned the hard way that before I teach my students *how* to be better writers, I must teach them *why* they need to be better writers. Knowing that many of my students lack confidence and motivation when it comes time to write, I begin by sharing with them reasons why they should develop their writing skills. I have found that the following eight reasons resonate with them.

Writing Reason #1: Writing Is Hard, but "Hard" Is Rewarding

Writing is rewarding, but the reward does not come easily. I bring to class and share with my students some writing I have struggled with over the years, including:

- the first article I wrote with my own byline for my junior high school newspaper
- the first letter-to-the-editor I wrote that was published in the newspaper. I was fifteen and was protesting a builder's proposal to construct homes in the local wetlands
- the first magazine article I wrote as an intern in college
- a column I wrote in the local newspaper
- a research paper I wrote in college
- the poem I wrote for my oldest daughter last year as she left home to go away to college
- an article I wrote for a teaching journal
- my first book proposal
- a speech I wrote to address the local school board

None of these pieces were easy to write. In fact, I reached high levels of frustration while writing every single one of them. This is the point: writing is not for the fainthearted. Writing is *hard*—so hard that it has been called the most complex of all human activities. I do not sugarcoat that message for my students. Instead, I highlight the difficulty as an opportunity for them to create something truly rewarding. Writing is rewarding *because* it is hard. I ask my students, "When was the last time you got a lot of satisfaction without trying hard?"

When my students have written something well, I want them to recognize the reward that comes from knowing that they have succeeded in "the most complex of all human activities."

Writing Reason #2: Writing Helps You Sort Things Out

When I was a senior in high school, my basketball coach, Lionel Purcell, died on campus from a massive heart attack one month before graduation. Coach Purcell was a father figure to me, and to say I was devastated would be an understatement.

I clearly remember coming home from school that day and sequestering myself in my room. I sat bewildered, crying. I did not know where to turn. I felt a strange, overwhelming mix of grief and rage, and I did not know what to do with it. I went for a run hoping to numb myself. I returned home and curled in the fetal position for over an hour. I went out and shot some baskets in the driveway. Finally, I walked to my desk and started writing a letter to the editor of our small newspaper. I poured my grief out into the letter, outlining what Coach meant to me. I wrote about the lessons I had learned from him, how much I was going to miss him, and why I was a better person for having known him. Writing the letter did not bring my coach back, but, for me, it was the first step in a long healing process.

Later, I clipped that letter from the newspaper and to this day I still have it in a scrapbook. Creating the letter taught me that in times of difficulty, writing could serve as a refuge, a place where I could sort out grief, pain, and frustrations. Now, almost thirty years later, I continue to write to help me work through tough issues.

It seems that with each passing year, more of my students are burdened with serious problems. I tell them the story of my coach because I want them to understand that writing is a good place to sort out your thoughts when the world seems to be crashing down.

Writing Reason #3: Writing Helps to Persuade Others

One of the traditions at my high school is that seniors celebrate their graduation by attending Grad Night at Disneyland. After our school's graduation ceremonies, they board buses and head to an all-night party inside the amusement park. It is a reward they look forward to throughout the year. Last year, due to an administrative error, students were told they were not having Grad Night because the reservation was submitted late and the park was already booked. Disappointed, the seniors asked if they could reschedule the event for the night after graduation (which still had availability). They were told that wouldn't work because by then they'd already be graduates and the teachers, their chaperones, would already be gone for the summer.

It just so happened that we were reading *1984* at the time, so I encouraged the students to challenge the powers that be. I wanted them to understand that they shouldn't give up at the first obstacle, so I encouraged them to voice their displeasure through a letter and petition. In the letter, they outlined reasons why Grad Night *could* be done later than usual, detailing why the tradition of only having it on the evening of graduation could be broken. In the letter they also listed the names of the teachers they had recruited to chaperone. Virtually, the entire senior class signed it.

It worked. The administration, to their credit, reconsidered, and Grad Night was saved—saved by a piece of writing. I want my students to understand that a time will come in their lives when they will need to use writing in order to persuade.

Writing Reason #4: Writing Helps to Fight Oppression

Recently, I explained the concept of oppression and asked my students if it still exists in modern American society. They overwhelmingly responded, "Yes." I then asked them who in this society is most likely to be oppressed. After some give and take, they decided that the poor and the uneducated stand the highest risk of being oppressed. I then asked, "Is there a relationship between being poor and being uneducated?" They responded that this is often, but not always, the case.

I then shared with them research conducted by The Education Trust, which found that three out of every ten students who start high school will not finish on time (Hall 2005). It is worse for people of color: one of every two African American and Latino students will not graduate on time. More to the point, I added, an alarming number of American children do not finish high school at all. See Figure 1.4 for recent graduation rates for every state and for the District of Columbia.

In sharing these statistics with my students, I want them to understand that developing a high level of literacy will be their best defense against oppression. You will struggle when you write the next essay, I tell them, but that struggle will pale in comparison to the struggle you face if you leave this school unable to read and write well. That will be a *lifelong* struggle.

Writing Reason #5: Writing Makes You a Better Reader

In *Because Writing Matters,* Carl Nagin discusses "the new understanding of how reading and writing are intertwined and inseparable language tools throughout a student's learning" (2003, p. 31). Nagin notes that fifty years of correlational and experimental studies investigating reading and writing have concluded the following:

- Better writers tend to be better readers (of their own writing as well as other reading material).

Average Freshman Graduation Rate

State or jurisdiction	2002–03	2003–04
United States[1]	73.9	75.0
Alabama	64.7	65.0
Alaska	68.0	67.2
Arizona	75.9	66.8
Arkansas	76.6	76.8
California	74.1	73.9
Colorado	76.4	78.7
Connecticut	80.9	80.7
Delaware	73.0	72.9
District of Columbia	59.6	68.2
Florida	66.7	66.4
Georgia	60.8	61.2
Hawaii	71.3	72.6
Idaho	81.4	81.5
Illinois	75.9	80.3
Indiana	75.5	73.5
Iowa	85.3	85.8
Kansas	76.9	77.9
Kentucky	71.7	73.0
Louisiana	64.1	69.4
Maine	76.3	77.6
Maryland	79.2	79.5
Massachusetts	75.7	79.3
Michigan	74.0	72.5
Minnesota	84.8	84.7
Mississippi	62.7	62.7
Missouri	78.3	80.4
Montana	81.0	80.4
Nebraska	85.2	87.6
Nevada	72.3	57.4
New Hampshire	78.2	78.7
New Jersey	87.0	86.3
New Mexico	63.1	67.0
New York	60.9	—
North Carolina	70.1	71.4
North Dakota	86.4	86.1
Ohio	79.0	81.3
Oklahoma	76.0	77.0
Oregon	73.7	74.2
Pennsylvania	81.7	82.2
Rhode Island	77.7	75.9
South Carolina	59.7	60.6
South Dakota	83.0	83.7
Tennessee	63.4	66.1
Texas	75.5	76.7
Utah	80.2	83.0
Vermont	83.6	85.4
Virginia	80.6	79.3
Washington	74.2	74.6
West Virginia	75.7	76.9
Wisconsin	85.8	—
Wyoming	73.9	76.0

See notes at end of figure on next page

Figure 1.4 *Average freshman graduation rates, by state: School years 2002–03 and 2003–04*

continued

Figure 1.4 *Average freshman graduation rates, by state: School years 2002–03 and 2003–04 (continued)*

State or jurisdiction	2002–03	2003–04
Bureau of Indian Affairs and outlying areas		
Bureau of Indian Affairs	—	—
American Samoa	81.0	80.2
Guam	56.3	48.4
Northern Marianas	65.2	75.3
Puerto Rico	67.8	64.8
Virgin Islands	53.5	—

— Not available.

Note: Enrollments for school years 1998–99 through 2001–02 and diploma recipients for school years 2002–03 and 2003–04 were used.

[1] The national estimate for 2003–04 does not include data from two states with missing diploma counts: New York and Wisconsin. The adjusted national rate with estimates for these two states included is 74.3 percent.

Source: NCES, Common Core of Data: State Non-Fiscal Data Files. 1998–99 Version 1c, 1999–2000 Version 1c, 2000–01 Version 1b, 2001–02 Version 1b, 2002–03 Version 1b, 2003–04 Version 0c, and 2004–05 Version 0c.

- Better writers tend to read more than poorer writers.
- Better readers tend to produce more syntactically mature writing than poorer readers.

If students are to fight oppression (see Writing Reason #4), they have to learn to read and write well. One cannot be addressed without the other. As stated in *Because Writing Matters,* "Reading development does not take place in isolation; instead a child develops simultaneously as reader, listener, speaker, and writer" (p. 32). The emerging research is clear: Writing makes you a better reader, and vice versa.

Writing Reason #6: Writing Makes You Smarter

All students understand what happens when a muscle is exercised and what happens when a muscle is neglected. I explain to them that the brain is no different. Mental stimulation improves brain function and actually protects against cognitive decline. Not only does writing sharpen the brain by providing mental stimulation, but different kinds of writing sharpen different kinds of thinking. As Langer and Applebee have noted:

> While all writing helps learning, it is important for teachers to be selective about the kinds of writing activities they ask their students to engage in, depending on the kinds of learning they are seeking. Analytic writing leads to a focus on selective parts of the text, to deeper reasoning about less information. Summary writing and note-taking, in contrast, lead to a focus on the whole text in more comprehensive but more superficial ways. Short-answer study questions focus attention on particular information, with little attention to overall relationships. (1978, p. 136)

Langer and Applebee note that each type of writing has its place in our schools, for all of them enhance a different part of our students' thinking and reasoning.

I share with my students something I have learned by writing three books. Even though I started writing each book by creating a detailed outline for each chapter, I have yet to follow any of the outlines point-by-point. Every chapter has deviated from its original outline. Why? Because the act of writing itself creates new thinking, and as a result, my writing changes direction midstream, pulling my brain into new territories. I have learned that writing requires me to think, and the thinking generated by writing opens the door to new thinking.

Writing Reason #7: Writing Helps You Get Into and Through College

Generally speaking, college admissions officers look at four criteria in trying to decide who gets in: (1) grade point average, (2) involvement on the high school campus, (3) involvement in the community, and (4) writing ability. Because college admission is more competitive than ever, the applications are beginning to look alike—lots of students with high GPAs and active involvement in their schools. The choice between one student and another is razor-thin, and often what separates the winners from the losers is the college application essay.

Once accepted, students will be called on to demonstrate their thinking through writing. This is problematic since the National Commission on Writing notes that "by the first year of college, more than 50 percent of the freshman class are unable to produce papers relatively free of language errors or to analyze arguments or synthesize information" (2003b, p. 17). The inability of students to write well has proved costly to colleges and universities. Commission chair C. Peter Magrath said, "The writing weaknesses of incoming college students cost our campuses up to $1 billion annually." When incoming freshmen do not write at a collegiate level, universities are forced to spend valuable resources on remedial writing courses.

I share these statistics with my college-bound students. For my seniors, I emphasize that this school year should be spent "sharpening the saw" rather than giving into senioritis. They have one year left to improve their writing before they find themselves competing at the collegiate level.

Writing Reason #8: Writing Prepares You for the World of Work

In *The World Is Flat*, Thomas Friedman makes the sobering point that our students will enter a job market that is very different from the one we entered. Technology has flattened the world, Friedman argues, and as a result, our students will be entering a workplace where the competition for jobs is global (2006).

When I was in high school, for example, there were American jobs. There were Japanese jobs. There were jobs in India. Not any more. Technology is flattening the world in a way that means our students will compete for work with students from around the globe. Oceans and mountains will no longer offer American workers refuge. This is reflected in my favorite anecdote in Friedman's book, in which he recalls his mother prodding him as a young boy to eat his vegetables. To turn up the guilt, she would remind him of the children starving in India. Now a father, Friedman prods his daughter to do her homework, reminding her of the children in India starving for the job both children might compete for some day.

Unfortunately, many students are leaving our schools unprepared to work in a flat world. According to a 2005 survey given to members of the National Association of Manufacturers, 84 percent of employers say K–12 schools are not doing a good job of preparing students for the workplace (up from 78 percent in 2002). Here are some other findings from the survey:

- Eighty-one percent of respondents answered that they are currently facing a moderate to severe shortage of qualified workers.
- Sixty-five percent of all respondents and 74 percent of respondents with more than 500 employees reported a moderate to severe shortage of scientists and engineers.
- When asked, "To what extent does the shortage of available skills impact your ability to serve customers?" 54 percent indicated a moderate to high degree of negative impact.
- Sixty-one percent of the respondents said that applicants with high school diplomas were poorly prepared; this figure drops to 19 percent for applicants with two years of college.
- When asked, "What types of skills will employees need more of over the next three years?" 51 percent checked "Reading/Writing/Communication Skills." (National Association of Manufacturers 2005)

My students have a tendency to believe that the entire world exists inside the walls of Magnolia High School. They suffer from tunnel vision and are often unable to see the big picture. When they start complaining about the amount of writing they are asked to do, I remind them that while they are home watching *American Idol,* students in other countries are working hard to compete in a flat world. I also remind them of some of the findings in *Writing: A Ticket to Work . . . or a Ticket Out* (2004a), a report by the National Commission on Writing. The following are among the study's findings:

- Writing is a "threshold skill" for both employment and promotion, particularly for salaried employees. Half of the companies indicated they take writing into consideration when hiring (p. 3).
- People who cannot write and communicate clearly will not be hired and are unlikely to last long enough to be considered for promotion (p. 3).

- Two-thirds of all salaried employees in large American companies have some writing responsibility (p. 3).
- Half of all companies take writing into account when making promotion decisions (p. 3).

I want my students to be aware that writing can be either "a ticket into work or a ticket out."

This book will outline how to build better adolescent writers, but the strategies outlined in subsequent chapters may become moot if our students remain unmotivated to write. You can teach students *how* to write, but if they don't understand *why* they should write, chances for success will diminish. Not one of these eight reasons to write has to do with getting a good grade in my class. All of them, however, appeal to my students' *intrinsic* motivation. I have found that sharing these reasons is time well spent; when students understand why writing is important, a foundation on which to begin teaching the six pillars has been set.

Overcoming "The Neglected 'R'": Establishing a Time and a Place to Write

If kids don't write more than three times a week, they're dead.

Donald Graves

When I started teaching twenty years ago, I learned the hard way just how little writing was expected from the students at my school. At the end of my first year I required my students to compile a portfolio, and as part of that assignment I mandated that they include writing samples from their other classes. When I explained this specific requirement to my first-period class, Adam, who sat in the front row, raised his hand, paused for effect, then proudly stated, "But, Mr. Gallagher, we do not write in our other classes."

By this time I had learned to take everything Adam said with a grain of salt. After all, he was the kind of student who would repeatedly use ampersands in his essays because for him to actually write "and" would require greater effort than it took to propel Lance Armstrong up and over the French Alps. I winked at him and said, "Surely, you are exaggerating. You might not have done much writing in your economics class, but surely you have written *something.*"

"Nope," he replied.

Crystal, the best student in the class, chimed in. "Adam's right, Mr. G. We haven't written a single paragraph all semester in that class. We are getting really good at multiple choice tests, though!"

Crystal's statement put a whole new spin on things. She was the kind of student we would all like to clone: hardworking, prompt, polite. She not only had beautiful handwriting, but she bathed on a regular basis, never forgot to give you a card and a new coffee cup come holiday time, and volunteered to baby-sit your children. *That* kind of student. If she was backing Adam's story, maybe this claim was not an exaggeration. Could it be possible that students spent an entire semester in an academic class without writing at all?

Looking back, I probably should have handled the situation with a bit more tact, but saddled with grading essays all weekend while my colleagues in other content areas lived actual lives angered me. To get my message across, I created a waiver form for my students to take to each of their teachers to sign off. It read as follows:

> As part of the final exam in senior English, students are being asked to produce a portfolio that contains writing samples from all their classes. To receive full credit, students must submit writing from each of their classes. Some of my students claim they do not write in some of their classes. In order for me to waive that part of their portfolio, I am asking students to verify with their teachers that they do not have any writing to submit for use in their portfolios. If this student has not done any writing in your class, please sign this form so I may waive them from that requirement. Thank you.

Granted, this was not the most tactful approach, and not surprisingly, it took less than ten minutes to receive feedback. Shortly after second period began, the economics teacher (who did not assign writing) ran into my room and started screaming at me in front of my students.

The good news occurred later in the day when the science department chair approached me and sheepishly said, "You caught me. My chemistry students do not have any writing to submit for your portfolio. But you will not catch me again." Today, her students write regularly in journals and complete science-related research papers. In fact, we spoke briefly yesterday, and I was pleased to hear her bemoaning the fact that she had a stack of essays to grade.

"The Neglected 'R'"—Then and Now

This experience during my rookie year prompted me to wonder: Was this dearth of writing a phenomenon only at my school? Or was it indicative of a far-reaching problem? Did I land at the wrong school? Or was lack of student writing at my school the tip of a much bigger iceberg? Shortly after my confrontation with the economics teacher, I received the answer to these questions when I began reading Judith Langer and Arthur Applebee's *How Writing Shapes Thinking*. Looking at a large cross section of schools across the country, Langer and Applebee came to some sobering conclusions about students' writing abilities. Among their findings were the following:

- Students' writing is often superficial, and "even the 'better' responses show little evidence of well-developed problem-solving strategies or critical thinking skills."
- A major conclusion to draw from the assessment of students' writing at all grade levels is that students "are deficient in higher order thinking skills." They have difficulty performing adequately on analytic writing tasks, as well as on persuasive writing tasks.
- "Because writing and thinking are so deeply intertwined, appropriate writing assignments provide an ideal way to increase student experiences with such type of thinking." As a result, "Students need broad-based experiences in which reading and writing tasks are integrated with their work throughout the curriculum." (1978, p. 4)

Langer and Applebee concluded that students were not getting necessary broad-based writing experiences. "Simply put, in the whole range of academic course work, American children do not write frequently enough, and the reading and writing tasks they are given do not require them to think deeply enough" (p. 4).

Langer and Applebee's sobering conclusions, written nearly twenty years ago, were published in the same year as Steven Krashen's *Writing: Research, Theory, and Applications*. In his book, Krashen cited a number of studies that detailed the benefits students received when they participated in rigorous writing programs. Among his findings were the following:

- The best incoming college freshmen writers are those who do the most writing in high school (McQueen, Murray, and Evans 1963).
- The best college freshmen writers are those students who do more expository writing in high school (Bamberg 1978).
- Students who write two essays a week do better in college than those who write one (Lokke and Wykoff 1948).
- Good writers are much more likely to do more writing outside of school (Stallard 1974 and Donaldson 1967, in separate studies).
- A higher percentage of college freshmen who entered as poor writers are those students who did no writing in high school (Woodward and Phillips 1967).

As Langer and Applebee were sounding the alarm that students in American schools were not writing enough, a mountain of research was emerging that clearly outlined the benefits received by those students who were fortunate enough to find themselves in rigorous writing programs. As Langer and Applebee noted, students were not writing, even after research clearly found that "in general, any kind of written response leads to better performance than does reading without writing. Within groups of students who complete the same tasks, students who write at greater length tend to perform better than students who write less, even after allowing for a general tendency for better students to do better at everything" (p. 130).

As a result of Langer and Applebee's findings and others that echoed their concerns, you might think that much of the educational reform over the past two decades has focused on bringing writing to the forefront in our schools. In an age when expectations have risen so that no child should be left behind, you might conclude that educators have heeded the call for more rigorous writing programs and that today's students are being taught those "broad-based" writing tasks necessary to develop their thinking and writing skills.

Unfortunately, the evidence suggests that very little has changed. Today, nearly two decades after Langer and Applebee revealed that our students simply were not writing enough, the writing front in America's schools remains bleak. Consider the following:

- Children today still receive little opportunity to write. In one recent study in grades one, three, and five, only 15 percent of the school day was spent in any kind of writing activity (National Writing Project 2003, p. 6).
- Two-thirds of the writing that did occur was word-for-word copying in workbooks (National Writing Project and Carl Nagin 2003, p. 6).
- Ninety-seven percent of elementary school students write less than three hours a week. This is 15 percent of the time they spend watching television (National Commission on Writing 2003b, p. 23).
- Compositions of a paragraph or more in length are infrequent even at the high school level (National Writing Project and Carl Nagin 2003, p. 6).
- Forty percent of twelfth graders report that they are "never" or "hardly ever" assigned a paper of three pages or more in length (National Commission on Writing 2003b, p. 23).

Clearly, the bar remains very low when it comes to the writing demands of the secondary classroom. As I write this paragraph, for example, I am in the last week of a school year and once again I am requiring students to submit writing samples from their other classes. Yesterday, a student informed me he has only one essay to choose from in his honors history class. Unfortunately, my school seems to be the norm—the National Commission on Writing (2003b) found that 75 percent of high school seniors are *never* given writing assignments in social studies. *Never.* Is it just me, or can you hear the hoof beats of the literacy stampede getting louder?

The situation in my own school seems to parallel a much wider problem. Sadly, two decades after the research made a compelling call for us to carve out more writing time for our students, the National Commission on Writing (2003b) has declared that writing remains the "neglected 'R'" in our schools. Only now, in our information-driven world, the stakes are higher.

A Writing Revolution

For years Donald Murray, author of *A Writer Teaches Writing* (2004), has advocated that we spend less time teaching writing and spend more time teaching the writer. What good is it, he asks, if we cover a lot of writing assignments but our students end the year without having internalized those essential skills that good writers possess? Teach the writ*er*, he argues, not the writ*ing*.

Teaching writers requires that we create extended writing time in our classes. I clearly understand the implications of this statement. If we create extended writing time to truly teach students how to write, doesn't that mean other parts of the curriculum will have to be sacrificed? In a word, yes. I know this flies in the face of the pressure we all feel to cover all the standards (standards, I might add, that have clearly been written for either Utopia Junior High or Nirvana High School). But consider the alternative: What good is a curriculum that is a mile wide and an inch deep? What good is it if a student can point out the symbolism found in *Lord of the Flies* if this same student leaves my class unable to write well enough for college admission or to secure worthwhile employment? If Langer and Applebee are correct—that good writing develops careful thinking and that writing is the cornerstone of producing literate human beings—then don't we have a responsibility that reaches far beyond simply covering our courses' content? Shouldn't we concern ourselves a little less with getting students to recite facts and figures and concern ourselves more with helping them develop these cornerstone skills they will need to lead literate lives? Shouldn't we teach the curriculum *through* writing?

If I recognize my duty to teach the writer, I must insist that writing activities be moved to the forefront in my classroom. In planning lessons, I am compelled to consider what kind of writing experiences I want my students to have and to work backward from that notion. Through this approach my students will learn less content over the course of one school year (simply put, there will be standards I won't teach). I hope, however, that by slowing down and going deeper into writing, the payoff will be longer lasting. I can't create deeper learning if I don't give my students the time they need to learn deeply. Twenty years from now I will not be concerned if my students have forgotten what foreshadowed Lenny's death in *Of Mice and Men*, but I will be worried if they are unable to write effectively in the workplace or if they cannot compose letters to their congressional representatives.

This commitment to teaching the writer is also found in recent recommendations put forth by the National Commission on Writing (2003b, p. 3). Among its findings are the following:

- Every state should revisit its education standards to make sure they include a comprehensive writing policy.
- More out-of-school time should be used to encourage writing.
- Districts should insist that writing be taught in all subjects and at all grade levels.
- Every district should require each teacher to successfully complete a course in writing theory and practice as a condition for teacher licensing.
- Schools should aim to double the amount of time most students spend writing.

In short, the commission is calling for nothing short of a writing revolution. As the commission notes, "American education will never realize its potential as an engine of opportunity and economic growth until a writing revolution puts the power of language and communication in their proper place in the classroom" (p. 14).

Consider the commission's recommendations and ask yourself the following questions:

- Does my school have a comprehensive, across-the-curriculum writing approach?
- Considering all of my students' classes, are they writing enough in school?
- Are my students writing enough out of school?
- Is writing taught at my school in all classes at all grade levels?
- Have the teachers at my site, in all grade levels and subjects, been given extensive writing training?

These are sobering questions, and thinking about them reminds me that the commission is not simply recommending that we squeeze in a bit more writing here and there. These are not window-dressing recommendations. The commission is calling for a *doubling* of the time our students spend writing. They recognize the underlying reason our students are not writing well— not enough time is being given, inside or outside of class, for students to competently develop their writing skills. Writing is not being given its "proper place" in the classroom. If our students are to realize their full potential in becoming literate adults, this must change.

Writers Need to Write Before They Write

When I coached high school basketball early in my career, I wanted my students to get as much practice as possible throughout the week so that they would be ready for the game on Friday night. In a typical week we might practice the following skills:

Offense	Defense
• Shooting	• Footwork
• Passing	• Seeing the ball at all times
• Rebounding	• Man-to-man defense
• Fast break transition	• Zone defense
• Dribbling	• Talking to each other
• Free-throw shooting	• Help side defense
• Set plays	• Screening out
• Out-of-bounds plays	• Rebounding
• Breaking the half-court trap	• Half-court trap
• Breaking the full-court press	• Full-court press
• Setting screens	• Defending out-of-bounds plays
• Back-door cuts	• Defending the screen
• Pick and roll	• Getting to loose balls
• Splitting gaps	

The idea, of course, was that my players needed to do a lot of playing before they actually were ready to play. It would have been crazy just to ask them to show up for the game Friday night without first giving my players a place to practice (the gym) and a lot of time to develop their skills (daily practices).

This same principle holds true for developing writers. In *A Writer Teaches Writing* (2004), Donald Murray suggests that writers need to do lots of writing before we can expect them to write well. Murray notes, "Writing is a skill, and students need to mess around with paints before they learn how to paint, plunk at a piano before they are taught scales, fool around with a basketball, get the feel of it, before they are put through a formal practice" (p. 17). Quite often, when students are asked to write formally in school, they haven't had enough previous writing practice to give them the competence to succeed. As Murray notes, "Inexperienced writers often write too soon" and as a result, "Much of the bad writing we read from inexperienced writers is the direct result of writing before they are ready to write" (p. 17). If we are going to require students to write complex essays, we need to give them the necessary time to develop their writing skills. They should be "messing around" and "playing" with writing every day to lay the foundation for the more challenging writing assignments that lie ahead. The idea of giving students time to practice writing before they are required to write in high-stakes situations is undoubtedly echoed in the National Commission on Writing's current recommendation that schools double the amount of time students currently spend writing. The commission recognizes that students are being sent directly into the game without adequate practice.

To help my students run with the literacy stampede, my class starts with the expectations that students will frequently "mess around" with writing.

Where do my students have this informal opportunity to "write before they write"? Through three components: (1) daily in-class writing activities, (2) weekly writing in their writer's notebooks, and (3) regularly scheduled first-draft, on-demand writing. Let's take a closer look at each of these components.

Daily In-Class Writing Activities

What is the value in having students write every day in class? Langer and Applebee propose three primary reasons (1978, p. 42):

1. Writing helps students to draw on relevant knowledge and experience as preparation for new activities

Writing can help frame new learning. By revisiting what they already know, students become better prepared to acquire new learning. Here are some specific examples in which I use writing as a warm-up before reading difficult text in my classroom:

- Before my students begin reading Elie Wiesel's holocaust memoir, *Night,* I write the word "holocaust" on the board and have them write as much as they can about this word in a five-minute period. If a student says he has nothing to write, I have him repeatedly write, "I know nothing about the holocaust." After a few seconds of this he will inevitably begin writing something relevant. At the end of the five minutes, we either share out as a whole group or pass the papers to be read in smaller circles. This not only activates prior knowledge but also teaches students new information about the topic, which, in turn, prepares them for reading *Night.*
- In Act 1, Scene 3 of *Romeo and Juliet,* Juliet's parents decide whom she should date. Prior to reading this scene, students do a quickwrite in response to the following focus question: "Should your parents have any say in who you date?" This writing activity leads to lively discussion, which, in turn, prepares students to better comprehend the upcoming scene.
- Early in *1984,* George Orwell introduces the idea of "thoughtcrime." Prior to reading this chapter, students are given the following two-point focus task: (1) "Please brainstorm a list of all the methods the government of Oceania has used thus far to control the thoughts and actions of its citizens" and (2) "In this chapter Orwell will explain the concept of 'thoughtcrime.' Before reading the chapter, predict what he means by 'thoughtcrime.'" Revisiting the text (in this case by writing a list) helps students predict what will happen and provides a focus for their reading (they read to see if their predictions will be accurate).

These activities share the same goal—to use writing as a means to draw on relevant knowledge and experience to prepare students for the learning at hand. Instead of starting with "cold" reading, writing is used to warm up students by framing the learning.

2. Writing helps students to consolidate and review ideas and experiences

Do you know the Grocery List Theory? It is based on the idea that if you write a shopping list of the groceries you need and then forget to take it with you to the store, you will still end up buying more of the items you wrote down than had you simply gone shopping without ever having written a list in the first place. This is because the physical act of writing helps imprint information in your brain and allows you to recall more. (I suspect this is also why when studying for an exam in college, I always did better when I wrote careful notes or made flash cards).

The traditional strategies of note taking, outlining, clustering, and creating double-entry journals remain effective in helping students to consolidate and review ideas. I have also used some of the following writing strategies in my classroom to help students review and retain their thinking:

Exit Slips Near the end of the period I stop to give students time to write exit slips. The directions may be as simple as, "We have five minutes left in class. Explain in writing what you have learned in class today." Students then conclude the class by reviewing the big ideas read or discussed in class that day. This writing serves as a ticket to be handed to me as they exit the room.

SDQR Chart This strategy can be used to capture thinking from a lecture or from reading a passage (fiction or nonfiction). Students are asked to complete the following chart:

Says	Doesn't Say	Questions	Reflections
Students record: • Facts learned • Facts confirmed	Students record: • What is not said/omitted • Inferential thinking	Students record: • Questions that arise	Students record: • Thoughts • Connections

See Figure 2.1 for Carlos's thinking after reading the "Born Bad" vignette in Sandra Cisneros's *House on Mango Street*.

Movie Reading Because of limited time, I do not show movies end-to-end in my classroom. I do, however, show a number of film clips. Unfortunately, for many students, "movie time" is a euphemism for "cognitive slumber party." When the lights are dimmed, so, often, are their brains. To avoid this I want my students to think and write while watching film. I might, for example, show the students three different film versions of Prince Hamlet's "To be or not to be" soliloquy (as performed by Laurence Olivier, Mel Gibson,

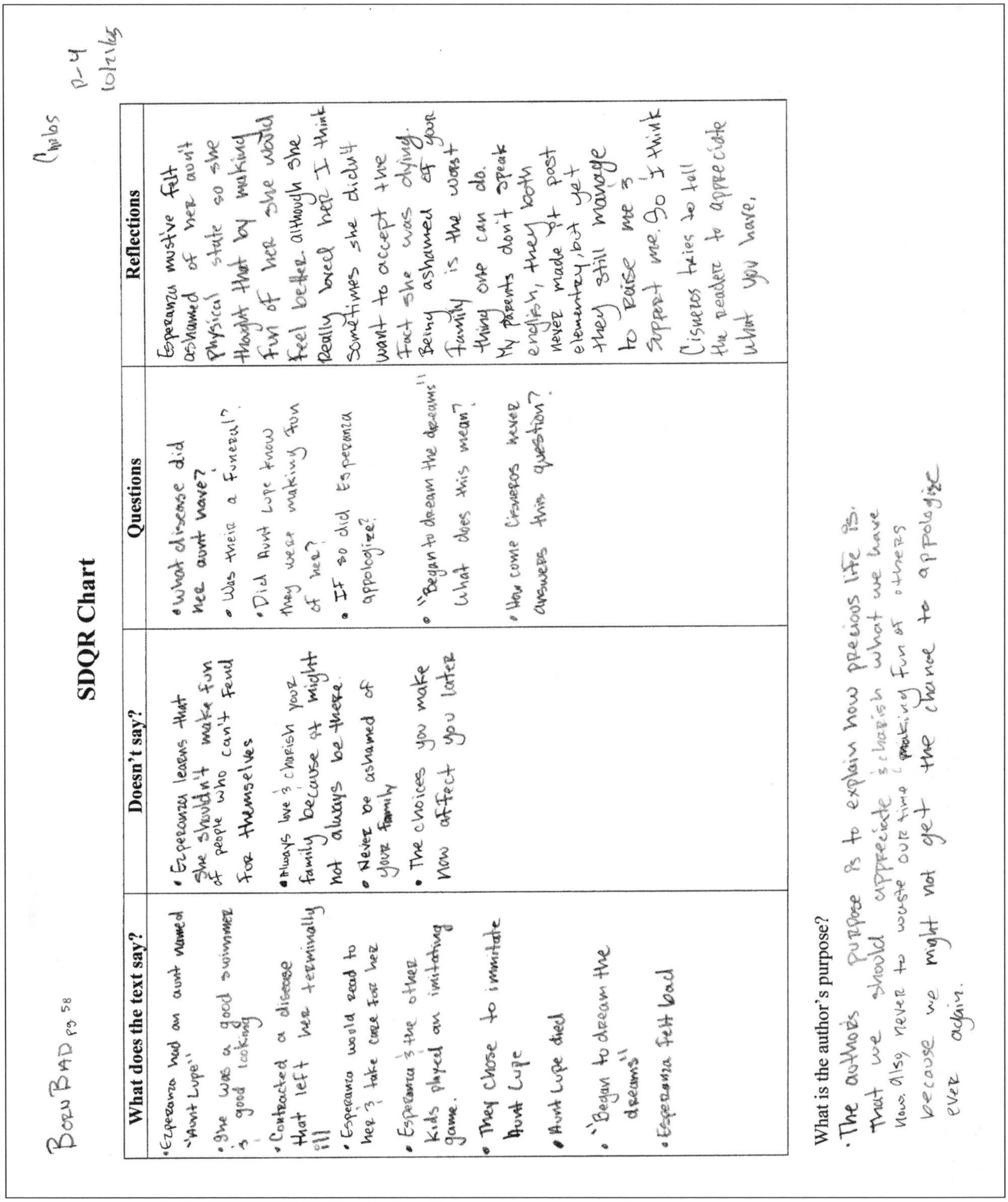

SDQR Chart

Bou Bad pg 58

What does the text say?	Doesn't say?	Questions	Reflections
• Esperanza had an aunt named "Aunt Lupe" • She was a good swimmer & good looking • Contracted a disease that left her terminally ill • Esperanza would read to her & take care for her • Esperanza & the other kids played an imitating game. • They chose to immitate Aunt Lupe • Aunt Lupe died • "Began to dream the dreams" • Esperanza felt bad	• Esperanza learns that she shouldn't make fun of people who can't fend for themselves • Always love & cherish your family because it might not always be there. • Never be ashamed of your family • The choices you make now affect you later	• What disease did her aunt have? • Was there a funeral? • Did Aunt Lupe know they were making fun of her? • If so did Esperanza apologize? • "Began to dream the dreams" What does this mean? • How come Cisneros never answers this question?	Esperanza must've felt ashamed of her aunt's physical state so she thought that by making fun of her she would feel better. Although she really loved her. I think sometimes she didn't want to accept the fact she was dying. Being ashamed of your family is the worst thing one can do. My parents don't speak english, they both never made it past elementary, but yet they still manage to raise me & support me. So I think Cisneros tries to tell the reader to appreciate what you have.

What is the author's purpose?

• The author's purpose is to explain how precious life is. That we should appreciate & cherish what we have now. Also never to waste our time & making fun of others because we might not get the chance to apologize ever again.

Figure 2.1 *Carlos's SDQR chart*

and Kenneth Branagh). While watching the film clips, students complete the following chart:

Notes on Olivier's Performance	Notes on Gibson's Performance	Notes on Branagh's Performance

Reflections:

See Figure 2.2 to see Mica's *Hamlet* Movie Chart. A reproducible version of this chart can be found in Appendix 2.

Figure 2.2 *Mica's movie chart*

Notes on Olivier's performance	Notes on Gibson's performance	Notes on Branagh's performance
•It's in black and white •What year was this made? •Performed outside above a cliff. Is he talking inside his head? •What is up with the close up of his head and the clouds? •The music swirls and is cheesy •He seems to old to be Hamlet	•It's in color •Takes place in a tomb. I like this setting better than the first film. What better place to film thoughts of suicide than in a tomb? •Mel Gibson also seems too old to play the prince. Isn't Hamlet supposed to be in his 20's?	•How come everyone who plays Hamlet is so old? •Takes place in the palace --- I like the use of the mirrors. That must have been hard to film without getting the reflection of the camera. •I like Branagh's performance --- he has a crazy look in his eye.

Reflections:
• Where's Ophelia?

I like something different in each version. In the Oliver version I like the idea that he might jump off the cliff. In the Mel Gibson version, I like that it takes place in the family's tomb. But the version I think captures the "to be or not be" scene the best is the Branagh version. I like the use of the mirrors and how these mirrors are used to deflect the truth. Also, if you look at the floor, the squares make it look like a chess game. This gives the viewer that a game of chess is being played, which if you think about it, it is!

What was the writer's purpose in this piece?	How does the author create this purpose?	Reflections

Generate Outrage— "There has been little outrage..."
 	
 To scare → recognize how serious spying / identity theft is
 	
 Inform us of the depth of the problem
 	
 Make the reader think about protecting his / her own privacy
	- Relates to the Readers - stories from her own life
	 - uses Everyday examples that you don't / wouldn't think about worrying about
	 - Reminds us / Brings up a warning about the situation we are going through Orwell's 1984
	 - Personal anecdotes
	  ATM
	  Google earth } Affect all
	  Credit card } Americans
	  I crew
	 - Audience
	  parents / students
	  Facebook
	 - invokes / Brings up 911 scares
	 - literary connection 1984
	 - circular arguement
	 - ends previous point "underware"
		As someone, an eighteen year old, female, getting ready to enter the "real" world out of high school, it is worrisome and scary to know what I'm walking into.
		 This issue about privacy is frightening to me, especially at this time of my life. I am about to become more independent, entering college, and maybe even moving out. I may be just the gold mine, along with my fellow classmates and our future graduates, for all the Big Brothers out there.
		 This article already makes me think about the conversations that I've already had on the telephone, my credit card transactions, and my home.
		 Most recently, Big Brother has shown up on my doorstep, literally. In addition to the gates and walls that have been around the complex, cameras have just been installed. Yes, they may be for safety reasons, but still, I'd rather not have someone watch my every move, everyday. I get enough at work anyway, although most of our McDonald's workers have found blind spots, I have yet to find where they are at my apartment complex.
		 However, through Reading literary works like Orwell's 1984, and other articles about our privacy, or lack of, opens my eyes and they at least gives me a heads up in entering the "real" world.

Figure 2.3 *Purpose chart*

Purpose Chart Another way I want students to use writing to demonstrate understanding is by having them give careful consideration to the author's purpose. In Figure 2.3, for example, you will see a chart I use to help students track the author's purpose. In this example, Jenny is considering Orwell's purpose in a passage from *1984*.

Teaching Adolescent Writers

The importance of recognizing the author's purpose, along with examples of student work, will be discussed in greater detail in Chapter 6. See Appendix 3 for a reproducible Purpose Chart.

3. Writing helps students to reformulate and extend knowledge

Many teachers I know have their students write for one main reason: to demonstrate what they know (and what they don't know) about the subject at hand. But there is another valuable reason why our students should be doing much more writing across the curriculum: the act of writing *extends* knowledge. Putting pen to paper (or fingers to keyboard) creates new thinking. The act of writing itself is generative.

The book you are holding in your hand, for example, is the third book I have written. As I mentioned in Chapter 1, I began this book by writing a complete outline, chapter by chapter, with a definitive finish line in mind. It is interesting to note that I have yet to write a single chapter that followed my outline point-by-point. Not one of them stayed true to the plan. Why? Because every time I sat down and began writing about a particular idea, the act of writing generated new ideas. As a result, each chapter took unforeseen turns. When this happens I am reminded of what E. M. Forster once said: "How can I know what I think till I see what I say?"

Marion Crowhurst, in *Writing in the Middle Years* (1993), reinforces the notion that writing generates new thinking when she writes the following:

> *Novice writers think that good writers plan what they want to say before they begin, write down what they planned to say, make the necessary corrections or revisions—and the job is done. However, except with routine writing tasks, the reality is far different.*
>
> *For example, finding out what one has to say may take a long, long time. The germ of an idea may be nurtured for weeks before a tentative beginning is made. The first draft of a piece based on this germ may be set aside for days or months before it is taken up again and completed and some first drafts are never finished.*
>
> *Planning is often incomplete when writing begins. In fact many experienced writers find out what they want to say by starting to write. (p. 14)*

Sometimes it is beneficial to have students write to help them figure out what they want to say. Recognizing that the thinking of my students can be generated and extended by writing has prompted me to implement the following strategies:

Free Response Have you ever read a complex passage with your students— something very thought provoking and powerful—only to have them stare at you blankly when you try to elicit some response from them? When this happens to me I ask myself, "Have my students had time to think before they can think?" When my students are a bit overwhelmed following an intense reading, I will ask them to take out their writer's notebooks and write whatever is on their minds for five minutes. This exercise allows them some cognitive breathing space—an opportunity for them to think before they have to think. Exploring their initial thinking through writing takes the onus off the teacher and gives students time to process heavy ideas. This five-minute investment of time is almost always paid back by the deeper discussions that ensue once the quickwrites are over.

Looping Looping, a term coined by Peter Elbow in *Writing with Power* (1998), is a useful strategy to help students explore their thinking through writing. This strategy enables a student to move from unfocused to focused writing. Here are Elbow's steps for looping:

1. Start by having students write their initial thinking on a given topic. For example, in an English class, students might be asked what they think of a particular character's behavior. In a history class, they might write their thoughts about an historical period or a major political event. Students' initial writings may wander.
2. Ask students to write nonstop for ten minutes. The key is to begin with the first thing that comes to mind and to not stop writing. If students get stuck, have them rewrite the last sentence. Students must be taught that their writing might take them in unforeseen directions. This is a good thing.
3. After ten minutes, have students reread what they have written thus far. As they read, they are searching for a "hot spot"—an emerging theme, a central idea—anything that stands out and creates a spark of thinking.
4. Have students highlight or circle this "hot spot." Skipping a line or two, have the students rewrite this hot spot into a complete sentence.
5. Beginning with this new sentence, ask students to write again for ten minutes.
6. At the end of ten minutes, tell students to find a new hot spot and again write a summary sentence.
7. Keep looping until a focus or thesis emerges. Sometimes this will occur in a single loop; sometimes it takes a few loops.

Pass-the-Reflection Have students write their thoughts on a given topic for two minutes. When the time is up, have students pass their papers to one another (this can be done in small groups or as a whole class). Each student receives someone else's quickwrite, reads the initial thinking, and then has two minutes to continue writing on the topic. The process is repeated until each student has responded to a number of papers. This activity encourages students to extend their thinking through both the written responses they produce and through the written responses they read.

Conversation Logs I mentioned this strategy in my previous book *Deeper Reading*, and it bears repeating here. It is an excellent strategy to help students

Teaching Adolescent Writers

> All I know is that the kids are in training right now (while they're young) So they probably get away w/ things. But I'm pritty sure that once they're old enough, they'll get the same treatment. I don't know what "Newsthink" is, but doublethink is when one argues w/ one's self about a beleif. I wonder, Can People move out? Why don't they do something about their situation? ♡ Per. 2 ━ ★
>
> Im in the same boat, what is "Newspeak? I have many questions too. Whats the deal with the coupons, did they have to earn them? Was there a certain amount they could have? If they had none, what would they have done? Plus In Chp 3 was
>
> it really mandatory to exercise? Does anyone have a choice? If so, what would have happened to Winston if he just felt tired and gave up or passed out? Other than that what trully happened to his family, did he even have a sister? 4/5/06 Per5
>
> 4/11/06, per 1
>
> To answer per. 2s, I think people are scared to try to do something about their situation. Everyone seems to be stupid & they just lister to everything Big Brother tells them. About the coupons they don't have to earn them they get it every time a month. yes, it's mandatory for them to exercise. In ch 6, I think it's so disgusting that he had sex with a 50 year old woman who didn't have teeth. what did you guys think about it?
>
> Love, per 1

Figure 2.4 *Conversation log pages*

extend their thinking through writing. Let's say, for illustrative purposes, that three of my classes—periods one, two, and three—are studying the same unit. For this activity I provide one set of composition books and number them. I then assign a number to each student in each class that corresponds with the number on one of the logs. As a result, each log is assigned to one student from first period, one student from second period, and one student from third period. Three different students will alternate writing in the same log. They are not allowed to put their names in the logs or to identify themselves in any way. This allows sets of students to explore their thinking anonymously with one another through daily written entries in their Conversation Logs. See Figure 2.4 for an excerpt from a conversation log between Leana, Brenda, and Peter.

Weekly Writing: The Writer's Notebook

If a painter needs an easel to play with painting, and a basketball player needs a gym to play with the basketball, then it reasons that writers—especially developing writers—need a place to play with writing. In my class the place to play with writing is the writer's notebook.

Students who do not write on a regular basis run the risk of being trampled by the literacy stampede. With this in mind, I require each student of mine to write regularly in a writer's notebook. At the beginning of the school year each student brings a spiral notebook to class (minimum 200 pages), and

I have the students number the pages. After the pages are numbered, I give students sticky notes to serve as tabs and I have them block out sections of their notebooks as follows:

Pages	Section Title	Purpose
1–3	Table of Contents	Students keep track of all mini-lessons taught so they can refer to them at a glance.
4–10	What Should I Write?	In this section students leave pages where we will do a number of brainstorming activities for those times when they claim they have nothing to write. Many of these brainstorming activities are listed in Chapter 5.
10–12	Writing/Literary Terms	These pages are where students write key writing and literary terms and their definitions. If they forget what "discourse" or "irony" means, for example, they refer to these pages. These terms are gradually added as we progress through the year.
13	Spelling Demons	Students keep these pages open to track their personal spelling demons (more on this in Chapter 7).
14–40	Craft	This section is reserved for "craft" mini-lessons. "Craft" is defined as those things good writers do (e.g., writing an effective introduction or combining sentences to gain more rhythm).
41–65	Editing	This section is reserved for editing mini-lessons. Editing lessons focus on mistakes writers make (e.g., run-on sentences or improper citations).
66+	Writing	This is the heart of the writer's notebook. Much like the artist's easel or the hoopster's gym, this is where the writer plays with writing on a daily basis.

Once the writer's notebooks are set up, I spend a couple of days helping students brainstorm some topics that they might be interested in exploring. (See Chapter 5 for a number of strategies to help students get started with daily writing and for details on moving students into writing in various discourses.) As we begin the year students are given some choice of writing topics; as the year progresses students are directed to write in specific discourses, which, in turn, help prepare my students for the SAT as well as for mandated state exams.

By the second week of school we are off and running with the writer's notebooks, and students are asked to produce a minimum of five pages of writing a week. These five weekly pages are *in addition* to the regularly assigned writing both inside and outside of class. From the get-go I want students to roll up their sleeves and have a place where they can regularly practice their writing.

For more in-depth discussion of the writer's notebook, I recommend Aimee Buckner's *Notebook Know-How* (2005).

Regularly Scheduled Writing: The ABCs (and D) of On-Demand Writing

As stated earlier in this chapter, students, on the average, are spending only 15 percent of their school time actually writing. That 15 percent includes all the various modes of writing that students are asked to do in a given school day (e.g., quickwrites, logs, journals, process papers). If all of these types of writing are included in the 15 percent figure, then we can reasonably infer that students are being given very little, if any, time on the one writing skill that may prove to be the most important of all: on-demand writing. Why is it crucial for our students to develop their ability to write on demand? Consider the following:

- Many state-mandated assessments now require students to produce on-demand writing. In California, for example, students are required to write an essay to pass the High School Exit Exam. Other states have, or are adopting, similar requirements.
- The new SAT has a written section. Students are required to produce an on-demand writing sample.
- Students who are university-bound sometimes take Advanced Placement exams. Nearly every one of these exams requires students to write on demand.
- Many employers are now asking for writing samples as part of the interview process. Why? Because they are finding huge writing deficiencies in their workforce. Today, 40 percent of firms "offer or require training for salaried employees with writing deficiencies. Based on survey responses, it appears that remedying deficiencies in writing may cost American firms as much as $3.1 billion annually." One executive reported sending between 200–300 people annually for writing training. Students who write well will have a leg up on the competition when it comes to applying for career jobs (National Commission on Writing 2004a, p. 1).

Writing on demand has become a gate-keeping issue. Students taught to write well have the key to unlock gates to better opportunities. Students who do not write well on demand risk being locked out.

Many of the skills needed to perform well when someone hands you a prompt and says, "Go," differ from those skills needed to do well on a multidraft process paper. To help students internalize on-demand writing skills, I teach my students the ABCs (and D):

Attack the prompt
Brainstorm possible answers
Choose the order of your response
Detect errors before turning the draft in

Let's look at each of these stages and how they help students write better when confronted with on-demand writing tasks.

Attack the Prompt
Here's a prompt found on a recent high school exit exam:

By the time students enter high school, they have learned about many moments in history that have influenced our world today. Think about a moment in history you studied and consider its importance.

Write a composition in which you discuss a moment in history. Share its importance in today's world. Be sure to support the moment with details and examples.

If students do not know how to attack a prompt, they may find themselves distracted by the verbiage. The above prompt, for example, is in two parts. Students need to recognize that the first half is essentially a warm-up, and that the actual writing prompt is to be found in the second part.

Once I clarify this, I have students attack the prompt. Here are the steps to attacking the prompt:

1. Cross out the words "Write a composition" in the prompt. We do not need these words because we already know our purpose for being here. Crossing these words out helps us prune the prompt, thus reducing the chances of becoming distracted.

2. Circle any word that asks you to do something. (In this prompt students would circle "discuss," "share," and "support." This immediately reinforces the notion that the prompt is asking for three things, not just one. This helps to avoid the problem some students have when they only partially answer the prompt.)

3. Draw an arrow from each circled word (those words that tell you to do something) to what it specifically tells you to do. (For example, students should draw an arrow from the word "discuss" to the words "moment in history."

4. Under the prompt, rewrite and number the circled words. Next to each word, rewrite what the word asks you to do. This now serves as your prompt—there is no need to look at the entire prompt anymore.

After attacking the "moment in history" prompt, Erika rewrote it in a simpler form (see Figure 2.5).

Students cannot answer a prompt if they don't understand the prompt in its entirety. I give students repeated practice in attacking prompts until they can demonstrate they understand all facets of the question. With practice, they can do this in under two minutes.

Brainstorm Possible Answers

Recognizing that the prompt was asking her to do three things, Erika began her mapping by brainstorming in the same order she numbered the prompt when she attacked it. She started by brainstorming moments in history. In Figure 2.6, you'll see that in a one-minute brainstorm she generated the following topics: the September 11 attacks, the Holocaust, the Declaration of Independence, the Iraq War, and World War II. After completing this brainstorm, Erika selected a

Teaching Adolescent Writers

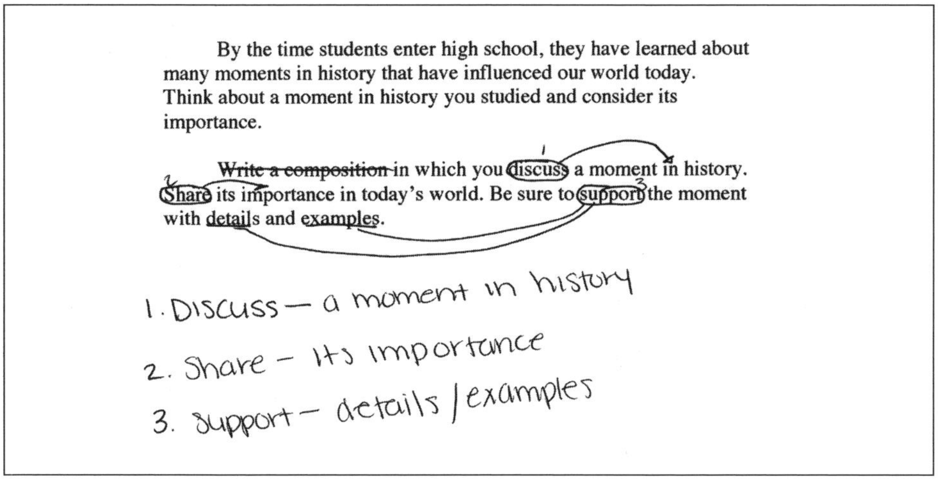

Figure 2.5 *Attack the prompt*

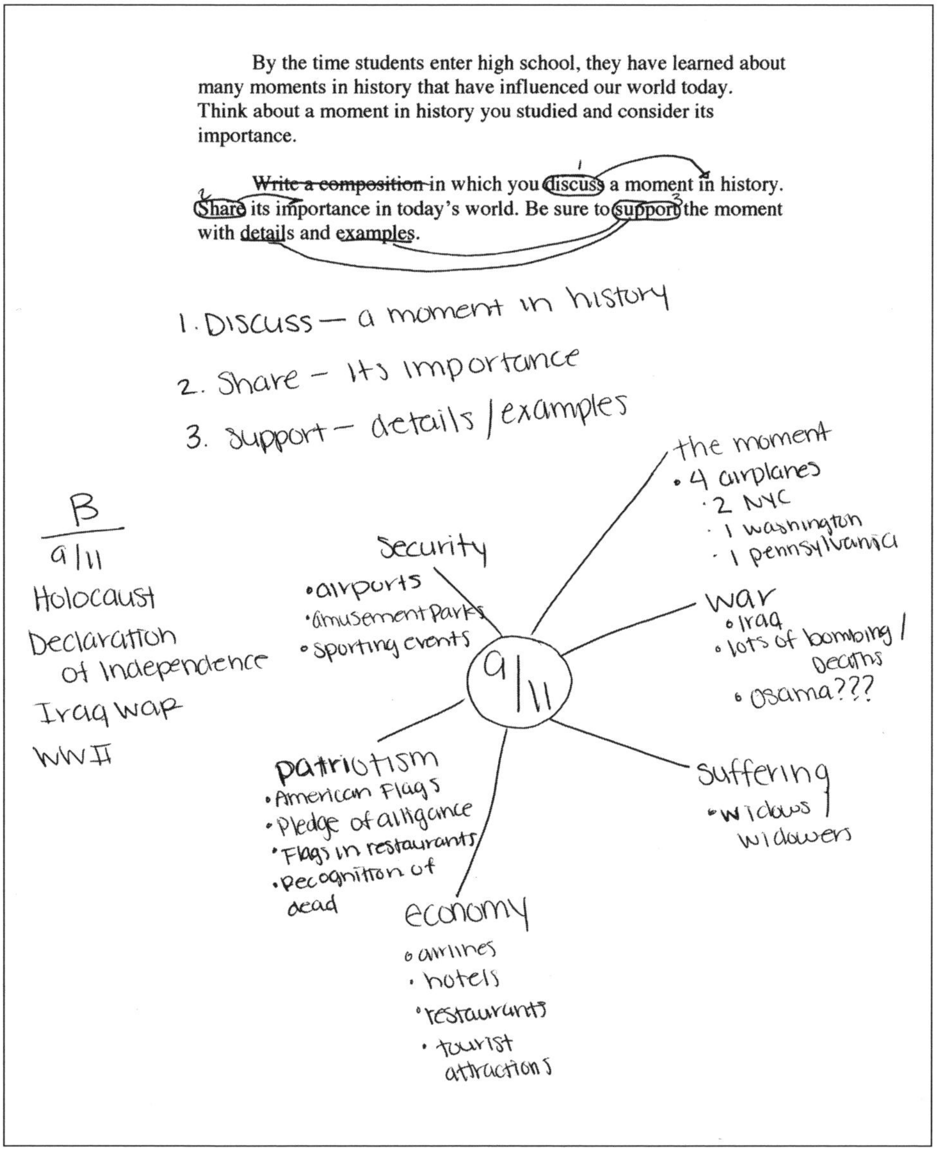

By the time students enter high school, they have learned about many moments in history that have influenced our world today. Think about a moment in history you studied and consider its importance.

Write a composition in which you discuss a moment in history. Share its importance in today's world. Be sure to support the moment with details and examples.

1. DISCUSS — a moment in history
2. Share — Its importance
3. Support — details / examples

Figure 2.6 *Brainstorm—9/11 with specific examples for each importance*

By the time students enter high school, they have learned about many moments in history that have influenced our world today. Think about a moment in history you studied and consider its importance.

Write a composition in which you discuss a moment in history. Share its importance in today's world. Be sure to support the moment with details and examples.

1. DISCUSS — a moment in history
2. Share — Its importance
3. Support — details / examples

B
9/11
Holocaust
Declaration of Independence
Iraq War
WWII

9/11

the moment
• 4 airplanes
• 2 NYC
• 1 washington
• 1 pennsylvania

war
• Iraq
• lots of bombing / deaths
• Osama???

suffering
• widows / widowers

Security
• airports
• amusement parks
• sporting events

patriotism
• American Flags
• pledge of alligance
• Flags in restaurants
• Recognition of dead

economy
• airlines
• hotels
• restaurants
• tourist attractions

Figure 2.7 *Choose the order of the response*

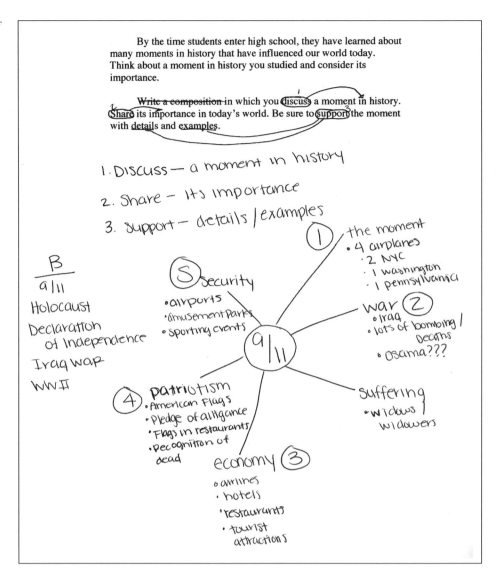

moment to write about (in this example, she chose the September 11 attacks). After choosing her topic, Erika began brainstorming the second layer of the prompt—why this event is still important today. Erika was then ready for the third layer of her brainstorm: adding supporting details to illustrate why this event is still important today.

With practice, students can complete these three layers of brainstorming in five minutes. Upon completion of the brainstorming phase, it's time to move on to "C," choosing the order of the response.

Choose the Order of Your Response

When I am driving in unfamiliar territory, it helps quite a bit to have a map. Having a map also helps students to negotiate their way through on-demand essays. How many times have you seen a student tear into writing an essay only to stop halfway through as she becomes unsure of which way to go? Or worse, how many times have you seen her start backtracking by crossing sections out or drawing arrows because she has decided to reverse directions midstream? This is far more likely to occur to a student who has begun her writing journey without a clear map of where she is going.

Students write better in an on-demand setting if they first take a few minutes to chart their courses. To help students create a map before writing, I ask them to revisit their brainstorms and choose the order of their responses. This not only means that students have to decide what goes first, what goes second, and so on, it also means they have to decide what parts of their brainstorm get cut and do not make it into the draft. I have students place numbers within their brainstorms to mark what they will write about first, second, and third, etc., and I have them cross out parts that don't make the cut. See Figure 2.7 for the order Erika chose for her essay.

Erika spent six minutes completing the ABCs of on-demand writing before beginning her essay. She now knows where she is going and is ready to thoroughly answer the question.

I start teaching my students the ABCs of on-demand writing very early in the school year. For the first quarter, my students do not actually write any on-demand essays; they practice only their prewriting—their ABCs. I start with teaching only the "A" step (attacking the prompt). I will give them opportunities to practice this skill until I feel most of my class are ready to move on. I then have my students practice both "A" (attacking) and "B" (brainstorming). When I feel that most of the class can complete these two steps, I add "C" (choosing the order). Being able to do A and B and C in a reasonable amount of time generally occurs somewhere near the end of the first quarter. Thus, the teaching of on-demand writing in my classroom is scheduled as follows:

Quarter I	Quarters 2–4
Students are given repeated practice with completing the ABCs of on-demand writing. By the end of the first quarter students will be expected to complete A, B, and C on a prompt in approximately seven minutes. They have not yet started actually writing on-demand essays.	Once students have the ABCs down, they are given an on-demand writing prompt every third Friday. At this pace every student will have written approximately ten on-demand essays using the ABC format by the end of the school year.

See Appendix 4 for twenty-five practice prompts I use to help students master the ABC steps.

Once students actually start writing the essays, it's time to introduce them to the last step in the process.

Detect Errors Before Turning the Draft In

It never ceases to amaze me that some students will spend forty-five minutes writing essays, but will not take one minute to reread them before handing them in. It's as if their papers have gathered radioactivity while they wrote them, and the minute they finish they *must get them off their desks.*

My students, especially the reluctant writers, must be taught that there is real value in revisiting their pieces before turning them in. Even the best writers make errors when completing on-demand writing tasks, and it is during the rereading of the papers that writers often uncover silly mistakes. I do not expect my students to write mistake-free essays in on-demand writing situations; I do, however, expect them to reread their essays carefully before turning them in, in order to detect at least some of their first-draft errors.

Final Thoughts

I began this chapter with Donald Graves' caution that if students don't write at least three times a week they are dead. Graves' warning echoes the research that strongly suggests that before our students are put into the "game" of writing, they need lots of practice playing developing their writing skills. We can provide practice in a number of ways, including daily in-class writing activities, weekly writing in writer's notebooks, and regularly scheduled on-demand writing. As it stands now, students are not getting the amount of writing practice they need to develop into effective writers. We must commit to giving writing its proper place in the classroom.

Once we make the decision to increase the amount of time and attention given to our students' writing practice, it becomes time to look at the second pillar of building young writers—the importance the teacher plays as a writing model.

Beyond the Grecian Urn: The Teacher as a Writing Model

Yesterday got off to a bad start. I was about to sit down for my morning bowl of cereal when I opened the refrigerator and found an unpleasant surprise. Overnight, the refrigerator's thermostat had gone haywire and all of my breakfast staples—milk, orange juice, strawberries—had frozen solid.

When the repairman arrived this morning, he was accompanied by a trainee. As the experienced repairman diagnosed the problem and fixed the thermostat, he stopped and demonstrated each step of that process to the rookie. I later learned that this was not the trainee's first day. Before being sent into the field, he had taken a basic training class. Having passed the class, he was now spending six weeks in the field learning firsthand from an experienced repairman before being allowed to answer calls on his own.

After the refrigerator was repaired, my wife, Kristin, and I went to a local restaurant for lunch. When the waitress took our order, we noticed that another waitress was shadowing her. It turns out that the waitress who greeted us was experienced, and she was training the new hire how to properly take an order. Over a week's time, the new waitress would gradually take over.

While eating lunch, Kristin, a freelance writer who regularly writes for a large automaker's in-house magazine, told me she was writing an article on what it takes to become an auto mechanic. She had learned that before becoming a certified auto mechanic, employees start by taking basic classes. Once they pass their classes, new mechanics work alongside master mechanics for an extended internship. Though the classes taken prior to the internship are helpful, she was told by a number of new mechanics she interviewed that it was seeing the master mechanics diagnose and repair problems that had best prepared them. This is why new mechanics are not awarded their own service bays until they have spent extended time watching the master mechanics doing repair demonstrations.

As the day unfolded I began to see a theme developing. In all three of these learning situations—involving the refrigerator repairman, the waitress, and the auto mechanic—the person learning the new skill benefited greatly by having the skill modeled by an expert. All three of them learned from somebody who didn't just tell them how to do the new skill, but who also *demonstrated* the new skill.

Reflecting on the importance an apprenticeship plays in the learning process reminds me of what the writer Ann Berthoff once said: "We aren't born knowing how to write, but we are born knowing how to know how." This chapter is built on the premise that when it comes to writing, the best way to know how to know how is by *seeing* the writing process consistently modeled by the best writer in that classroom—the teacher. Telling the students what constitutes good writing is not enough. As apprentices, students must see the process in action. Much like the new auto mechanic, our students need to see how the work is done "in the field." They don't need a teacher who assigns writing; they need a teacher who demonstrates what good writers do.

When the teacher becomes a writing model by actually writing alongside the students, many benefits, for both teachers and students, emerge:

Why Teachers Should Write Alongside Their Students	
Benefits to Teachers	**Benefits to Students**
Teachers better understand the writing task when they do it themselves. There is no substitute for doing when it comes to understanding.	Students will better understand the task at hand when the teacher better understands the task at hand.
Teachers, when they write, uncover the hard parts and are thus better able to see which mini-lessons will most benefit their students. Writing done by the teacher drives better instruction.	Students receive better instruction from focused, meaningful mini-lessons.
Teachers can model that writing is challenging. This demonstrates to students that good writing is almost always the product of multiple revisions.	Students see the teacher struggle with the complexity and chaos of writing. This helps demystify the writing process. Students no longer maintain the false impression that good writing just flows at will.
Teachers who complete a specific writing task develop a clearer sense of how to assess that writing task.	When the assessment is clearer to the teacher, students gain a better understanding of how the writing will be assessed. This, in turn, drives better writing.

It has been my experience that my students write better when I roll up my sleeves and write alongside them. With this in mind, this chapter will focus on specific modeling strategies teachers can use to help students internalize the things good writers do. It might be helpful to break these strategies into two categories: (1) modeling strategies teachers can use to promote better first-draft writing, and (2) modeling strategies teachers can use to help drive better revision.

Modeling Strategies That Promote Better First-Draft Writing

For many of my students, getting started is the hardest part of composing. Why? Because writing is hard, and beginning a writing task creates a formidable cognitive hurdle for inexperienced or reluctant writers. Unfortunately, many students continue year in and year out with the mistaken notion that writing is easy for some and difficult for others (generally speaking, they think writing is easy for the teacher and difficult for the students). My guess is that they have reached this erroneous conclusion primarily due to one of two reasons:

1. They have teachers who do not actively write. As a result, these teachers may have forgotten how hard they themselves struggled as developing writers. When teachers do not write, students lose the opportunity to see adults successfully struggle through the writing process.

or

2. They have teachers who do actively write but who have become expert at hiding the work it takes from their students. Often when teachers share their own writing, it is only after extensive revising and polishing that has been done out of the sight of the students.

Students' anxiety is reduced when they come to understand that everyone—students, teachers, professional writers—has to work hard when they sit down to write. Even Stephen King, one of the most prolific writers working today, has to fight self-doubt when he sits down to write, as he recounts in *On Writing*:

With the door shut, downloading what's in my head directly to the page, I write as fast as I can and still remain comfortable. Writing fiction, especially a long work of fiction, can be a difficult, lonely job; it's like crossing the Atlantic Ocean in a bathtub. There's plenty of opportunity for self-doubt. If I write rapidly, putting down my story exactly as it comes into my mind, only looking back to check the names of my characters and the relevant parts of their back stories,

I find that I can keep up with my original enthusiasm and at the same time outrun the self-doubt that's always waiting to settle in. (2000, p. 209)

Rather than hide the fact that writing is a constant struggle against the "self-doubt" King refers to, teachers serve their students better when they reveal their own writing doubts. What better way to model how to handle these doubts and the various challenges of writing than to compose in front of the students? Though students already know that writing is hard, they do not realize that more experienced writers often struggle as much as they do. Our students stand a greater chance of internalizing and embracing the complexity of writing when they see their teachers struggle to internalize and embrace the complexity of writing.

Beyond the notion that writing is hard, a second reason surfaces to explain why my students have a difficult time diving into a first draft: they are often afraid their writing will be lousy. Writing is personal and risky, and many of my students are paralyzed by the notion that the writing they produce will be sub-par (especially when it comes to sharing their writing with their teacher and peers). They often feel they have nothing interesting to say, or if they do have an idea, they are unsure how to get it down on paper. My response to students faced with writing apprehension is simple and straightforward: Join the crowd.

Students do not understand that most first-draft writing, *for everyone*, is lousy. But a good writer recognizes that a lot of lousy first-draft writing must be done before better writing can occur. To help get students over the fear of failure, I begin our writing year by sharing the following poem:

Don't Be Afraid to Fail
Author unknown

You've failed many times,
although you may not
remember.
You fell down
the first time
you tried to walk.
You almost drowned
the first time
you tried to
swim, didn't you?
Did you hit the
ball the first time
you swung a bat?
Heavy hitters,
the ones who hit the most home runs,
also strike

out a lot.
English novelist
John Creasey got
752 rejection slips
before he published
564 books.
Babe Ruth struck out
1,330 times,
but he also hit 714 home runs.
Don't worry about failure.
Worry about the
chances you miss
when you don't
even try.

After sharing the poem I remind my students that Peter Elbow (1998) once said a person's best writing is often mixed up with his worst. I tell them it is a requirement in my class to produce a lot of bad writing. From bad writing, I tell them, the seeds of good writing will eventually grow. Bad writing is necessary before good writing emerges. To better encourage them to take risks in first-draft writing and to understand that first- and second-draft writing are not the same thing, I share with them the chart depicted in Figure 3.1.

This chart, developed by my friend and mentor Mary K. Healy, who was an early leader in the Bay Area Writing Project, reinforces the idea that before writers can get it right they first have to get it down. Ralph Fletcher, in *What a Writer Needs* (1993), calls getting the first draft down "the sneeze." He encourages students to blast out their thoughts without fear of how the writing will turn out. Once students recognize that first-draft writing is tentative and exploratory in nature, their trepidations begin to dissipate. This is the first step in breaking down their reticence.

Figure 3.1 *MK's first- vs. second-draft comparison chart*

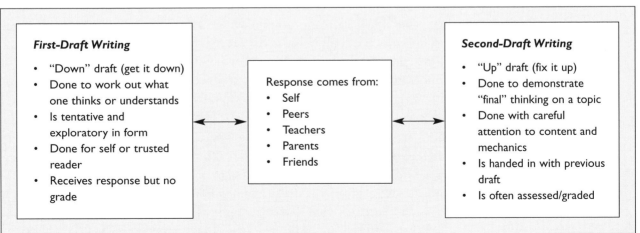

First-Draft Writing
- "Down" draft (get it down)
- Done to work out what one thinks or understands
- Is tentative and exploratory in form
- Done for self or trusted reader
- Receives response but no grade

Response comes from:
- Self
- Peers
- Teachers
- Parents
- Friends

Second-Draft Writing
- "Up" draft (fix it up)
- Done to demonstrate "final" thinking on a topic
- Done with careful attention to content and mechanics
- Is handed in with previous draft
- Is often assessed/graded

Beyond getting students to embrace the difficulty of writing and helping them accept the notion that it's okay for first-draft writing to be lousy, here are five additional ideas to consider. When implemented, these ideas help lower student anxiety about first-draft writing.

1. Move Beyond the "Grecian Urn Approach"

I remember clearly the moment in my first year of teaching when I was preparing to assign my students an analytical essay on the novel they had just finished reading. Because this was the first big essay I was teaching, I felt unsure how to explain the assignment. When I shared my hesitance with the veteran teacher next door, she told me that my students would write better essays if I wrote a sample essay first—a model—and then shared it with them. This sounded reasonable to me, so the night before assigning the essay, I sat down at home and carefully wrote a draft. Because I wanted to make sure my students had a good model, I then spent some time revising it. And then I revised it a few more times. Since my writing would serve as THE MODEL, I wanted to make sure the students saw a highly polished final product—something to which, if they set their writing hearts to it, they could aspire.

Unfortunately, that's not how it turned out. My model seemed to scare my students away as much as it inspired better writing. I had succumbed to what Ron Strahl, the director of the South Basin Writing Project, calls the "Grecian Urn Approach." It's the idea that simply showing students a Grecian urn will be enough to inspire them to produce Grecian urns of their own. There is only one problem with the "Grecian Urn Approach": it doesn't work.

What I have now come to realize is that the value is not in showing my students the Grecian urn; the value is in showing them the process, step-by-step, that is used to construct the urn. When I brought in my model essay for my students, I was doing nothing more than showing them the Grecian urn. However, I had hidden from them the most valuable part—the steps, often torturous, I took to get to the polished product. I would have been better off helping my students to understand the process of writing by showing them the steps in my process. Modeling is particularly important in the first-draft stage, when reluctant writers are more likely to give writing a shot if they see that struggling with the complexity of the process is normal for all writers—even for their teacher. Handing out polished final drafts at the beginning of the school year does not sharpen my students' writing skills; the polishing of my students' writing begins when I explicitly write, step-by-step, alongside my students.

When I assign a complex writing task now, I write alongside my students. While I write, I project my work on a screen for all to see. I am fortunate enough to have a projection system that allows my writing (either handwritten or typed on a computer) to be projected on a large screen in front of the classroom. Before I had this system, I simply composed on transparencies on an overhead projector. When I write with my students, I demonstrate the messiness of first-draft writing by doing all the things writers do when they put their initial sneeze onto paper (e.g., stop and start, cross words out, consider different approaches). I think out loud as I begin composing and ask students to chart the number of decisions I make while writing my first paragraph. Most important, I model letting go of the idea that this first draft has to be the best thing I have ever written, reminding them constantly that lousy first-draft writing is a prerequisite for this class.

Instead of presenting my students with a polished, finished product, students are given an extensive look at the many steps that go into creating a polished, finished product. Rather than show them an urn, I show students the steps involved in creating the urn. There is a big difference between the two.

2. Adopt a 4:1 Grading Philosophy

Another way to encourage students to start writing is to let them know up front that you, the teacher, will not be grading everything they write. I cannot think of one approach more likely to freeze an adolescent writer in his tracks than knowing that whatever he puts down on paper will be scored. Imagine being a painter and every time you try a new medium or new brush stroke technique someone looms over you with a grade book. Imagine picking up a new musical instrument and every time you experimentally hit an incorrect note someone records your shortcomings. This approach is ridiculous. Every painter and every musician has good days and has bad days. This is true for writers as well—especially for those trying to gain a footing in the skill. In fact, going through numerous writing experiences, both good and bad, are prerequisites to elevating a novice's writing.

Students will become more open to writing when they know that not everything they will write will be scrutinized under the grading microscope. I will discuss assessment in greater detail in Chapter 7, but let me preview that chapter here by suggesting two guiding assessment philosophies in my classroom that encourage adolescents to start writing:

1. Students need coaches more than they need critics. As a result, I do not grade everything they write. As a general rule of thumb, students are asked to write four times more than I can physically assess. In the initial writing stages, I concentrate on being a coach, not a grader.
2. First drafts should not be graded. Outside of timed writing, I never grade first drafts. Students are given credit, not grades, for their effort in first drafts. Once they have written a number of different pieces, (usually between three and five), students select one of their pieces to move into the revision process. This paper will eventually be assessed at a determined point in the process—not always at the end. Sometimes, for example, I might stop the paper before it has gone completely through the process so that I can score the degree of revision; other times I will grade after the editing process.

Having students write more than I can grade gives them permission to write crummy first drafts; this, in turn, lowers their anxiety, freeing them up to get started. Again, tips on providing feedback that drives better writing will be discussed in greater detail in Chapter 7.

3. Talk the Paper Out

Sydney Sheldon, author of a number of very long best sellers, "writes" his novels by first dictating them into a tape recorder. When he is finished talking a novel out, he has the dictation typed up, and it is at this time that he begins his revision process. I think of Sheldon's process every time a student says to me, "I know what I want to say, but I don't know how to start writing it." At this point I encourage my students to verbalize their thinking, to talk out their essays. For some of my students it's easier to start talking the paper out than it is to start writing it.

At the beginning of the year I have every student talk out at least one paper, usually by asking them to tell an autobiographical story. I model this by first talking out my own story. As I talk, I model taking notes about the key points using the screen for everyone to see. I then pair students, and as one is talking out his or her story, the other takes careful notes. When the first student is finished talking, the partner hands over the notes. These notes serve as an outline for the first student's essay. The roles are then reversed.

After this assignment, students can sign out the classroom's handheld tape recorder if they have an easier time getting started by first dictating what it is they want to write.

4. Model How to Create a Map Before Writing

Similar to the way the ABC (and D) exercise (discussed in Chapter 2) helps a student chart her writing course for on-demand writing, taking time to map their thoughts will help many of my students to write better first drafts. To help facilitate this thinking process, I often provide students with various graphic organizers to help them with their mapping. In Figure 3.2, for example, you will see Katherine's writing map, created in response to the question, "Who shares responsibility for the deaths of Romeo and Juliet?" This map then becomes an outline for a literary analysis essay.

In Figure 3.3, you will find a graphic organizer completed by Beatriz when her ninth-grade class read *Animal Farm*. The class was asked, "Which animals played key roles in the liberties being lost on the farm?" In this particular organizer, Beatriz was asked to choose which animals were culpable and to support each choice with passages from the text. This organizer served as an outline for Beatriz's essay (after she had chosen the order of her response).

When my students take the time to organize their thoughts before writing, they almost always write more fluent first drafts.

Who is responsible for the deaths of Romeo and Juliet?

Name	Benvolio	Friar Laurence	Nurse	Paris	Apothecary	Old Man Capulet
Why Responsible?	Benvolio was always aware of the grudge between the Capulets and the Montagues. When he tryed to help Romeo he knew that it would cause problems if he took him to the Capulets party. He is responsible for taking Romeo to the party	Although it was an innocent act, he married Romeo and Juliet. •Helping Juliet out he gave her the idea to drink a potion that could help her fake her death. This idea lead Juliet and Romeo to kill each other.	The nurse is responsible because she knew too much and didn't tryed to stop it. She knew that Romeo was a montague and that all this doing was teenagers "hormones" thinking. She is not to blame for but is in a way responsible for the death of the youngians.	It wasnt his fault that he was in love with Juliet but after blowing his change to gain her love, Paris asks again for her hand in marriage to her father. If he would of gone himself and proposed to her personal things would of been difficult. But they wevent.	Not having any intention to hurt Romeo and Juliet he sold the potion to Romeo. He was in need of the money when he sold it, but he is responsible for the death of the two lovers.	In a way, old man capulet forced Juliet to use Friar Laurces plan. Old man capulet put her against the way when he said that she was to marry Parish or else she will be disowned. Juliet couldn't bare living without Romeo or being disowned by her family.
Textual evidence	Act I, scene II "At this ancient feast of capulets sups the fair Rosaline whom thou so lovest. With all the admired beauties of Verona : Go thrither, and with un attcaned eye .Compare her face with that I shall show, And I make thee think thy swan a crow"	Act II, IV "In one respect I'll thy respect assistant b Act II, VI "So smile the heavens upon this holy act, that after-hours with sorrow chide us not" Act IV, I "Hold daughter, I do spy a king of hope, which craves as desperate an execution" "A thing like death to chide away this shame, that coppest with death himself to scape from it, And thou darest t'll give thee remedy	Act I, V "His name is Romeo, and a Montague, the only son of your great enemy?" Act II, VI "Then hie you hence to friar Laurence cell. There stays a husben to make you a wife.	Act III, IV "Monday my lord" Act II "But now my lord what say you to my svit?" "Yonger than she are happy mothers made"	Act V, I "Such mortal drugs I have, but Mantuas Law is death to any he that utters them." "Put this liquid thing you will, And drink it off, and if you had the strength of twenty men, it would dispatch you straight."	Act III, IV "A quaint him have of my son Paris Love." Act III, V "To go with Paris to Saint Peter's church or I will drag thee on a hurdle. thither. Act. III, V "And that we have a curse in having her

Figure 3.2 *Student writing map: Who is responsible for R/J deaths?*

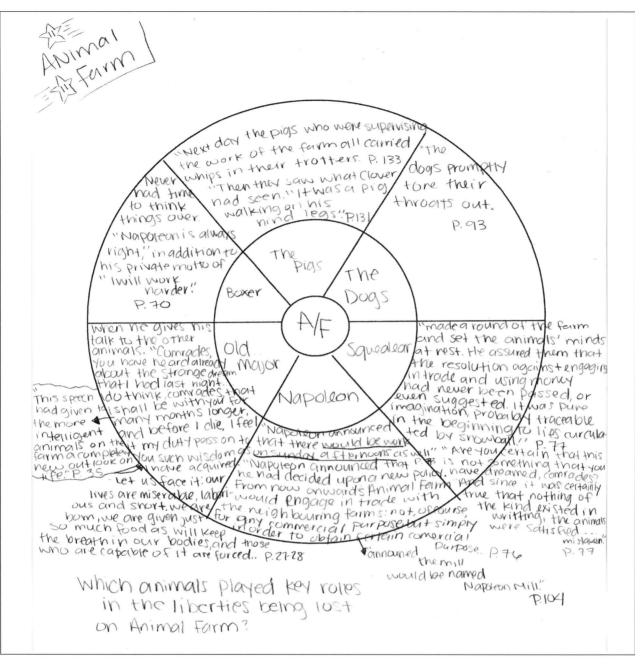

Figure 3.3 Animal Farm
target notes

It is important to note that I do not simply begin the year by handing these organizers to my students and asking them to complete them. When introducing them, I complete the organizers myself (as I, too, write the essay) so that they can hear the thinking that goes into creating effective writing maps.

5. Allow for Choice Within Given Topics or Discourses

Almost every state has writing standards that spell out which discourses students will be expected to write. One way to encourage students to begin writ-

Figure 3.4 *Iraq players chart*

Players in the Decision to Invade Iraq			
George W. Bush	Dick Cheney	Condoleeza Rice	Colin Powell
John Kerry	A U.S. infantryman	Saddam Hussein	Tony Blair
A store owner in Baghdad	An insurgent	French President Jacques Chirac	Al Gore
Richard Clarke	Saudi Arabian prince	Usama bin Ladin	Saudi oil baron

ing in these discourses is to give them choices *within* each discourse. For example, I recently visited a history class that had completed a unit titled, "Was the United States justified in invading Iraq?" The teacher had a list of "players" who held various opinions about America's involvement (see Figure 3.4). Students were asked to choose a player and to write a persuasive piece from the point of view of that person. Because they were given some choice, they were much more willing to invest the necessary time and effort into their papers. On the due date, students stood up and read their papers to the class from the point of view of the person they had chosen. It created quite an interesting oral collage of opinions.

Although the choice in the Iraq assignment was limited, it helped motivate students to begin writing. Additional ideas for giving students more open choices and for generating interesting writing topics will be discussed in detail in Chapter 5.

I have found these five steps ([1] moving beyond the Grecian urn, [2] adopting a 4:1 philosophy, [3] talking the paper out, [4] modeling map making, and [5] providing students with choices) helpful in getting students on track when faced with first-draft writing. Now let's turn our attention to modeling strategies that teachers can use to help drive better revision.

Modeling Strategies to Help Drive Better Revision

E. B. White once said, "The best writing is rewriting." Unfortunately, many of my students come to me with an "I wrote it once; I'm done" philosophy. I immediately start to break this notion down with an activity I learned from Patti Stock, the former director of the National Writing Project. Standing in front of the class, I tell students that when I say, "Go," I want them to observe my behavior carefully and continue to do so until I say the word "Stop." After I say, "Stop," they are to write one sentence describing what they have just witnessed. When the students are ready I pause in the doorway of the classroom, say, "Go," and then stride across the classroom and sit down in my chair. Once seated, I say, "Stop," and ask the students to write down their one-sentence observations.

When they finish writing, we snake around the room and each student reads his or her sentence aloud. This is always fun because in a room of thirty students, no two answers are the same. This establishes the idea that writing is artistic. I tell the students that if we all sat around and made ceramic pots, they would all be different as well, that each of us would put our own artistic touch to the pots. The same is true with writing, I tell them. Writing is artistic, and through this exercise I want them to see themselves as artists when they sit down to write.

After we share the sentences on the first day of this activity, I have students hold on to them until the second day. When they return on day two I have them take out their sentences and I do a mini-lesson on the importance of strong verbs. I share the sentence I wrote on day one: "The teacher walked across the room and sat in the chair." Then I revise my own sentence by making my verbs stronger: "The teacher strode across the room and plopped in his chair." By replacing weak verbs with strong verbs I elevated my sentence. I ask the students to consider revising to upgrade their verbs (which presents a great opportunity to introduce the thesaurus). When they have added strong verbs to their sentences, I tell them to hold on to their papers until day three. When the students return on day three I conduct a new mini-lesson (e.g., turning a simple sentence into a complex sentence) and have them revise their sentences again. I repeat this process for five days until each student has five rewrites. Here, for example, are Alex's five sentences:

> Monday: The teacher walked across the room and sat into the chair.
> Tuesday: The teacher sauntered across the room and sat into the chair.
> Wednesday: The teacher sauntered across the room and collapsed into the chair.
> Thursday: The teacher, Mr. Gallagher, sauntered across the room and collapsed into the chair.
> Friday: Tired and cranky, Mr. Gallagher sauntered across the room and collapsed into the chair.

This lesson only takes five minutes a day, but by the end of the first week I have established E. B. White's idea that the best writing is rewriting and that any student serious about creating worthwhile writing needs to understand the futility of an "I wrote it once; I'm done" mentality.

Pimp My Write

With the importance of rewriting established, I ask my students to write for fifteen minutes about something that bothers them. Below is my first-draft sneeze on this topic (written in front of the students):

Draft 1
The way some things are packaged bothers me. For example, it is physically impossible to open a pack of graham crackers without splitting the entire cello-

phane wrapper. I defy you to open a box of cereal without mangling the bag. Cheese-its? Forget opening those with your bare hands. But when it comes down to torturous packaging, one product hovers above all: the packaging of CDs. I hate CD packaging.

It wasn't always this difficult to listen to music. For those of us who grew up listening to records, we simply made a quick tear on the side of the album, and presto! In five seconds the record was in your hands, ready to be played. Today, you have a horrendous fight on your hands to get that little CD out of its packaging.

I am thoroughly convinced that the person who designed CD packaging also designed the bank vault at Fort Knox, where the nation's gold supply is kept. That's because I can't get to the CD—the packaging is impenetrable.

Pretty good job of modeling a lousy first draft, wouldn't you say? Before students start thinking about a second draft, I ask them how many of them seen the MTV show *Pimp My Ride*. (For the uninitiated, *Pimp My Ride* is a show in which someone who drives a junky car is chosen and their car is completely "pimped," or customized. The remodeling is often extreme. For example, one person, a surfer, had the trunk of his car fitted with a customized clothes dryer so as not to have to drive home in wet swimming trunks. The remodelers do not stop at customizing the trunk, however; they continue "pimping" the car until it is overhauled bumper to bumper.) Most of my students have seen this show, and it doesn't take much to get them to enthusiastically discuss their favorite episodes. They are amazed at how junky cars can be transformed into a beautiful new "whips."

I tell my students that we are going to start our own show, entitled *Pimp My Write*. Much like the artists who take a junky car and make it much better, we are going to do the same thing with our junky first drafts. Just as there are a number of ways of transforming a car, I tell them, there are an equal number of ways of transforming an essay. I place a crummy first draft of mine up on the screen so the entire class can see my "pimping" process, and as I begin my revision, I think aloud. During the think-aloud I make sure I alert the students to the four major ways a writer can transform an essay (dubbed "STAR" by Richard Cornwell, a colleague in the South Basin Writing Project):

Substitute
Take things out
Add
Rearrange

When introducing STAR, I had the class brainstorm specific actions a writer might undertake for each letter of the acronym. I helped them shape the language as we brainstormed, and we produced the following list:

S (Substitute)	T (Take things out)	A (Add)	R (Rearrange)
Replace: • overused words • weak verbs with strong verbs • weak adjectives with strong adjectives • common nouns with proper nouns • "dead" words	Take out: • unnecessary repetitions • unimportant or irrelevant information • parts that might belong in another piece	Add: • detail • description • new information • figurative language • development • clarification of meanings • expanded ideas	Rearrange: • the sequence to produce a desired effect • the order for a more logical flow

With the steps of STAR in mind and still in front of my students, I create a second draft of my CD essay, again thinking aloud, discussing my revision decisions. Here is the second draft of the CD essay:

Draft 2

The way some things are packaged irks me.

For example, it is physically impossible to open a pack of graham crackers without splitting the entire cellophane wrapper. I defy you to open a box of Life cereal without mangling the bag. Cheese-its? Forget it! You cannot open those with your bare hands unless you have been working out daily with The Rock and have been gulping a daily dose of Barry Bonds' steroids. But when it comes down to torturous packaging, one product wins the grand prize: CD packaging.

It is so hard to open a CD that I am thoroughly convinced that the person who designed CD packaging also designed the bank vault at Fort Knox, where the nation's gold supply is kept. That's because I can't get to the CD—the packaging is impenetrable.

It wasn't always this difficult to listen to music. For those of us who grew up listening to records, we simply made a quick tear on the side of the album, and presto!—in five seconds you were holding Led Zeppelin in your hands, ready to be played. Today, you have to have the patience of Mother Teresa to get that little CD out of its packaging. If you stick to it, you may finally get the CD out—the only problem is that by the time you finally get to the actual CD, chances are you will have aged so much that your musical tastes will have changed.

This second draft is an improvement on the first draft and models all four elements of revision: (1) substituting, (2) taking things out, (3) adding, and (4) rearranging. To help students see that I revised using all four elements, I distribute copies of both of my drafts. Through whole-class discussion, we review and mark up the draft, indicating specifically where I used each STAR element. Figure 3.5 depicts my draft after the class discussion. The handwritten letters show where each element of STAR was used.

Figure 3.5 *Students recognize STAR in my CD revision*

Mr. Gallagher's 1st draft	Mr. Gallagher's 2nd draft

The way some things are packaged bothers me. For example, it is physically impossible to open a pack of graham crackers without splitting the entire cellophane wrapper. I defy you to open a box of cereal without mangling the bag. Cheese-its? Forget opening those with your bare hands. But when it comes down to torturous packaging, one product hovers above all: the packaging of CDs. I hate CD packaging.
 	
    It wasn't always this difficult to listen to music. For those of us who grew up listening to records, we simply made a quick tear on the side of the album, and presto! In five seconds the record was in your hands, ready to be played. Today, you have a horrendous fight on your hands to get that little CD out of its packaging.
 	
    I am thoroughly convinced that the person who designed CD packaging also designed the bank vault at Fort Knox, where the nation's gold supply is kept. That's because I can't get to the CD---the packaging is impenetrable.
	The way some things are packaged irks me.
	    For example, it is physically impossible to open a pack of graham crackers without splitting the entire cellophane wrapper. I defy you to open a box of Life cereal without mangling the bag. Cheese-its? Forget it! You cannot open those with your bare hands, unless you have been working out daily with The Rock and have been gulping a daily dose of Barry Bonds' steroids. But when it comes down to torturous packaging, one product wins the grand prize: CD packaging.
	    It is so hard to open a CD that I am thoroughly convinced that the person who designed CD packaging also designed the bank vault at Fort Knox, where the nation's gold supply is kept. That's because I can't get to the CD---the packaging is impenetrable.
	    It wasn't always this difficult to listen to music. For those of us who grew up listening to records, we simply made a quick tear on the side of the album, and presto! ---in five seconds you were holding Led Zeppelin in your hands, ready to be played. Today, you have to have the patience of Mother Theresa to get that little CD out of its packaging. If you stick to it, you may finally get the CD out---the only problem is that by the time you finally get to the actual CD, chances are you will have aged so much that your musical tastes will have changed.

After I have modeled this process, I ask the students to use the same process. I pass back their first drafts written about something that bothers them and ask them to "make them better." For many students, "make them better" is often interpreted as recopying them neatly or typing them up. I caution them not to make this mistake by explaining that making your paper better is not the same thing as making it correct. I tell them, "We will work on correctness later. Right now I want you to revise your paper, like I did. When you finish your second draft, you should be able to point to specific places in your essay that show how your second draft is better than your first. The 'stuff' of your second-draft essay should be better than what is found in your first draft. When you lay your second draft down next to your first draft, you should be able to show the reader where your paper has *moved.* Your second draft should move away from your first draft in a way that makes it better. As

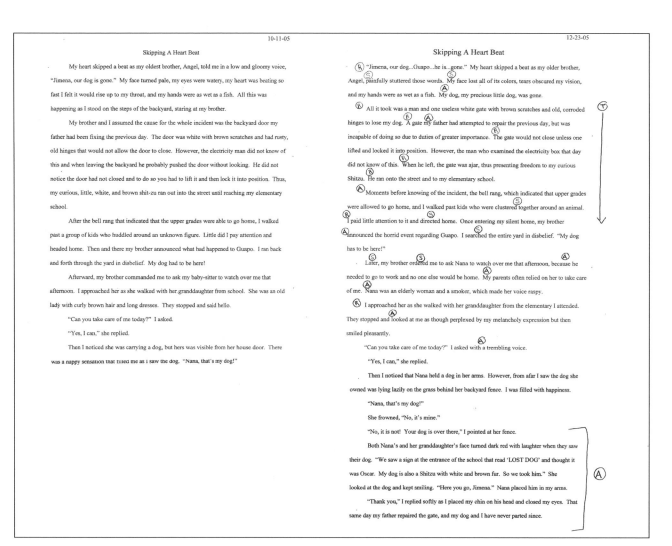

Figure 3.6 *Students identify STAR in their own revision (Portfolio)*

you revise, consider the four things good writers do (STAR) when they rewrite."

After students have written second drafts, I have them repeat the process that they had done earlier with my model. They lay their two drafts next to each other and indicate which STAR steps they employed to improve their initial drafts. In Figure 3.6 you will see a first and second draft written by Jimena, a freshman, and her markings of the four STAR elements she used while moving her first draft through revision.

Surface Versus Deep Revision

When students understand the importance of revision and the elements involved in moving an initial draft to a better place, I use the *Pimp My Ride* metaphor again to introduce the idea that within the STAR framework, there are two levels of revision—surface revision and deep revision. When overhauling a car, there are surface-level improvements and deep-level improvements:

Surface-Level Improvements as Seen on *Pimp My Ride*

- Giving the car a new paint job
- Reupholstering the ceiling lining
- Replacing the tires

Deep-Level Improvements as Seen on *Pimp My Ride*

- Ripping out the back seats and replacing them with a movie projection system
- Putting a more powerful engine in the car
- Outfitting the car with hydraulics

We can make these same levels of improvement with our writing. I introduce this concept by sharing the following chart:

Levels of Revision	
Surface	*Deep*
Changing a	Changing the
• word	• focus of the piece
• phrase	• purpose of the piece
• sentence	• sequence of the piece
	• discourse
	• point of view

I then bring out my two drafts of the CD packaging essay and as a class we examine my revisions through a new lens by asking ourselves which revisions were surface and which revisions were deep. I record their responses on a t-chart up on the screen. An example of a class chart follows:

Examples of Surface Revision in the CD Essay	Examples of Deep Revision in the CD Essay
Substituted words • "bothers" became "irked"	Isolated the first sentence into its own paragraph for effect.
Took things out • removed the sentence: "I hate CD packaging."	Added significant development, moving the piece from two paragraphs to three.
Added details • Life cereal • The Rock/Barry Bonds' steroids • Led Zeppelin	Rearranged the sequence of the piece, moving paragraph two in the first draft to the last paragraph in draft two.
Rearranged sentences • combined two sentences to create the following sentence: "You cannot open those with your bare hands unless you have been working out with The Rock and have been gulping a daily dose of Barry Bonds' steroids."	

Students are then asked to revisit their own drafts and chart the levels of their own revisions. In Figure 3.7 you will see Jimena's reflection on her levels of revision.

Figure 3.7 *Student identifies own surface versus deep revision*

Surface Revision	Deeper Revision
Substitute	**Re-arrange**
• My face lost all its colors	• Completely re-wrote the introduction.
• painfully stuttered those words	• Moved some writing from paragraph four and created a new paragraph (see paragraph five).
• Kids who were clustered together around an animal	• Added more dialogue (see second page of essay).
• I searched the entire yard in disbelief.	• Added more details to the end of the essay. (see after, " Mana, thats my dog!")
Add	
• Added a new sentence to the forth paragraph.	
Take Out	
• Took out one sentence from introduction.	
• Took out words here and there. (Ex: "little" in paragraph two)	

Let's conclude this chapter with specific classroom strategies I have found helpful in moving students through both surface revisions and deep revisions. Here are four strategies that promote better surface revision.

Surface Revision Through Sentence Branching

Many first-draft papers have a lack of rhythm. I will often read papers that have the same monotonous structure: Six words, period. Eight words, period. Six words, period. Seven words, period. With such a lack of sentence variety, a droning sensation sets in.

To get more sophisticated sentence variety from students, I teach them the three places a sentence can be branched: front, middle, and end. Take the following simple sentence, for example:

I drove my car to the beach.

By adding blank lines to indicate the branches, I show my students visually where each of the three branches my be added to this sentence:

_____, I drove my car to the beach.
I drove my car, _____, to the beach.
I drove my car to the beach, _____.

Teaching Adolescent Writers

Taking each sentence, I have the class brainstorm possible front, middle, and end branches. For example:

Front branch:
Hurriedly, I drove my car to the beach.
After getting off work, I drove my car to the beach.
With my girlfriend sitting next to me, I drove my car to the beach.

Middle branch:
I drove my car, radio blasting, to the beach
I drove my car, a '68 Chevy, to the beach.
I drove my car, without a driver's license, to the beach.

End branch:
I drove my car to the beach, hoping to find a good parking spot.
I drove my car to the beach, unaware of the policeman behind me.
I drove my car to the beach, praying the waves would be good.

To introduce this strategy in a longer piece of writing, I put up a first draft of my writing on the overhead and have the students identify the simple sentences. (To help this process I pick a draft where I have intentionally written many simple sentences.) We pick a sentence in the sample draft and I begin molding it in front of the class, connecting various branches to see what effects they create. After turning simple sentences into sentences that contain various branches, I have students revisit their second drafts and highlight their simple sentences. This gives them an instant visual of what kind of sentence variety they have (or don't have) in their papers. They then begin creating more sophisticated sentences in their own drafts.

In *Image Grammar,* Harry Noden identifies a number of ways to modify sentences. Playing off the metaphor of writers as artists, Noden identifies the following "brush strokes" as methods writers use to enliven sentences:

Brush Stroke	Basic Sentence	Revised with Brush Stroke
Paint with participles.	The player dribbled through the defense to make the winning basket.	Slicing and dicing, the player dribbled through the defense to make the winning basket.
Paint with absolutes (a two-word combination—a noun and an *ing* or *ed* verb).	The surfer braved the cold water.	Lips trembling, knees knocking, the surfer braved the cold water.
Paint with appositives (a noun that adds a second meaning to the preceding noun).	John surprisingly voted for the Republican candidate.	John, a Democrat, surprisingly voted for the Republican candidate.
Paint with adjectives shifted out of order.	The sleek, long, red automobile was beautiful.	The red automobile, sleek and long, was beautiful.

Adapted from Noden, H. Image Grammar. *1999.*

Surface Revision Through Elimination of Some "Be" Verbs

It's a cliché, but it's true: weak verbs drive weak sentences. Conversely, strong verbs drive strong sentences. One way to improve student drafts instantly is by having them replace weak verbs with stronger verbs. When I introduce this idea I start with the "be" verbs:

be
being
is
am
are
was
were

Considering the following sentence and its revision:

The clouds were in the sky.
The clouds hung in the sky.

Replacing the "be" verb ("was") with a stronger verb ("hung") instantly elevates this sentence. Using a stronger verb also drives the revision to produce a more active sentence.

I begin by having students find the "be" verbs in a piece of my writing. After I model how to replace some of them with stronger verbs, I have students search out their "be" verbs in their first drafts and challenge them to replace some of them with stronger verbs.

Surface Revision Through Use of Synonyms for "Said"

When students use dialogue in their papers, they often lazily resort to the word "said" when it comes to attribution. Consider how the different attributions in the following sentences bring different shades of meaning into each sentence:

The man said, "I am next in line."
The man bellowed, "I am next in line."
The man whined, "I am next in line."
The man threatened, "I am next in line."
The man admonished, "I am next in line."

When dialogue is present, have students create different shades of meaning for "said." To find lists of synonyms, Google the phrase "synonyms for said."

Surface Revision Through Limiting Dead Words

Over the course of my years of teaching, I have generated a list of "dead" words—words that my students overuse to the point that they lose their meaning. Here is my dead word list:

good	very	thing(s)	really	a lot
etc.	gonna	got	kind of	like
so + well (at beginning of sentences)			totally	I think
I feel	I believe	in my opinion	in conclusion	
+	@	&	#	

For example, a student might write, "The pizza was good." I ask my students for suggestions to replace the dead word "good":

The pizza was scrumptious.
The pizza was delicious.
The pizza was mouth watering.
The pizza was delectable.
The pizza was fresh.

All of these sentences are improvements. If time permits, I might ask them to revisit the sentence again with a focus on replacing the "be" verb (e.g., "The pizza tasted fresh"), or have them revisit it again with sentence branching in mind (e.g., "The pizza, piping hot from the oven, tasted fresh" or "Piping hot from the oven, the pizza tasted fresh").

Replacing dead words in a second draft often raises the level of the paper. However, a word of caution: it is important that students not concern themselves with dead words during the initial drafting stage. To illustrate this, I show them a first draft of my writing that contains dead words. This is normal, I tell them. In fact, I add, I do not think about dead words while I am drafting because doing so inhibits my creativity and motivation. I have a strict rule: *Dead-word hunts are reserved for late drafts only.* I will not hunt for dead words in my own writing until after I have moved through a number of drafts. It is also important to note that dead words are always permissible in dialogue or in any piece where the writer is trying to capture the authenticity of speech.

Modeling Deep Revision

I begin nudging students toward deep revision after they gain confidence in surface revision strategies. Julie Lecesne-Switzer, a colleague in the South Basin Writing Project, discusses deep revision with her students in terms of the following priorities:

Priorities in Revision	
Content	What has the writer chosen to write about?
Elaboration	How has the writer expanded on the topic?
Organization	How has the writer organized the material?
Language Use	How has the writer used language?

The following sections describe four strategies that have proved helpful in getting students to revise with these priorities in mind.

Modeling Deep Revision by Changing the Content

One frequent problem with first-draft writing is that it is often too broad and unfocused. One remedy for this is to have students revise, as Ralph Fletcher suggests in *What a Writer Needs* (1993), with the intent of writing smaller. This does not mean reducing the size of your handwriting or font; writing smaller means focusing on and illuminating something small in the story as a means of helping the reader understand the big picture. To introduce this idea to my students, I share the following two pieces of writing about the September 11 attacks on the World Trade Center. I ask them to read the two pieces and tell me which one they feel is the better piece of writing:

Version One	Version Two
At 8:46 AM (local time), the terrorists piloted the first plane into the north tower of the World Trade Center in New York City. The huge twin towers (completed 1970–72) were designed by Minoru Yamasaki (1912–1986). At 1,368 ft (417 m) and 1,362 ft (415 m) tall, they were the world's tallest buildings until surpassed in 1973 by the Sears Towers in Chicago. The towers were notable for the relationship of their simple, light embellishment to their underlying structure. In 1993 a bomb planted by terrorists exploded in the underground garage, killing several people and injuring some 1,000. A much more massive attack occurred on Sept. 11, 2001, when first One World Trade Center and then Two World Trade Center were struck by hijacked commercial airliners deliberately flown into them. Shortly thereafter both of the heavily damaged towers, as well as adjacent buildings, collapsed into enormous piles of debris. The attacks—the deadliest terrorist assault in history—claimed the lives of some 2,800 victims. Thousands more were injured.	With Tommy Knox (who died in the World Trade Center) it was often the little things. The way he put toothpaste on his wife's toothbrush when he got up before her, almost every day. He'd leave it on the vanity ready for her before he left his home in Hoboken for his job as a broker at Cantor Fitzgerald. Or perhaps it was how he made the oldest gag in the book funny again. At weddings, parties, any place, really, he slapped in a set of grotesque false teeth and worked the room in his gregarious, antic style, which never failed to make everyone laugh. The youngest of six children, Mr. Knox, who was 31, was always the first to grab the attention of his siblings' 11 children at family get-togethers with a joke or some routine to keep them laughing. Or maybe it was the way he listened—attentive, alert, compassionate. "I guess it was all the little things," said his wife, Nancy Knox. "All these little, special things that made Tommy who he was and made us all love him."
Source: Encyclopedia Britannica Premium Service (2006)	*Source: New York Times (2003)*

The following is a transcript of an audiotaped discussion I had about the two pieces with my second-period class (I am KG):

KG: Why did you like the second piece better? Why is it more powerful?

Gerardo: It flows better and gives us a sense of what the people were actually like.

Brenda: Version one just describes what happened.

KG: How can version two be more powerful? Look at version one—2,800 people died! In version two, only one person died. How can that be more powerful?

Katherine: The second one gives you little details that make you care.

KG: Right. (*KG covers the essay so the students can no longer see it.*) Without looking at the second version, what detail sticks in your head about Tommy Knox?

Luis: He put toothpaste on his wife's toothbrush every day.

Linda: He made everybody laugh.

KG: How old was he?

Many students: Thirty-one.

KG: That's young, right? Maybe not by your standards, but by mine it is.

Students: (*laughter*)

KG: Notice how the small details carry more power than the large details. Small details make it personal. As you begin writing today, remember this. Try to write small whenever possible.

Once students understand the power of writing smaller, I have them choose a piece of their own writing they feel might be too broad. With the September 11 example in mind, I challenge them to write a "smaller" version of their piece. Additional discussion on moving students into more powerful, "smaller" writing is found in Chapter 5.

Modeling Deep Revision Through Elaboration: Creating a Question Flood

To help students who have written underdeveloped first drafts, I ask them to submit their papers to a *question flood*. I model a question flood, starting by showing students the following five-minute draft, which I have intentionally underwritten:

> *I have a really embarrassing story to tell you. I was on a television game show and I was playing for big money. At exactly the wrong moment, my brain froze. I said something really embarrassing, right in front of twenty million Americans (not to mention my fiancée, who was in the studio audience). Though it happened a long time ago, thinking about it today still causes me embarrassment.*

I place the draft on the overhead, and as a class, I have students brainstorm questions that have been left unanswered in my initial draft. In Figure 3.8, you can see that Alicia has flooded my paper with thirteen questions. Though I certainly will not respond to every single question written on my

Figure 3.8 *Question flood on my game show piece*

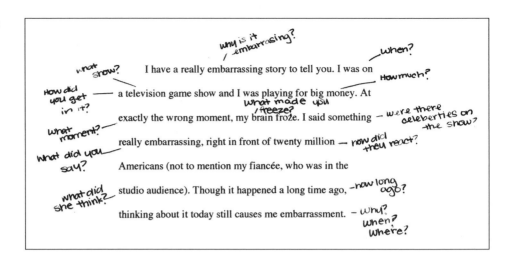

draft, enough good questions have been generated to give me some new direction when it comes to revising my story. I rewrite the draft in front of the students, integrating answers to some of their questions. After seeing how this process drives better writing, students trade papers and repeat the process.

Modeling Deep Revision Through Reorganization

Once students have completed a draft, I give them scissors and mandate that they cut their essays into pieces by paragraph. This activity forces students to consider rearranging the order of information in their essays. I cut up my own essay and model rearranging the pieces, thinking aloud regarding what effect might be created if I move this piece here or that piece there. Some students are initially taken aback by this activity, but I like the physical act of cutting up our writing because it sends a strong message to the students that we, as writers, should not fall in love with the ordering in our first drafts. When students cut their essays into segments and shift the pieces around, they are forced to consider various organizational structures. This, again, reemphasizes the artistic side of being a writer.

Deep Revision Through the Use of Language: Finding Your Voice

Have you ever been bored reading a stack of your students' essays only to have one jump out that you really enjoy reading? When this happens to me, I ask myself, "What is it about this paper that makes it stand out from the rest? What illuminates it?" Often the answer is one word: voice. Vibrant student papers are filled with rich voice—you can hear the authors in their papers. Peter Elbow, in *Writing with Power*, writes:

> *In essence, writing with voice is writing into which someone has breathed. It has that fluency, rhythm, and liveliness that exist naturally in speech of most*

people when they are enjoying a conversation. Moreover, writing with real voice has the power to make you pay attention and understand—the words go deep. (1998, p. 299)

When I come across a piece of writing with strong voice, whether written by a student of mine or by a professional writer, I share it with my students. Sometimes I will rewrite the passage without voice to show the contrast. Below, for example, is an excerpt from Brianna, a ninth-grade student, who had written about a frustrating trip to the movies. Paired with Brianna's excerpt is my rewrite, written with its voice removed:

Brianna's Excerpt	Revised Without Voice
"That'll be ten dollars," you hear the cashier demand. Ten dollars! Can you believe it? Ten dollars to see a movie that is not really original. Ten dollars to see some hour-and-a-half-knock-off-wannabe-remake. "Digitally remastered!" my rear end. I am paying ten dollars to see a new version of *Cinderella* so that I can see that her foot isn't white; it's peach. All of these waste-of-time remakes are exactly the same characters and plotlines as they were twenty years ago. The only new things about them are the one-hit-wonder actors doing what they call "acting" in front of cheesy green screens. Whatever happened to the classics? Keyword here: classics.	Recently I went to the theater to see a digitally remastered new version of *Cinderella*. When I paid for my ticket, I was shocked that they were charging ten dollars! Ten dollars to see a movie that is not even original. Like many of the remakes out there today, the stories are the same as they were twenty years ago. They don't even get very good actors. These remakes make me miss the classics.

When students were asked which one was better, they unanimously chose Brianna's piece. This led to a rich discussion on the importance voice can play in elevating an essay. Unlike the voiceless example, Brianna's writing has the power to make you pay attention.

I might also add that students are much more likely to write with a rich voice when they care about their writing topic. The importance of providing students leeway when choosing writing topics will be discussed further in Chapter 5.

"What Are You Doing Here?"

I like teaching ninth graders because they sometimes come up with the wackiest notions. Early in this school year one of my freshmen, Christina, asked, "Mr. Gallagher, I heard that you have written a couple of books. Is that true?"

"Yes," I answered.

"If that's true, what are you doing *here*?" she asked, genuinely curious about why a writer could be found teaching in an urban high school.

Christina's question is revealing—it tells me that many of my students have developed the notion that writers exist "out there" in the world somewhere. She reminds me that my students have not completely accepted the idea that they, themselves, are writers, too. She also reminds me that my students need to be taught that writing well is not something reserved solely for those who write books, but that all students, with the right motivation and work ethic, can become writers. Honing writing skills is not something that only writers should do; practicing writing is a worthwhile pursuit for anyone wishing to lead a literate life. I want my students to stop thinking of writers as "them" and to start thinking of writers as "us."

To do so, I need to work from the first day of school to demystify their notions of what real writers do. I do this by modeling my own writing for my students, by writing alongside them, by making visible all the difficulties and rewards that come with the act of writing. It is important for teachers to write, Donald Murray says,

> so they understand the process of writing from within. They should know the territory intellectually and emotionally: how you have to think to write, how you feel when writing. Teachers of writers do not have to be great writers, but they should have frequent and recent experience in writing. The best preparation for the writing class, workshop, or conference is at least a few minutes at the writing desk, saying what you did not expect to say. If you experience the despair, the joy, the failure, the success, the work, the fun, the drudgery, the surprise of writing you will be able to understand the composing experiences of your students and therefore help them understand how they are learning to write. (2004, p. 74)

If You Are Going to Walk the Walk . . .

As we write alongside our students, we can serve as writing models in one other way—by continually speaking the language of writers. If you want to teach surfing, for example, you must use the language of surfers. If you want to teach lacrosse, you must use the language of lacrosse. Writing has its own language as well. In writing classrooms you will hear both teachers and students using words like *recursive, revision, discourse,* and *author's purpose.* Peter Johnston, in *Choice Words,* reminds us that the language we use in our classrooms is "constitutive." In other words, "Children grow into the intellectual life around them" (2004, p. 2). If we want our students to grow into being writers we should speak the language of writers to them. Talking like writers, argues Johnston, helps to "position" our students as writers. In Appendix 5 you'll see a glossary of some of the writing terms used frequently in my classroom.

This chapter has advanced the idea that students are more likely to develop as writers when teachers lead by example. When we compose alongside our students, when we speak the language of writers, when we make the struggle all writers face visible, we demystify the process, thus making writing more approachable for students. Once my students begin internalizing the writing practices I have modeled for them, it becomes time to expand the modeling by having them closely examine what professional writers do.

Teaching Adolescent Writers

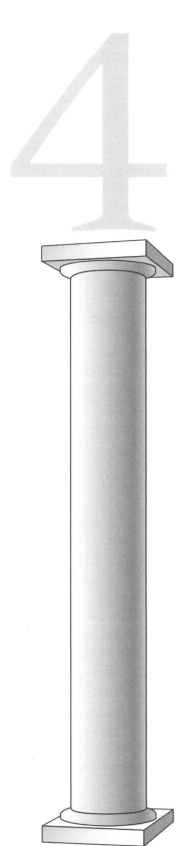

Elevating Student Writing: Using Real-World Models

I started this school year with a theory about the role that reading plays in my students' writing lives. As I walked into class on the first day of school, my theory went something like this: before knowing my students, I would be able to predict with a reasonable degree of accuracy which of them were readers simply by closely examining their writing.

I put this theory to the test during the first week. Each of my thirty-eight freshman students completed a timed writing piece on the second day of school and turned them in without their names on the papers. As I read their pieces, I placed them in three predictive piles: (1) those students whom I suspected were heavy readers (defined as those who frequently read for fun), (2) those students whom I suspected were moderate readers (defined as those who occasionally read for fun), and (3) those students whom I suspected were light readers (defined as those who rarely or never read for fun). To decide into which pile to place each paper, I looked closely for clues that might help. I asked myself some questions:

- What is the maturity level of the diction?
- How sophisticated is the sentence structure? Are the sentences predominantly simple, or is there evidence of compound and complex sentences?
- How developed is the essay?
- Is there evidence of craft in the essay (e.g., interesting introduction and/or conclusion, strong voice)?
- Is there use of advanced punctuation and editing skills?

After I had sorted the essays into the three piles, I administered a reading survey to my students (again, without names) asking them how much they read (frequently, occasionally, rarely/never). My theory was that I'd be able to match the best writing with the students who read frequently; the average writing with the students who read occasionally; and the least sophisticated writing with the students who rarely or never read.

This informal, in-class research wouldn't pass muster in the *Journal of Adolescent Literacy.* For one thing, I made the predictions after I examined only one piece of writing (on the second day of school, no less!). Nevertheless, I find the results telling:

- Eighty-five percent of those essays I placed in pile A (the predicted frequent readers) were indeed written by frequent readers.
- Only 15 percent of my students who read frequently had essays that were not placed in the "good writers" pile.
- None of the essays by my students who said they were infrequent readers were placed in the pile designated as good writers.

From this informal survey, I have drawn a central conclusion that my students who read the most are better writers. I wish I could say the correlation was that simple—that just getting our students to read will immediately boost their writing prowess. If that were true, we would be able to summarize an effective writing approach in one simplistic formula: lots of reading = better writing.

My experience, however, tells me that it's not that simple. Yes, reading does broaden vocabulary. Yes, reading does help students to get a feel for crafting more sophisticated sentences. And yes, reading does enable students to see how different writers approach different discourses. This is evident in the essays written by my readers. But I suspect there is more to the picture than can be found in the simple formula: more reading = better writing. For one thing, I had two students who described themselves as frequent readers who did not write well. Why hasn't their frequent reading transferred into better writing?

My experiment brings to the forefront an idea I have long suspected of being true, that although reading is foundational to the development of young writers, reading *alone* does not explain why some of my readers write well and other don't. This suggests that something else is at play and brings a new formula to mind:

lots of reading + exposure to intensive hands-on writing instruction = better writing

What do I mean by "intensive hands-on writing instruction"? Students need teachers who:

- demand from their students a lot more writing practice;
- demystify the writing process by writing alongside their students;
- often give students choice when it comes to writing topics;
- teach students to write for authentic purposes and to authentic audiences;
- give students meaningful feedback from both the teacher and the students' peers;
- model that writing, though hard, is a valuable, intrinsically rewarding endeavor;
- help students to overcome the "I wrote it once; I'm done" mentality.

It is the *coupling* of extensive reading with hands-on writing instruction that generates effective adolescent writers. Students who read a lot come to class better prepared to bloom when writing instruction is introduced. They have begun internalizing the things that good writers do so that when they receive instruction they have the necessary foundation to implement what they have learned. Voluminous reading alone does not make the writer, but those students who are readers come to the writing task with a marked advantage.

Think of it in these terms: if my task is to teach you how to effectively shoot basketball free throws, my job would be much easier if you came to the lesson having watched a lot of basketball growing up. Because you would have seen many others attempt free-throw shooting, you would arrive at the task with some notion of how to attempt the skill—where to place your feet, how to position the ball in your hands, how to follow through on the shot. You might start off as a lousy free-throw shooter, but coming to the first lesson with a strong foundation would create favorable conditions for rapid learning. You come to the court with a certain degree of readiness.

Now look at the flip side. You show up to the first free-throw lesson without any basketball experience. You have never watched a game, so you do not know what a free throw looks like. There is no basketball foundation on which to build; you come to the task of shooting free throws "cold." With you, I will have to start my instruction from scratch—a much more difficult teaching task. You arrive without any degree of readiness, and as a result, the unfamiliarity of the task is already working against you.

The students I receive each year comprise a mixed bag of reading experience. Some have had extensive reading experience, but more often than not, I am finding many of my new students to be aliterate. They are capable, but for one reason or another, have not adopted a reading habit. It is the aliterate students more than anyone else in the classroom who benefit most from models prior to writing, because they have come to the writing task with little degree of readiness. They have not internalized very many, if any, of the things good writers do. In essence, they are trying to shoot free throws without ever having seen the game.

When I stand in front of my students, many of whom are nonreaders, I am reminded of what Stephen King once said: "If you want to be a writer, you must do two things above all else: read a lot and write a lot. There's no way around these two things that I'm aware, no shortcut" (2000, p. 145). If I want my students to acquire the skills that good writers possess, I start by placing a number of exemplary models to read in front of them. In Chapter 3 I make the point that my students benefit from seeing models written in front of them by the most experienced writer in the classroom—their teacher. In this chapter, I will take the modeling notion one step further by suggesting that students are more likely first to recognize and then to acquire effective writing skills when they have teachers who model by bringing professional writing into their classrooms. I do not want my students, especially those who are inexperienced in reading, to come to their writing task cold. Instead, I have them begin the task by seeing how the "pros" do it. Students who see how other writers shoot their free throws will be more likely to succeed when it becomes time for them to shoot their own. Reading these models will give our students a foundation—a context—so that when writing instruction does occur they will be more likely to infuse into their writing those things good writers do.

Feeding Writing

To get my students to understand the idea that we can learn much by studying what professional writers do, I begin with a topic of interest for all adolescents: food. I ask my students to consider a restaurant experience they have had, and intentionally without giving them much instruction, I ask them to write a restaurant review. When I assigned this essay early in the year in one of my freshman classes, Suzy raised her hand and asked, "How long should it be?"

"How long is a piece of string?" I answered.

"As long as you cut it," she replied.

"Exactly," I said. "When you feel like you have reviewed the restaurant, covering the main points of interest, you are finished. That's when you cut the string." They moaned. They would, of course, like me to tell them exactly how long they should write. I avoid this at all costs, because it inhibits their writing. If I tell a student to write 300 words, I'll get an essay of 303 words.

We spent some time in class discussing some of the elements that might be found in a restaurant review. Students were then asked to draft for the rest of the period and to come to class the next day with a first draft. After collecting all the first drafts (and without reading them), I handed out a restaurant review culled from the *Orange County Register* entitled, "Adding Up the Pluses at Soma Café." I prepared the text in two ways: (1) I cut and pasted the review to leave note-taking space in the right-hand margin of the paper; and (2) I chunked the text by drawing lines to create sections of the review (see Figure 4.1).

After students read the review, I placed it on the overhead, and as a class we revisited each section of the review with one central question in mind: What is the main topic addressed by the writer in each of the eight sections? (Laura Robb, teacher and author, calls this "reading with an author's eye.") Using the review as a model, the students brainstormed the following:

Section 1: The writer told a personal anecdote to introduce the review.
Section 2: The writer gave an overview of the menu.
Section 3: The writer shares the restaurant's history.
Section 4: The writer discusses the children's menu.
Section 5: The writer describes in detail the specific meal she ate.
Section 6: The writer details other visits and the different dishes she tried on these visits.
Section 7: The writer discusses a regret.
Section 8: The writer concludes with a thesis statement, which in this case is positive.

Once the students had recognized these eight sections as a model used by a professional restaurant reviewer, I handed back their first drafts and asked them to revise. I did not mandate that they follow the model section by section; I simply told them that this was one of many ways to write a restaurant review and that they were free to refer to any or all of the sections as they set off to improve their first drafts. In Figure 4.2, for example, you will find a first and a second draft from Jesus, a reluctant ninth-grade writer.

Though Jesus's paper is still in rough-draft form, it is clear that studying a professionally written restaurant review helped elevate his writing. I particularly liked how he modeled his introduction after the professional piece of writing ("I am a sandwich eater") and how mapping the original review into chunks enabled him to more than quadruple his development. For students who always say they don't know what to write, providing a model helps them over this hurdle.

Models do not only benefit reluctant writers. Carlos, another ninth-grade student in Jesus's class, has no reluctance when it comes to writing. But even though Carlos has little trouble warming up to writing, his first draft, written without any model, remains underdeveloped and unfocused. Like Jesus, his writing took off after he had a chance to analyze a model. In Figure 4.3 you'll find Carlos's two drafts—one written before the model was introduced and one written after he had a chance to dissect the model.

Adding Up the Pluses at Soma Cafe

By Chantal Lamers

The Orange County Register

What did the writer do?

I'm a calorie counter. But not having the option of knowing how many calories are in my turkey burger or side of vinaigrette is a professional hazard when you spend time reviewing restaurants.

So when I opened the menu at the Soma Cafe and found the protein, fat, fiber, carbohydrate and calorie content listed with just about every item, I let out a huge sigh of relief. Finally someone has caught on and is kind enough to tell me, the customer, what I'm about to put into my body.

① *Tells a personal anecdote to introduce the review*

Although I was happy that the nutritional information was at hand, I assumed that would mean an array of bland dishes. As I sipped my iced tea, I envisioned boring alfalfa sprouts on an even more boring slab of bread. Or something like that. I pictured a slew of salads served with corn and low-fat ranch dressing.

But the tasteless menu I anticipated was far from the reality. Instead, I found whole-wheat flat bread "pizas," sandwiches, burgers and wraps. There were banana pancakes, turkey-bacon and egg breakfast wraps, and green salads such as the edamame pasta salad and seared ahi tuna salad. And for dinner, there was pork tenderloin in ginger plum sauce, lean caramelized beef tenderloin or New York prime strip.

② *Gives an overview of the menu*

The restaurant is a new addition to the Newport Coast shopping center just off the San Joaquin Hills (73) Toll Road in Newport Coast, and is the second Soma Cafe in the country. The first was opened more than two years ago near Phoenix, and the third will open later this year in Laguna Beach. Soma's innovative menu, created by a team of doctors, nutritionists and professional trainers, might be made for athletes, but at Soma, everyone, from the person who takes brisk daily walks to an Olympian, is considered an athlete.

③ *Shares the restaurant's history*

Along with the full-menu restaurant, there is a coffee and smoothie bar. If you're not craving a meal, you can choose from healthy-minded pastries or bowls full of fresh berries and/or melon.

The children's menu at Soma, dubbed "Future Athletes," proves that children aren't an afterthought here. It includes chicken strips and pancakes, but the chicken strips are baked, not fried, and the pancakes are made with whole-wheat flour. The cheese "piza" is made with whole-wheat flat bread and the grilled cheese sandwich is made with whole-grain bread and cheddar cheese.

④ *Discusses the children's menu*

After carefully scanning the menu, and adding and dividing the calories in menu items, I finally settled on the lettuce wraps appetizer, and the grilled salmon sandwich for my entree. (Together, the dishes totaled 517 calories and about 12 grams of fat).

The wraps were some of the best I've had. Tender slices of chicken were mixed with dainty snow peas, toasted almonds, cucumber slices, red onions and shredded carrots. The mixture was served inside a delicate piece of iceberg lettuce and topped with a tangy, kick-to-it vinaigrette, made with ginger and rice vinegar.

⑤ *Describes in detail a specific meal she ate*

The grilled salmon sandwich was served in the whole-wheat flat bread, which is made from scratch daily at Soma. A thick strip of fresh salmon came with arugula, tomato and red onion.

After this meal, I popped into Soma for the next two days. My friends and I tried the grilled pineapple "piza," which comes on that hearty whole-wheat flat bread and is topped with a tangy tomato sauce, low-fat mozzarella, grilled chicken, pineapple and red onions. (For six decent-size slices, you're looking at about 600 calories and 7 grams of fat.)

We also tried the soy balsamic portobello chicken pasta (which was a little heavy on the marinade but good nonetheless). The whole-wheat pasta comes with generous portions of marinated portobello mushrooms, artichoke hearts and roasted bell peppers. The pasta was mixed with fresh basil and olive oil. The entire serving is just over 700 calories, and is so generous, it could feed three people.

⑥ *Details other visits and the different dishes she tried on these visits*

My next visit to Soma was for breakfast. My regular latte was joined by a turkey bacon, egg and cheese breakfast wrap (once again, wrapped in a fresh, warm whole-wheat roll). My only complaint: It was good but slightly dry, and I needed much, much more of their fresh salsa.

My only regret in visiting Soma Cafe is that it spoiled me terribly. Whenever I eat at another restaurant, I crave knowing how many grams of fat and carbohydrates will be in the dish I order.

⑦ *Discusses a regret*

But maybe Soma's way is a sign of good things to come. Maybe eateries everywhere will start to change their menus to include nutritional information, and restaurant patrons will no longer have to eat in blissful ignorance. Until that day comes, Soma has you tastefully covered.

⑧ *Concludes with a positive thesis statement*

Figure 4.1 *Chunked restaurant review*

Jesus's First Draft (Written Before Seeing a Model)	**Jesus's Second Draft (Written After Seeing a Model)**
Don't know what too eat? Tired of arguing with your friends or family because you want to eat different things. Then go to home town buffet where you can eat till you drop for a low price. You can eat anything from their freshly sliced fruit to their hot crisp crispy chicken. And if you don't feel like eating food then go to their desert section where you can chose anything from cold ice cream to hot baked cookie.	I am a sandwich eater. And I also like knowing whats in my sandwich. So that's why I go to subway, where I know it will be prepared fresh right in front of my face. Getting there is only half the battle for once you get there you have to choose from their freshly made chicken Bacon Ranch, their OMT, or their Carne Asada. After you have chosen your meal you have to choose your beverage, and then you are in heaven. This heaven is located in Gilbert and Lincoln. It went under new management in 1996, and it was built in _____, since then Subways have been opened in _____ locations around California. Sure other food restaurants have their own kids menu. Who really needs a kids menu? When you can get a fresh sub. You aren't in the mood for a sub. Then you can always enjoy fresh cookies with milk. After hearing the many chooses I had, I settled with the Carne Asada. Made with Carne Asada, lettuce, tomatoes, pickles, bell pepers, olive, and on top or everything salsa. This delecasi is then wraped up and served to the costumer. For the next couple of day I decided to head back and try other choises. The first day I went for the Chicken Bacon Ranch (which had chicken, Bacon, cheese lettuce, tomatoes, pickles, bellpepers, olives and ranch) Then afrere everything is put in they put it in the oven for 15 to 20 sec until its nicely cooked Then it was the BMT which was made of pepperoni, sauumy, ham, lettuce, tomatoes, pickles, bell pepeper, and olives. And like the chicken Bacon Ranch it was also pot in the oven for 15 to 20 sec. Sure every body else can go to Mc Donalds and get there chese hamburgers with fries. But not me I'll go to a place where I know the food will be served fresh in front of my face.

Figure 4.2 *Jesus's restaurant review drafts*

I often teach a variation of the restaurant review assignment. After having students write restaurant reviews, I have students transition into writing movie reviews. When I search for professional movie reviews, I start with Roger Ebert, syndicated columnist and co-host of *Ebert and Roeper at the Movies*. I like to use Ebert because his writing is direct and easy to understand (I am not fond of movie reviewers whose sole purpose is to wow us with their superior wit, often to the point where I get to the end of the review and find myself still not sure what the reviewer thinks of the film. Ebert's reviews, which are straightforward, can be found at www.rogerebert.com).

When my students sit down to write essays, many of them have trouble getting out of the starting gate. They simply do not know how to start.

Carlos's First Draft (Written Before Seeing a Model)

What is fast food? Can I actually trust to eat a cheeseburger that was made thirty seconds after I ordered it? For some reason I think that should be a law If you want the Rolls Royce of burgers I strongly suggest Farmer Boys is the place to be. Farmer Boys delivers you quality and authentic food. Even their slogan assures you the best quality "Worlds Greatest Burgers"

This fast food restaurant's atmosphere is great. It gives you the feeling of a small town great burger while leaving the city. The prices are great as well. I would prefer paying an extra dollar or two for the pure satisfaction that McDonalds can't provide. The bottom line is this, if you want the best burger you can find just go to Farmer Boys.

Carlos's Second Draft (Written After Seeing a Model)

I love fast food, but when a place like Mc Donald's serves your cheeseburger thirty seconds after you've ordered it you have to ask yourself, "Wut's too fast?" Sometimes I swear they have your food ready before you even order it. That's why whenever your'e craving a burger or some freshly made food look past Mc Donalds, Jack in the Box and all the other fast food joints and drive directly to Farmer Boys.

When I first walked into Farmer Boys I thought it would just be another dull burger joint. Filled with an even more bland menu. I imagined burgers such as the cheeseburger, the double cheeseburger and the bacon cheeseburger with each being overly expensive. But as soon as glanced at the menu, my options varied from zucchini to burgers to tacos. I love food, and seeing the wide variety of choices I had to select from made my stomach grinned.

As I walked into Farmer Boys for the first time I instantly loved the atmosphere. There were no loud and obnoxious children that nearly set the place on fire begging for another toy on the happy meal. Their service is also outstanding. Ive been to three Farmer Boy locations and every waiter and cashier reminds me of family. Whenever a restaurant or any business establishment makes me feel as if I'm part of the family I immediately fall head over heals for it.

The best thing about Farmer Boys is their side orders. They range from fried zucharini to chilly cheese fries. The first time I ate their I had chilly cheese fries. Im not easily impressed with food, but when a restaurant gives me food that looks exactly like the advertised ones in the windows I am overwhelmed with awe. Other great side orders include their chicken strips. These chicken strips would even make the great Kentucky Fried Chicken fearful of competiton.

Farmer Boys, like other great restaurants, started out as a family owned business. The first Farmer Boys first opened it's doors in 1981 in Perris California. Since its opening the family business has turned into a franchise and now owns over 51 restaurants in the Southern California Inland Empire. Two of which are found here in Anaheim. Due to their high success in Southern California the franchise has decided to expand nation wide with new locations such as New York, Miami, Chicago and San Francisco. I think it's safe to say that this business will thrive in any area.

In my numerous visits to Farmer Boys I've found out that their "Farmer's Burger" has been the best. This

Figure 4.3 *Carlos's restaurant reviews*

Carlos's First Draft (Written Before Seeing a Model)	Carlos's Second Draft (Written After Seeing a Model)
	combination is simple, all beef patties with lettuce onions and tomatoes including bacon and avocado and of course their secret sauce. The difference though, is that their food makes you feel almost as if it had directly been picked off the farm, hence the name Farmer Boys. As I took my first bite into the burger the freshness of the lettuce combined with the melted cheese and oozing avocado with the sauce made it all worth while. Other great foods include their fish tacos. Being a Latino I've had a lot of fish tacos in my life. And these were as close to the real thing as you can get. The secret to Farmer Boys is that they serve fresh food fast. This has been their recipe to success. They need no public ads or do they need to spend their time on advertising billions of dollars. Their success has been spread out through word of mouth. The only thing that I regret though, is going their in the first place. Now a Mc Donald's run simply doesn't do the job anymore. It's like driving in a Honda after you've driven a Rolls Royce. It just doesn't get any better than Farmer Boys. After all their slogan is no lie, "World's Greatest Burgers."

Figure 4.3 *Carlos's restaurant reviews* (continued)

Analyzing models helps them get out of the gate. When we write movie reviews, for example, I provide them with the first paragraph of a number of Ebert reviews and ask them to identify the introduction technique, or hook, used by the writer to start each review:

Film: *8 Mile*

Hook technique: Start with summary

First paragraph of the review:

Pale, depressed, Jimmy Smith Jr. (Eminem) skulks through a life that has been so terribly unkind to him. His girlfriend has gotten pregnant and broken up with him, and although he did the right thing by her—he gave her his old car—he now faces the prospect of moving back into his mother's trailer home, with her boyfriend who hates him. Jimmy carries his clothes around in a garbage bag. He has a job as a punch press operator.

Film: *Harry Potter and the Chamber of Secrets*

Hook technique: Start with a straight thesis statement

First paragraph of the review:

The first movie was the setup, and this one is the payoff. Harry Potter and the Chamber of Secrets *leaves all of the explanations of wizardry behind and plunges quickly into an adventure that's darker and scarier than anything in the first Harry Potter movie. It's also richer: The second in a planned series of seven Potter films is brimming with invention and new ideas, and its Hogwarts School seems to expand and deepen before our very eyes into a world large enough to conceal unguessable secrets.*

Film: *Star Trek: Nemesis*

Hook technique: Start with humor

First paragraph of the review:

I'm sitting there during Star Trek: Nemesis, *the 10th* Star Trek *movie, and I'm smiling like a good sport and trying to get with the dialogue about the isotronic Ruritronic signature from planet Kolarus III, or whatever the hell they were saying, maybe it was "positronic," and gradually it occurs to me that* Star Trek *is over for me. I've been looking at these movies for half a lifetime, and, let's face it, they're out of gas.*

Film: *Flightplan*

Hook technique: Start with a question

First paragraph of the review:

How can a little girl simply disappear from an airplane at 37,000 feet? By asking this question and not cheating on the answer, Flightplan *delivers a frightening thriller with an airtight plot. It's like a classic Locked Room Murder, in which the killer could not possibly enter or leave, but the victim is nevertheless dead. Such mysteries always have solutions, and so does* Flightplan, *but not one you will easily anticipate. After the movie is over and you are on your way home, some questions may occur to you, but the film proceeds with implacable logic after establishing that the little girl does not seem to be on board.*

Film: *Swept Away*

Hook technique: Start with sarcasm

First paragraph of the review:

Swept Away *is a deserted island movie during which I desperately wished the characters had chosen one movie to take along if they were stranded on a deserted island, and were showing it to us instead of this one.*

I asked my students to revise the introductions to film reviews they had written by using the Ebert hooks as models. In Figure 4.4, you'll find Joanna's movie review introduction to the film *Mean Girls*. Notice how her review echoes Ebert's review of *Flightplan*.

Had I simply handed to the students a professionally written restaurant or movie review and then told them to write one on their own, this assignment would probably fall into the Grecian Urn trap. The key to this assignment, however, is taking the time to have the students dissect what the professional writer did. When my students create maps to understand how the professional writer tackled the writing task, they begin to understand how to approach the task on their own.

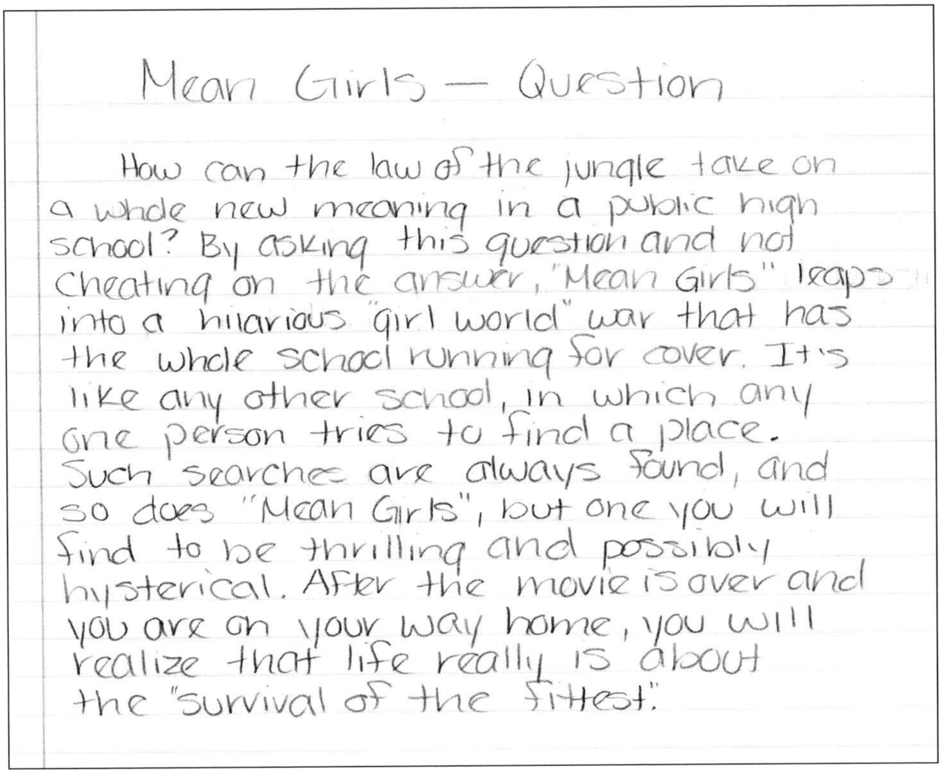

Figure 4.4 *Revised movie review hook(s)*

> ## Mean Girls — Question
>
> How can the law of the jungle take on a whole new meaning in a public high school? By asking this question and not cheating on the answer, "Mean Girls" leaps into a hilarious "girl world" war that has the whole school running for cover. It's like any other school, in which any one person tries to find a place. Such searches are always found, and so does "Mean Girls", but one you will find to be thrilling and possibly hysterical. After the movie is over and you are on your way home, you will realize that life really is about the "survival of the fittest."

Magazines as Models

Once students have written in areas where they feel comfortable (restaurant and movie reviews), we transition into writing more difficult argument. An excellent modeling source for this is *Newsweek*'s "My Turn" essay, which is found in every issue. In Figure 4.5, you will see an essay written by Patricia O'Hara entitled, "Charity Means You Don't Pick and Choose." I use this essay as a model with my high school freshmen. After we read this piece, I ask my students what the central question is that the author wants us to consider. After some discussion, they decide she is asking whether she should give handouts to the homeless.

Using the Yes/No graphic organizer depicted in Figure 4.6, I place that question at the top of the page and have the students then revisit the essay to find the pros and cons ("What is the author's argument?"). I then ask the students to revisit the essay a third time to find specific details to support each reason ("How does the author support the argument?"). Finally, given the weight of the arguments on both sides, I ask the students to determine the author's answer to the question, "Should we give handouts to the homeless?" I ask them to paraphrase the answer or to answer it directly by citing a line from the piece and write the answer beside "Author's Thesis" at the bottom of the graphic organizer. In one year, after some discussion, they chose the following line as the thesis for the essay: "It's better to set the needle of his

Figure 4.5 Newsweek *essay*

My Turn

Charity Means You Don't Pick and Choose

I know the arguments against giving handouts, but who am I to decide who deserves kindness?

BY PATRICIA O'HARA

IF YOU'RE NOT GOING TO EAT THAT, little boy, I will," said the man sitting on the sidewalk to my son, who was holding a doggie bag of restaurant left-overs. It was the first time my son had ever seen a homeless person. He was 5 years old, and we were spending the weekend visiting museums in Washington, D.C. It was a March night of unusually raw weather—not a night to be sitting on a cold, hard sidewalk. I tightened my grasp on my son's hand as I made eye contact with the man.

"Spare anything, ma'am?"

My son looked up at me uneasily, so I left him with my husband and went over to the man, dollar extended. He thanked me and asked my son again for his doggie bag. I motioned him over, nodding my assurances. "I didn't finish my steak sandwich," my son told him proudly, as he handed the man his bag. The man thanked him and said, "Be good to your mommy."

At just that moment a father and his two teenage sons walked past and, without breaking his stride, barked out: "It'd be better if they got a job!"

I was startled by the intensity of the man's disapproval, but I, too, have had doubts about offering handouts to the homeless. Under the watchful eyes of my child, I chose the action that I hoped would speak to my son about the principles of charity I hold dear, but the truth is, my decision to give has seldom been so clear-cut.

Like most people, I'm more comfortable giving when the people on the receiving end are anonymous. I happily participate in the clothing drives sponsored by my son's school, and I drop my spare change in the big metal kettle at the mall, where a man dressed like Santa Claus rings his bell and smiles at shoppers.

Giving directly to the street person shambling across my pathway—well, that's another matter. Hollywood tends to portray the homeless as lovable rogues (think Eddie Murphy in "Trading Places"), but in real life, the person asking for money is often suffering the effects of mental illness or addiction. I'm not proud to admit it, but even the few seconds it takes to look the other person in the eye, extend my hand and offer some change can feel like more of a connection than I want to make.

I've heard the intellectual arguments against giving handouts: the money will be used to buy drugs or alcohol, handouts breed dependency, giving money discourages the homeless from going to shelters. I don't want to undermine the efforts of the mental-health professionals who work to get the homeless off the streets. But what I know in my head doesn't square with what I feel in my heart. Pretending that people don't exist and withholding a couple of quarters or a dollar bill feels like the wrong thing to do.

Several years after our encounter with the homeless man in Washington, my son and I visited New York City. As we walked down the street, a thin, drugged-out young man approached us and asked us for change. It was midtown at midday, so there was nothing particularly threatening about the circumstances. Nevertheless, the man was, by anyone's standards, unsavory-looking with his dirty clothes and unhealthy skin. I passed him by. Half a block later, my son stopped walking and asked: "Why didn't you give him anything?" I fumbled through a rationale about how we hadn't had time to stop and why we couldn't possibly give to everyone. My son interrupted and said, "Yeah, I don't think you should give money to people like that."

"People like that."

In his words and his tone of voice were echoes of the man who told the panhandler to get a job. I had shown my son that it was acceptable to classify people as the deserving and the undeserving poor.

Last spring I traveled to London to do some work-related research. Each day on the way to the library, I passed a group of homeless men lying on the steps of St. Pancras Old Church. Perhaps spending time in one of Charles Dickens's old neighborhoods set me thinking about his righteous anger at society's neglect of its poor. Or maybe I finally accepted that I'm in no position—and who is?—to judge another person's worthiness of a small act of kindness. Whatever the reason, I decided that I would always give when asked, even when it means weathering the sidelong glances of those who think I'm a fool or worse.

My son is now a teenager and will have to decide for himself if and how he'll give to the poor. For all of my inconsistencies, I hope that I've taught him that it's better to set the needle of his compass to the magnetic pull of kindness than to contempt. But time alone will tell.

O'HARA lives in Strasburg, Pa.

 Check out My Turn at 30, highlights from three decades of the column, on Newsweek.MSNBC.com

DECEMBER 23, 2002 NEWSWEEK **13**

---

compassion to the magnetic pull of kindness than to contempt." Upon completing this exercise, students are left with a graphic organizer that shows them an argumentative outline used by a published writer. I then distribute a blank copy of the Yes/No Chart (see Appendix 6), and while the model is still fresh in their minds, I ask students to outline their own arguments.

Having our students closely examine real-world writers helps them to see the craft behind good writing. Let's face it, our students will not be spending the rest of their lives reading *Beowulf*. But, hopefully, they will spend their adult lives reading books and magazines. By getting them to analyze real-

Figure 4.6 *Graphic organizer to chart* Newsweek *arguments pro/con*

Central Question the Author is Exploring:

SHOULD WE GIVE $ TO THE HOMELESS?

Yes	What is the Author's Argument?	How does the Author Support the Argument?
	SETS A GOOD EXAMPLE FOR HER SON	SHE TELLS THE ANECDOTE OF HER TRIP TO WASHINGTON D.C. W/ HER SON.
	KINDNESS IS A BETTER WAY TO GO THAN CONTEMPT	THERE IS NO SUCH THING AS DESERVING AND UNDESERVING HOMELESS PEOPLE
	SHE HAS A REALIZATION (AN EPIPHANY)	LONDON ANECDOTE — COMING TO THE IDEA SHE WOULD ALWAYS HELP

No	What is the Author's Argument?	How does the Author Support the Argument?
	HOMELESS PEOPLE MAY BE LAZY	"IT'D BE BETTER IF THEY GOT A JOB" INCIDENT
	WHERE DOES THE $ GO?	DRUGS? ALCOHOL? AM I FEEDING DEPENDENCY? HOW DO I KNOW WHAT THEY USE THE $ FOR?
	AM I MAKING THE PROBLEM WORSE?	AM I DISCOURAGING THE HOMELESS FROM SEEKING HELP? SHELTER?

Author's Thesis: "IT'S BETTER TO SET THE NEEDLE OF HIS COMPASS TO THE MAGNETIC PULL OF KINDNESS THAN TO CONTEMPT."

world text, not only are we preparing them for their adult reading lives, but we are also providing them with interesting, relevant models. This is not a call to abandon core literature; it is a call to augment our core literature with as much real-world text as possible. What better coaches are there than those writers who have risen to writing prominence?

Read-Around-Groups: Real-World Peer Models

Though students benefit immensely by examining professional writing, there is also another opportunity for students to learn by reading other writers, and that opportunity presents itself in our classrooms daily. I am speaking of the benefit that arises when we have students read each other's writing. Getting students to willingly share their writing with one another, however, is not always an easy task given the fact that sharing writing involves risk.

How do I get my students over this fear of sharing their drafts? I tell them that every time I send a new chapter I have written to my editor, I cringe. I tell them that when I work with college-educated adults, they often have the same level of anxiousness when it comes to sharing their writing. In short, I tell them, this feeling is normal and the sooner we can work our way past it the sooner we will begin improving as writers.

One way I have students work through the nervousness of sharing their writing with one another is to set up read-around-groups, in which students are given the opportunity to read each other's papers anonymously. There are various versions of RAGs out there; here are the rules for my classes:

Rules for RAGs

1. Students bring clean drafts to the RAGs. They do not put their names on the paper. Instead, they identify themselves by writing five-digit numbers or code words at the top of their papers.

2. Students are *randomly* placed in groups of four or five. The papers are collected in one pile for each group. It is better to not have all the best (or worst) writers at the same table.

3. At the start, on the teacher's signal, the papers are passed from one group to the next. Students do not read papers by members of their own group. Each student receives one paper and reads it for one minute. Not all students will finish all papers, but in one minute they have an opportunity to get a strong feel for the paper.

4. At the teacher's signal, papers are passed clockwise *within* the groups. Each student now has a new paper and has one minute to read the paper. This process is continued until everyone in the group has read all four or five papers.

5. Once everyone in the group has read the set, each group is charged with the task of determining which paper is the "best." They have two minutes to do so. The hope is that this will produce arguments, because it is through these arguments that students think deeply about the merits of good writing.

6. One student in each group is designated as the recorder. This student records the five-digit number or code word of the winning paper.

7. Once the winner is recorded, the papers get passed again and the process repeats itself. This is continued until all students have read all papers. Remember, each group is not to score their own papers.

Teaching Adolescent Writers

Figure 4.7 *Focus areas for using read-around-groups*

> **Variations of RAGs**
>
> Have students do a RAG focused solely on a specific feature of the essay. Here are some examples of possible focus areas:
> - Introductions
> - Thesis statement
> - Conclusions
> - Transitions
> - Supporting detail
> - Sentence variety
>
> Adjust the reading time accordingly. For example, if students are focusing solely on introductions, cut the reading time to twenty seconds before passing the papers.

Once these seven steps are complete, the teacher asks the recorders for the winning entries and charts all the winning numbers (or code words) for the students to see. Generally, two or three papers in the class will receive the most votes. These papers are read aloud (again, no names are identified). As they are being read, students are asked to take bullet notes as to what made the papers the "best." The lesson is completed by students sharing their bullet notes through a whole-class discussion, thus giving everyone in the class a clear idea of what features made these good essays.

I have found that RAGs are more beneficial to students if they do them *before* their final drafts are due. What good does it do them to identify features of good writing if they do not have an immediate opportunity to implement some of these discovered features into their own writing? Often I will collect essays on the due date (without names on the papers), but instead of taking them home, I will place students in RAGs. Once they have completed the process and have seen some examples of good writing, I give their papers back to them and allow one additional night for them to revise with the features of good writing fresh in their minds.

Once my students have begun sharing their writing in RAGs, I find they are more willing to begin sharing their writing in other settings as well.

Final Thoughts

Earlier in this chapter I noted one of my favorite Stephen King lines: "If you want to be a writer, you must do two things above all else: read a lot and write a lot. There's no way around these two things that I'm aware, no shortcut" (2000, p. 145). If we want our students to develop the tools needed to write well, we must provide them with numerous models to read and study—models from both inside and outside our classrooms. Getting students to internalize what good writers do is critical, and for students to have any chance to do this, they need modeling, modeling, and more modeling.

Beyond Fake Writing: The Power of Choice

When my seniors walked into my classroom the first week of the school year, I asked them to jot down what came to their minds when I said the word "writing." Todd, seventeen, wrote:

During the course of our school years we are forced to write essays on topics that we care nothing about just to make our teachers look good.

The bad news is that Todd's response is typical. The worse news, I am afraid, is that his lament contains much truth. By the time students reach their last year of high school, many of them have come to see writing as just another school-induced hoop to jump through—an obstacle that must be circumvented in order to reach the high school finish line. Any desires they once may have had as writers have long been buried under too many formulaic book reports, too many standardized research papers, too many attempts to analyze the author's use of . . . (fill in the technique). They have had years of writing tasks thrust upon them—writing tasks they often find uninteresting and irrelevant. In some cases, writing has even been used to *punish* them (e.g., writing one hundred sentences for misbehaving).

In my first book, *Reading Reasons,* I make the point that students have also lost sight of the value of reading. I argue that, as teachers, we need to help students to understand the intrinsic reasons why reading is more than just another school requirement. In that book, I proposed ten reasons why students should be readers. Unfortunately, we are faced with the same level of opposition when it comes to motivating young writers. Many of our students have lost sight of the real value that comes from writing well. Like reading, students often see writing as just another painful obstacle they must overcome to earn a diploma. This is unfortunate, because we, as teachers, know that the value of writing extends far past school. We know, for example, that:

> Writing helps you to be a better reader.
> Writing makes you smarter.
> Writing helps you in the workplace.
> Writing prepares you to get into and through college.
> Writing helps you to persuade others.
> Writing enables you to fight oppression.
> Writing is a necessary skill to have in the dawn of an information age.

In short, writing anchors a literate life, and we know that students who write well will reap the rewards long after high school is over. With this in mind, we have one year to get our students to discover the value of writing; we have one year to help them understand that we don't assign writing just to make the teacher look better. If we are to be successful in getting our students to turn the corner as writers, we must put them in a position to see that writing is much more than a school-induced hoop to jump through to reach graduation. For literate adults, writing is one of life's staples.

Beyond Fake Writing

One reason students don't write well is that they do not care what they are writing about. If you think about it, we often ask students to do the kind of writing that we, as adults, *never* do. When was the last time you sat down at home and wrote a draft analyzing Shakespeare's use of biblical allusions in *Hamlet*? Or wrote a letter that aligned perfectly to a rigid, five-paragraph format? It seems to me that we spend a lot of time preparing students for "fake writing"—the kinds of writing they will never do once they leave school.

Does this mean that we should stop teaching students to write literary analysis essays? No. I want all of my students to be able to analyze literature at a deeper level because I believe doing so gives them the cognitive underpinnings to analyze the world outside of the novel. What I am suggesting, however, is that before we plunge our students into some of the traditional "school" writing, maybe we should invest some time in having them write about things they actually care about. If we first get our students up and running as writers, they will be better equipped when the time does come for them to write about Golding's use of symbolism in *Lord of the Flies*.

Choice Is Where It Starts

It has been my experience that students write a whole lot better when they care about what they are writing. I have also found that they are much more likely to care about what they are writing when they are given choice in writing topics. Choice generates a welcome chain reaction: it creates student buy-in, which in turn generates writing motivation, which in turn causes students to write better. Choice is where it starts for reluctant writers, and if we want them to warm up to writing, we need to structure our classes so that our students have some say in what they write.

Allowing Students to Choose Writing Topics
Creates Two Immediate Benefits

1. Choice fosters a feeling of ownership in the writer. When a student develops ownership, she is much more likely not only to start a paper, but to maintain a stronger work ethic while in the drafting process.
2. Choice drives better revision. The number-one determiner in whether a student of mine will spend meaningful time revising a first draft is whether she cares about the paper. A student who cares about her paper is much more likely to closely revise; a student who does not care about her paper will treat the revision process lightly, if at all.

Choice is good, but we are living in the age of standards, and I can hear you thinking as you read this, "But what about the standards? I have many different discourses I must teach! How do I balance the demands of my grade-level standards with the notion of allowing students to choose their writing topics?"

I certainly feel these same pressures. In California, where I teach, I am expected to teach the following discourses to my ninth-grade students:

*   Biographical and autobiographical narratives or short stories
*   Literary analysis essays
*   Expository compositions, including analytical essays and research reports
*   Persuasive compositions
*   Business letters

On the one hand I am advocating that students will write better when allowed to choose their writing topics; on the other hand the state requires that I teach a number of very specific discourses. This creates a delicate balancing act for English teachers (see Figure 5.1).

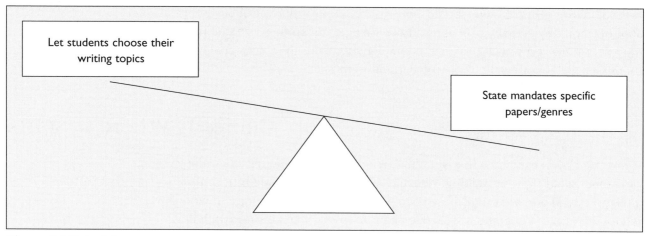

Figure 5.1 *Teeter-totter*

In the rush to meet the numerous writing standards, how do we infuse choice? How do we allow students to select their writing topics and still make sure that we teach all the required writing discourses? Can this balance be managed in this age of testing concerns?

Two Guiding Principles of a Writing Classroom

I will make the case in this chapter that student choice can be generated in our classrooms without sacrificing the goal of teaching the mandated discourses. In order to maintain this delicate balance, I advocate two guiding principles:

1. Sometimes we have to take a step backward before we can move forward.
2. Teachers can work students into the required discourses slowly by designing writing assignments that allow for partial student choice.

Let's explore these two guiding principles. I will briefly elaborate on why each principle is important and will share a number of effective writing strategies I have used to help establish each of them in my own classroom.

Principle #1: Sometimes We Have to Take a Step Backward Before We Can Move Forward

Imagine that your state has passed a mandate that every student in your third-period class must play in a varsity basketball game. Many of your students tell you that they don't see the point of playing basketball and tell you they would rather not participate. You scoff at this notion, telling your students there is much beauty in the game of basketball, that basketball is important, and you reassure them that the game is good for them. To illustrate the greatness of basketball, you randomly choose a student and insert him into Friday night's game. Without much experience or confidence going into the contest, the student immediately finds himself overwhelmed. He plays poorly, and is relieved when the game is over. He leaves the game hoping he will not have to play basketball again.

No one would teach adolescents to play basketball this way. It would be cruel. But isn't this how we teach our teenagers to write? We tell students that writing is worthwhile. They tell us they don't like to write. We scoff at that, telling them that the big game is coming (the state-mandated writing exam). We insert them into pressure writing situations (their efforts will be scrutinized and graded). When they finish the "game" they are grateful that it is over and hope not to write again any time soon.

Before I can concern myself with any of the specific discourses, I must first work on breaking down the negativity that many of my students carry with them regarding writing. It doesn't matter what writing standards our students are being held accountable for if they come to us with an aversion that is so strong they won't take any ownership of their writing. This is a bigger issue than simply a testing issue. Tests come and go, but attitudes about writing can be *lifelong*. This may be one of the more controversial stands I make in this book, but *I am advocating that we ignore the mandated discourses until we have had a chance to help students warm up to writing.* We have to work students through and beyond their anti-writing bias before we worry whether every standard is taught. It is unconscionable for me to feel satisfaction about teaching every standard if I get to the end of the school year and find that my students still dislike writing.

Job one is to get students interested in writing. Until students warm up to writing they will never work hard developing their writing skills. Think about it: when was the last time you took a strong interest and worked hard on something you really hated doing? Can you think of one example? I can't. (Well, maybe one. Doing my taxes. But I only do those to avoid an up-close and personal meeting with the IRS. If any employee of the IRS is reading this, let me reiterate what a fine job you are doing and recognize how under-appreciated you are in your line of work). Generally speaking, however, people do not work hard on tasks they hate doing. This is the very problem writing teachers confront year in and year out. Many of our students come to us with a strong distaste for writing, yet we unrealistically expect them to immediately roll up their sleeves and get into the writing flow of our classrooms. Though writing generates in them the same feeling that I get every year when faced with doing my taxes, we remain surprised and disheartened when they balk at completing their writing assignments.

Before we can get reluctant students to write well in any mandated discourse, we first have to warm them up to the notion of writing. Before I insert my students into the writing "game," I want them to have tons of safe practice under their belts. I want them to write daily for an extended period of time before we focus on any specific discourse. In my ninth-grade classes, this means I will spend much of the first quarter of the school year breaking down their resistance to writing. I focus on building up their interest and motivation in writing before entering them into serious competition (e.g., mandated genres or state testing). I do this not only by suggesting some interesting writing possibilities, but by allowing my students some choice as they begin to get their feet wet as writers.

In short, sometimes we have to take a step backward before we can move students forward. I am not going to stick a kid into a basketball game who does not how to dribble the ball. With this in mind, here are ten writing assignments I use early in the year to help ease my students into writing. These are assignments that even reluctant adolescent writers like doing.

1. Find the Fib

Below you will find six statements about me. Five of the statements are true; one is a fib. Can you guess which one is the fib?

1. Tiger Woods was a student of mine when he was in high school.
2. I was once an extra in a Dustin Hoffman movie.
3. I almost ran over a famous NFL quarterback with my car as he was jogging down the street.
4. In Italy, I was robbed at gunpoint. The gunman took my passport.
5. I had a terrible brain freeze on national television as a contestant on a television game show.
6. I once shook hands with the president of the United States.

Five are true; one is a fib. After students try to guess the correct answer, I have them generate four statements about themselves. They exchange papers and have their peers guess which one of their statements they believe to be false. The student who fools the most classmates is recognized at the end of the activity. Students are then asked to choose one of their truths and tell the story in writing. Very rarely do they shy away at this writing assignment; in fact, just the opposite occurs—by the time we get to the end of the activity, students are eager to write their stories.

My falsehood, by the way, is number one. Although Tiger did attend high school in Anaheim, he was never a student of mine. The other five statements are true, though I'd rather not relive three of them.

2. Establish Writing Territories

Nancie Atwell, in her seminal work, *In the Middle,* introduces the idea that every student has territories from which good writing can spring. We are all experts in specific territories. In Figure 5.2, you'll see my writing territories, which I share with my students.

Once their writing territories are established, students are asked to produce various "sneezes"—short, twenty-minute writing explorations into a given territory. Because students have generated their own territories, there is much more buy-in on their part. It also helps that I "sneeze" alongside them.

My Writing Territories

My children	Learning to drive	Playing HS basketball
Wife	Two auto accidents	Coach Purcell
In-laws	Scuba diving	Coaching HS basketball
My sister's troubled history	My 1st year teaching	Political activism
The ravages of drug abuse	Vegas boys' trips	Photography
My dog, Beezus	Europe	Jumping off bridges
Boogie boarding	NYC	Hunting sharks
Body surfing	Washington, D.C.	Broken bones
Umpiring	Florida	Getting stitched up . . . again
Reading	Maui	Emergency room visits
Writing	Berkeley	My 99-year-old grandmother
Music	Mexico	My Aunt Dolores
My car history	River rafting through Grand Canyon	Kobe
My pet history	Field trips	OJ
My hair history	Public speaking	JFK assassination
My concert history	Frisbee golf	Why Apples are better than PCs
Traffic tickets	Skateboarding (old school)	Ipods
Psycho ex-girlfriends	College stories	Airplane stories
Dating stories	Politics	Airplane food
Waiting tables	Being a congressional intern	Mapquest hell
Memorable baseball games	Talking to famous people	Picketing
Baseball cards	Meeting Jackson Browne	Toilet papering houses
Volleyball tournaments	TV game show appearance	Illnesses—my uncle's Parkinson's
Teaching stories	My movie "appearance"	Standing w/out pants on a runway in Miami
Memorable students	Practical jokes	
Memorable teachers	Football road trips	Photography
Memorable principals	Death in waves	Breakfast cereal history

Figure 5.2 *Gallagher's writing territories*

I have them explore a new territory daily for the first four days of the week, and on Friday they choose their best initial draft and revise it. We do this for a couple of weeks early in the school year and then periodically revisit and add to their writing territories as the year progresses.

3. Funneling a Writing Territory

Ralph Fletcher, in *What a Writer Needs* (1993), writes about the importance of getting students to narrow their focus before they write—to write "smaller" (p. 49). The smaller a student writes, Fletcher argues, the more interesting a piece of writing often becomes. I was reminded of this when I read a piece in *Newsweek* about the AIDS crisis in Africa (Zeitz 2003). The article was laden with startling facts (8,000 die every day due to the disease; the U.S. is spending $2.4 billion annually to help solve the problem [p. 14]), but the image I will always remember from the article is one of a young man standing on a street corner selling coffins. More than the statistic of 8,000 deaths every day, it is the image of that lone person selling coffins on the street that I find deeply touching. It's an image that is seared into my brain and a testament to the power of small writing.

One of the dangers when students are given choice is that they will often write large—so broadly that their essays drown in blandness. Jesus, a fan of Disneyland, indicated to me in a writing conference that he'd like to write about "going to Disneyland." I recorded our conversation (I am "KG"):

KG: Disneyland, huh? Okay. What, specifically, are you going to write about?
Jesus: I told you, Mr. G—Disneyland.
KG: I know your topic is going to be Disneyland, and I look forward to reading your paper, but what about Disneyland are you going to write about?
Jesus: It's my favorite amusement park.
KG: Okay, I am good with that, but what is the focus of your essay going to be?
Jesus: That Disneyland is a great place to visit.

It was clear that Jesus, a reluctant writer, needed a little help in finding a focus point for his essay. With Fletcher in mind, I guided Jesus into "funneling" his topic (see Figure 5.3).

The conversation continued:

KG: Before you begin writing, let's try a strategy that good writers often use to help narrow their topic. I call it funneling. [I show Jesus the funneling chart.] Do you know what a funnel is?
Jesus: Yes, it helps pour liquid.
KG: Right. You pour a lot of liquid in the top, but at the bottom only a little comes out. In a way, a funnel narrows the liquid.
Jesus: Okay.
KG: Instead of putting water into the top of the funnel, let's put in your topic, a trip to Disneyland, and see if we can narrow it down a little.
Jesus: Okay, but how do I do that?
KG: Write "Disneyland" in the largest box. Let's think about your experiences at Disneyland. Have you been to the park more than once?
Jesus: Yes, I have been there many times.
KG: Does any particular visit stand out? When you think of your visits to the park, which visit is most memorable?
Jesus: My first visit.
KG: Good. That's a bit narrower. Write that in the next box. Now, when you think of your first visit to Disneyland, what memory first comes to mind?
Jesus: Trying to get on the Indiana Jones ride.
KG: Good. Put that in the next box. Now what was memorable about trying to get on the Indiana Jones ride?
Jesus: They had this sign with a line drawn on it, and you had to be as tall as the line or they would not let you on the ride. I was, like, an inch too short.
KG: So what did you do?

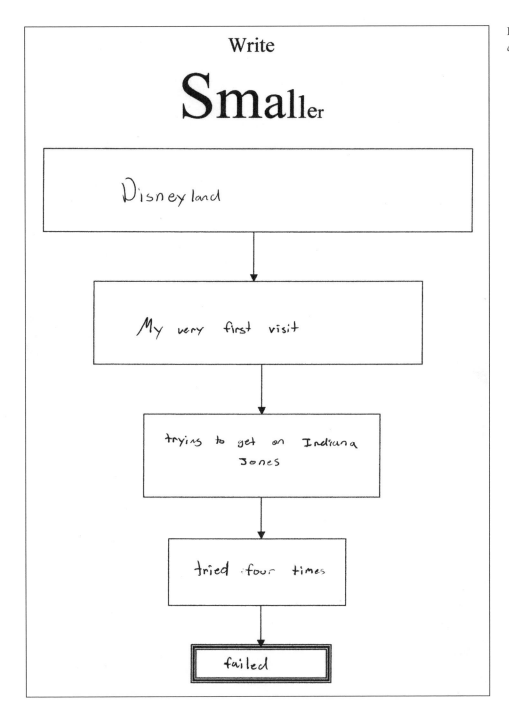

Figure 5.3 *Funnel graphic organizer*

Jesus: I tried to get on the ride four different times and each time they wouldn't let me on. I tried different strategies, but none of them worked.

KG: What do you mean when you say you tried different strategies?

Jesus: Well, the first two times I just tried to walk on all normal. After the guy wouldn't let me on, I waited until there was a new guy working the line. I tried it again, but he wouldn't let me on either.

KG: So what did you do?

Jesus: The third time I tried walking through the line on my tiptoes.

KG: (*laughs*) Did that work?

Jesus: Nah, he figured out what I was doing.

KG: Did you give up at that point?

Jesus: No, I tried once more. This time my uncle lent me his boots. I put them on and walked through the line again.

KG: Did it work?

Jesus: No. I was still too short. Just barely.

KG: How'd you feel when you were denied the fourth time?

Jesus: It sucked. They should of let me on. It was my first trip to Disneyland and all I wanted to do was ride that ride.

KG: You have a great story here—the day you tried to get on Indiana Jones. It's funny. It's interesting. Do you think you could try to capture this story in writing?

Jesus: I can try.

KG: Great. Go for it. When you finish your sneeze bring it back and we'll play with it.

When we had finished, Jesus had completed his funneling of the story. Before the funnel, Jesus was intent on writing about "going to Disneyland," an incredibly broad topic sure to produce a bland piece of writing. After finishing the funnel, he had narrowed his topic down to a more interesting, narrower topic: his mission to get on the Indiana Jones roller coaster. See Figure 5.4 for Jesus's "smaller" Disneyland first draft. In Appendix 7 you will find a reproducible copy of the funnel handout.

4. Topic Blast

Another way to encourage smaller writing is to have students choose one writing territory and "blast" it into as many pieces as possible. In Figure 5.5 you will find Joanna's topic blast for her quinceañera (fifteenth birthday), which in Mexican tradition represents the passing from childhood to adulthood for girls. The celebrations are elaborate and reminiscent of weddings. I sat down in a writing conference with Joanna and in a five-minute discussion she blasted her quinceañera into a number of smaller writing topics.

Had Joanna simply been asked to "write about your quinceañera," I have no doubt she would have produced a bland paper. Blasting the topic led her to a number of smaller, more interesting topics. See Appendix 8 for a reproducible Topic Blast chart.

5. The Myth of the Boring Topic

Bruce Ballenger, in *The Curious Researcher* (2001), introduces the idea of the myth of the boring topic. Ballenger argues that any topic is interesting if one takes a moment to scratch under its surface.

Too Short

Ever since I was little, I wanted to go the magical place I had never been to but had seen many times on television—Disneyland. I can still remember the commercials, with Cinderella riding in her carriage and the castle with the fireworks exploding behind it. I was looking forward to going on the teacups and the bumper cars and some of the other rides but I wanted the go on the ride with the most excitement, Indiana Jones.

As I passed through the gates it seemed almost like a dream to good to be true. There was a big parade going on and I almost got run over by a rhino. None of this bothered me, though, because I was on my way to ride the Indiana Jones ride.

Suddenly, I ran into it. The door was big, dark, and was covered with spider webs. Around the door was spears and at the tip of the spears there where human skulls. I knew this was the ride for me.

Then my uncle said, "Let's go on this ride it looks like it will be a good one." We walked down a dark hall which was covered in spider webs. It seemed to go on for ever. We were tired when we got to the end. The place looked just like the movie where Indiana Jones tries to out run the giant boulder. We were lucky because we were there early and we didn't have to wait long.

As I was about to get on the ride a tall man came out of nowhere and asked me to put my back against a sign with an arrow which was barely above my head. Then he said the words that would ruin my day, "I'm sorry, but you are too short for this ride." I was furious! The only ride I really wanted to go on and this man says I was too short.

I got out of line, waited a few minutes, and re-entered thinking I could make it the second time. But as I reached the front of the line my mortal enemy saw me again and told me I was too short and to leave the line. Normally, if someone tells you that you are too short to get on a ride you would most likely give up and leave before you get even madder. But not me.

While my uncle was finishing the ride I started to think of a new plan. When he got off the ride I asked him to come with me as I tried to get on again. This time I walked faster and more confident that he would let me on the ride. As I reached the sign, I put my plan into action. I stood on my tip toes sure that he wouldn't notice. It didn't work. He took one look at me and said, "Stand up straight and put your feet flat on the ground." Busted again.

After leaving I told my uncle I wanted to try one last time. As we approached the front of the line I asked my uncle to take off his boots.

"Why?" he asked.

"I am planning to use your boots to look taller," I answered.

I put his boots on. They felt warm and wet I'm guessing sweat.

When I got to the boarding area I was again told to stand with my back to the side. This time I was really sure they would let me on the one ride I really wanted to ride.

"Sorry," said the Devil Man. "You are too short. Please exit."

I was happy to finally visit Disneyland, but I will always remember the Indiana Jones ride as "the one that got away."

Figure 5.4 *Jesus's Disney essay*

To illustrate Ballenger's concept, I stood at my door one morning as my ninth-grade students entered the classroom. As they walked in the room, I said, "Good morning," and handed each student a dollar bill. (I am reasonably sure that this had never happened to them before!) When they had settled into their seats, I asked how many of them had ever seen a dollar bill before. They laughed. I then began the lesson by explaining that even though they had all seen dollar bills, my guess was that few, if any, of them had actually carefully *considered* a dollar bill. "A dollar may appear to be a common, boring, everyday item," I told them, "but if you think about it, that's not true at all. Dollars are fascinating."

"How so?" asked Kenny.

Figure 5.5 *Topic blast example (Joanna)*

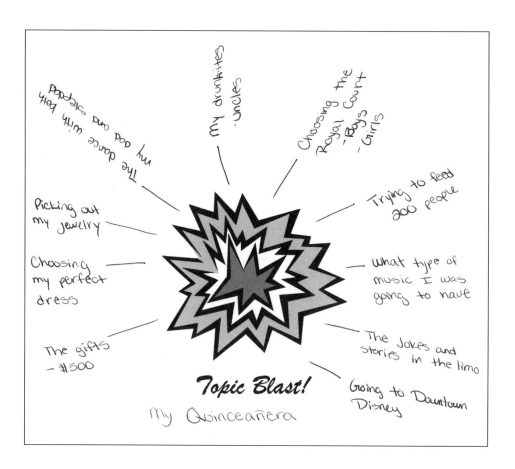

"Think of all the interesting facts, stories, and history behind a dollar," I responded. "Think of all the questions a single dollar generates. Can anyone in the room think of one interesting question that spins out of a single dollar?"

"How do people counterfeit them?" asked Adam. The class laughed.

"Great question," I responded. "Let me put that question on the overhead. Adam's question is interesting, and if you start thinking about that dollar in front of you, I'm sure other interesting questions will begin to flow. I am going to give each group ten minutes to generate a list of interesting questions about your dollars. I challenge each group to write the most interesting set of questions. Go."

Ten minutes later, I brought the groups back together and created a classroom list on the overhead projector. Below is the list generated by my fourth-period ninth-grade class.

Why George Washington?

How do you get a job making money?

What are the serial numbers for?

Who signs the dollar?

What is the history of this dollar?

What is the life span of a dollar?

What is the Federal Reserve?

Who makes the dollar? Where?

Why the phrase, "In God We Trust"?

What kind of paper is used? Ink?

What steps are taken against counterfeiting?

Why paper instead of a coin?

How much $ does it take to make a dollar?

Is it really a crime to destroy a dollar?

Why does the pyramid have an eyeball?

Why not more color?

Why only white people on our money?

Why letters in the serial number?

Why are there 13 parts to the pyramid?

Why these specific denominations?

Can you photocopy a dollar?

Who designed the dollar?

Why green as primary color?

Is there a hidden spider on the dollar?

What do the Latin words mean?

Why are there "hairs" inside the dollar?

Who decides who is pictured?

Why not a three-dollar bill?

What is the penalty for counterfeiting?

Has the design ever changed?

This exercise helps students to see that there is no such thing as a boring topic. Once the classroom brainstorm has been generated and shared, each student takes out a sheet of paper and is asked to choose a really "boring" topic. The new topic is written at the top of the paper, then passed around the room. When students receive a new paper with a "boring" topic on it, they are asked to try to generate an interesting question for it. After the papers have been passed throughout the class, students receive their topics back, each with a number of interesting questions written below it. Gerardo, for example, chose the topic "rocks." When he got his paper back, he found the following questions:

How many types of rocks are there?

What makes them different colors?

Why do people collect them?

What are they made of?

Why are some rocks more valuable than others?

Where do rocks come from?

How can you figure out how old a rock is?

Where is the largest rock?

What shapes them?

Where did the word *rock* originate?

Crystal's topic was "water." She was asked:

Which drinking water is best?

How do you clean water?

Where does our drinking water come from?

Why does some water make you sick?

What lives in water? How many organisms live in a single drop?

Is water organic or inorganic?

Why is water clear?

Has water been found anywhere else other than earth?

Is there enough water for everyone?

Why does our body need water?

Is it true that of our bodies are mostly made up of water?

Is flavored water bad for you?

Students are then asked to choose one question that particularly intrigues them and go find the answer. (It helps if they have been taught some research skills; I do a mini-lesson on how to use Google.) They bring their notes to class the next day and write their explanations. Upon completion, the students then pass their questions and answers around the class, providing not only a valuable opportunity for students to read each other's writing, but also providing the students (and teacher) with lots of interesting information.

A Variation of This Exercise The "Myth of the Boring Topic" exercise can be varied using objects other than a dollar bill. For example, fill up a brown grocery bag with everyday items (e.g., a baseball, a bottle of water, a key, a sock, and a candy bar). Make sure there are enough items in the bag so that each student in the class will be able to draw out one item. Each student then reaches into the bag blindly and pulls out an item. Once he or she has taken an item, the student then brainstorms as many interesting questions as possible. Eventually, he or she chooses one question from the brainstorm and goes to find the answer.

And, in case you're wondering, the answer is yes—I do collect my dollars before the end of the period.

6. What Bugs Me

In *A Writer's Notebook: Unlocking the Writer Within You* (1996), Ralph Fletcher has his students list things they find irritating. Here is my list, inspired by Fletcher:

- Talking loudly on cell phones at inappropriate times and places
- People who drive "cell phone drunk"
- Squeezing the middle of the toothpaste tube
- CD packaging
- The following expressions: "free gift," "totally destroyed," "no problem," and "You go, girl!"
- Local "news" broadcasts
- "Reality" television (especially MTV's *My Sweet Sixteen*)
- Standing in line—any line
- Filling my car with gas
- Subscription cards that fall out of magazines
- "Dumb" traffic signals
- Students who do not return books to my classroom library
- South Coast Plaza (local shopping mall) on December 26
- Telephone sales calls
- Leg cramps
- Liver
- Rude service in restaurants

- Fans who switch allegiance to other teams when their team is struggling (a.k.a. frontrunners)
- Car door dingers in parking lots
- People with fourteen items in the ten-items-or-less line at the grocery store
- Paying by check in a cash-only line
- Ticketmaster fees
- Parents who take ten-year-olds to R-rated movies
- Dangerous freeway drivers
- The rule in the NFL that says the ground cannot cause a fumble
- Baseball's designated hitter rule
- Hallowed baseball records broken by steroid users
- Using the last of the toilet paper roll and not replacing it
- Placing a milk carton back in the refrigerator when it has five drops of milk left in it
- Bags in cereal boxes that cannot be opened without completely mangling the bag
- Haggling with car salespeople
- Choosing a new cell phone plan

Students love to write about things that annoy them. There is something about this topic that brings out strong voice in my students' writing, as evidenced by the following excerpt from Brianna's essay (note: this excerpt is still in the revision stage; she has not edited it for errors):

When the lights dim, I think the movie is about to start. Nope, more previews. Now that "The Twenty" is over and I know what Whoopi Goldberg's real name is and how much Oprah makes in a year (not that I give a rat's tail), I finally get to see previews of movies that should be coming out within the next decade or so. Ten minutes of this insanity creeps by and throughout it the couple sitting two rows behind me are exchanging spit and the person three seats to my right who has already seen the movie is talking obnoxiously loud about all the good parts, ruining what's left of my anticipation. To make matters worse, Snow White and her seven dwarfs are on the screen showing off their anniversary edition DVD right before the movie Saw 2. *Nothing like seven dwarfs before seven deaths.* Saw 2 *finally starts and I'm sitting there out of money and out of Junior Mints. The people in back of me put their smelly feet onto the seat and open their bottled soda unleashing a fizzle that scares my organs into not functioning.*

When students care about what they are writing, their voice emerges.

7. Good Ideas/Bad Ideas

Another way to interest students in writing is to begin by having them brainstorm good and bad ideas they have encountered. I begin by sharing my list with them:

Good Ideas	Bad Ideas
Our International Week assembly	Removing the lockers from our school
Juice smoothie	McRib sandwich
Televisions in the back of airplane seats	Televisions in cars
Developing a daily reading habit	Cutting back the hours of our community's library
Freeway dots to divide lanes	Neglecting upkeep on our highways
IPod	Beta-Max
MADD	Blanket "zero tolerance" school policy
In-line skates	Skates built into tennis shoes
Cup holders in cars	"Pimping your ride" so that your car has a fish tank in the trunk
"Old school" Mr. Potato Head toy	New plastic Mr. Potato Head toy
Printing airline boarding passes online	Airlines have stopped serving meals
Disposable mop heads	Robotic vacuum cleaners

Once their brainstorms are completed, I have students choose one idea and complete a "topic blast" (see page 100). They are then ready to start drafting.

8. Explorations

A few years ago I heard Dan Kirby, co-author of *Inside Out: Developmental Strategies for Teaching Writing* (Kirby, Kirby, and Liner 1988), speak about the importance of memoir writing. In his presentation, Kirby suggested a number of places writers can explore for interesting writing topics. I share Kirby's ideas below, with my adaptations, which I have put into a first-quarter writing plan:

Week	Category	Areas to Explore for Writing Ideas
Week 1	Names	• Origins of your name • History of your name • The story of how you were named • Advantages and inconveniences about your name • Why you like/dislike your name • Teasing about your name
Week 2	Snapshots	• A photograph that first comes to mind • Your most treasured photograph • The photograph you wish you had never taken (or been in) • A photograph that taught you something • The photograph you most associate with loss; Happiness; A change in your life
Week 3	Boundaries	• Maps in your mind of special places • Home(s) • Neighborhood(s) • School(s) • Countries
Week 4	Artifacts	• Treasured items • Most treasured possession • Artifacts passed from generation to generation • Memories that come from holding a treasured item • An item that is of no monetary value but is priceless
Week 5	Family	• Family stories/legends • How people in your family met (or parted) • Characters in your family • Special family occasions • Family rituals/traditions • Roles and responsibilities in your family
Week 6	Ethnicity, Race, and Culture	• Immigration stories • Racism anecdotes • Overcoming language barriers • Overcoming cultural barriers • Strangers-in-a-strange-land stories
Week 7	Mysteries	• Secrets among family members or friends • Unsolved crimes or practical jokes • Things that are puzzling; riddles • Unexplained occurrences

Week	Category	Areas to Explore for Writing Ideas
Week 8	Parents	• Relationships • Tensions • Joys • Intense times/struggles • Learning something unexpected about your parent(s) • Seeing your parent(s) in a new light
Week 9	Celebratory Times	• Weddings • Births • Memorable parties • Overcoming a problem • Awards and recognition • Achieving a new level • Winning unexpectedly
Week 10	Difficult Times	• Life in crisis • Death • Illness • Family problems • Neighborhood problems • Coping with loss • Coping with uncertainty; doubt

If your goal in the first quarter is to get your students into writing, these have proven to be successful motivators. One year I introduced one of these places to explore each week and asked my students to write five weekly pages in their writer's notebooks. By the end of the first quarter they had fifty pages of interesting memoir writing and were well on their way to overcoming their disdain for writing.

9. I Remember . . .

Another effective strategy useful to help students write about their experiences is to introduce Edward Montez's poem, "I Remember." After reading through it a number of times, I have students write their own "I Remember" poem. In Figure 5.6 you will find a poem written by Stephanie, a ninth grader. Once Stephanie had written her "I Remember" poem, each stanza became a potential writing topic to explore on future writing days.

10. Pass the Portrait

As students walk into the room, I hand each of them an unusual photograph cut from magazine advertisements. Students study the photographs and begin writing stories about them. They write for three minutes and then each student passes both the photograph and partial draft clockwise to the person sitting next to him or her. When a student receives the next photograph, he or she studies it before reading the partial draft, and then picks up writing where

Figure 5.6 *Stephanie's poem*

> **I Remember**
>
> By Stephanie Castro
>
> I remember the scent of rice pudding cooking on cold winter nights.
>
> And tossing and turning under thick blankets in the summer heat.
>
> I remember my hair blowing wildly into the air from the ceiling fan.
>
> And my cousins dumping grass in my hair while I played with dolls on the porch.
>
> I remember the screaming siren of an ambulance siren in the dark, knowing it was a cry of death.
>
> And chasing the ice cream truck down the street when it drove through my neighborhood.
>
> I remember Grandma sitting in her favorite plastic chair in the sun.
>
> And lying on the edge of the swimming pool, baking in the sun like we had just come out of the oven.
>
> I remember father toiling in the garden while I swung back and forth on my swing set.
>
> And going to the movie theater with $10 in my pocket, $7.50 for the ticket and the rest was mine.
>
> I remember eating ice cream and popcorn, rooting for the villains to win, and they never did, but that was yesterday.

the draft left off. This process is repeated a number of times until, eventually, every student gets his or her initial draft back. Students are then placed in small groups and asked to share their stories. They nominate the "best" one and each group picks one person to read the story to the class.

This exercise has never failed to interest my students in writing. For homework, students can finish the draft (if it is, indeed, unfinished), or they may begin revising it.

Principle #2: Teachers Can Work Students into the Required Discourses Slowly by Designing Writing Assignments That Allow for Partial Student Choice

After my students have begun to warm up to writing, I begin leading them into the various required discourses through writing assignments that still allow for partial student choice. Here are some partial-choice assignments for the four most common discourses (autobiographical narratives, responses to literature, expository essays, and persuasive compositions):

Limited Choice Assignment for Autobiographical Narratives: The Introduce Yourself Notebook

This assignment, developed with my colleague John Powers, requires each student to write a number of autobiographical sketches. The project is broken down into two parts; part one contains required assignments; part two allows for student choice. Below are the directions I give my students for the Introduce Yourself Booklet:

Part One (cover page plus three essays)

Part one of your booklet must consist of the following four items:

1. **Booklet Cover**: Your booklet cover should convey something about you. The cover can be literal or metaphorical, and you may use drawings, pictures, or symbols that relate to your personality or interests. Your name should appear prominently on the cover. Also include the teacher's name, the period, and the date.

2. **Myself, the Writer**: Write a reflective piece about yourself as a writer. Consider some or all of the following questions/prompts: What are your thoughts about yourself as a writer? Do you like to write? If yes, why? If no, why not? Discuss a memorable writing assignment (good or bad). What are your strengths and weaknesses as a writer? Which writer(s) do you admire? What goal(s) do you have as a writer this year?

3. **Myself, the Reader**: Write a reflective piece about yourself as a reader. Consider some or all of the following questions/prompts: Do you like to read? If yes, why? If no, why not? Do you read much? What materials interest you? Why do you like to read (or why do you dislike reading)? Discuss a memorable reading experience (good or bad). What are your strengths and weaknesses as a reader? What goal(s) do you have as a reader this year?

4. **My Biographer and Me**: *This is the only piece in the Introduce Yourself Booklet not written by you.* Choose someone who has known you for a long time and who knows you well (e.g., a parent, grandparent, uncle, or older sister, etc.) and have them write a one- to two-page biography of you. The purpose of this piece is to get to know you through the eyes of another.

Part Two (three essays)

For part two of the booklet, choose any three of the suggested topics below and write a multiparagraphed reflection for each of the three. Consider any or all of the questions/prompts:

College and Me: Are you planning to attend college? Where will you apply? Which is your number one choice? Why? What steps will you take this year to get accepted to this college? Do you want to attend college locally or do you want to move away to attend school? What do you think you might study? What are the college experiences you most look forward to?

The Questioning Me: Consider a question about your life that is important to you. What are your dreams? Hopes? Worries? Explore a "big" question.

My Accomplishments: Describe a challenging project you completed at some point in your life, along with an explanation of how you became interested in the project. (e.g., sewing a dress, writing a story, building a shed, or learning to use a photography darkroom). If possible, include something to help the reader understand your project, such as a photograph, a photocopy, a map, or a blueprint.

My Goals: Describe a goal (or series of goals). Why is this your goal? What drives you to reach it? How do you plan on attaining your goal(s)? What steps do you need to take to achieve your goal(s)?

The Future and Me: What are your short-term and long-term plans for a job or a career? What leisure-time activities, travel, or hobbies do you anticipate for the future? Do you plan to start a family? Where will you live?

My Family and Me: Describe your family members and what you like about each one. Include pictures if you wish. What has each member of your family taught you?

The Relaxing Me: What do you do for relaxation? How do you eliminate stress? What do you do to unwind? Discuss your favorite form(s) of entertainment.

People (or Person) I Admire: Explain who your role models are (living or dead, famous or anonymous) and why. Make sure the reader understands the qualities of this person (or people) that you admire.

Humor and Me: Describe your sense of humor. Give examples of your jokes and cartoons, television shows, movies, or books that have made you laugh. Share stories in which your sense of humor came into play. Share a practical joke story.

Me Back When: Share anecdotes from your past. Choose a single incident you believe had an impact on your life. Discuss how you have changed—how you were back then and how you are now. What, specifically, changed you?

Nature and Me: Describe how you relate to the natural world and what you enjoy seeing or doing outdoors (e.g., camping, hiking, surfing). Why is this activity important to you?

Sports and Me: Describe your love affair with sports. What sport do you love playing? Watching? Write about an intense moment you had in athletic competition. Which team has your undying allegiance? Why? What is the most memorable game you have ever seen?

Art and Me: Are you artistic? Where do your artistic talents lie? What does art mean to you? What art do you admire? Why?

Music and Me: What music "gets inside" you? What does music mean to you? What are your favorite types of music? Who are you favorite singers/bands? Do you play music? What does playing music mean to you?

The Movies and Me: Write about any of the following: your favorite films, scenes, actors, directors, or genres. What is that one movie you don't mind seeing many times? Why?

Animals and Me: Write about an important animal (or animals) in your life. Why is this animal special? What interesting story can you share about this animal?

Regret(s) and Me: What regrets to you have? Consider both past actions and "the road(s) not taken." If you could have a do-over for anything you have said or done in your life, what would you do differently? Why?

Myself and _____: Can you think of a category that is not listed here? If you'd like to write about an element of you not listed here, go for it! One request: please run the idea by the teacher before you begin writing.

When students complete the assignment, their booklet contains six written sketches (three chosen by the teacher; three chosen by the students). They are encouraged to add artwork, photographs, drawings, or any artifacts that enrich their writing. (Grading Note: Because I do not want to start the school year by having to grade 700 essays, I only score two of the six pieces—one they choose as their "best" writing and one that I choose randomly. I do not tell students that only two of pieces will be scored until *after* the project is turned in. Assessment will be discussed in greater detail in Chapter 7.)

Capture Your Community

One of the advantages I have with my thirty-eight freshman students is that they are part of a program in which they will return to me as sophomores. Being their English teacher for two years enables me to make sure they have work to do over the summer. In addition to assigning recreational readings, I also require them to participate in a Capture Your Community project.

Through on-campus fund-raising, I purchase a disposable camera for each student (though many students do not need one because they already own or have access to digital cameras). With cameras in hand, I ask my students to capture their community on the 4th of July. I prompt them to look for the people and places that encapsulate the spirit of the community on the holiday. The photos can show the holiday in a positive light (e.g., a community picnic) or a negative light (e.g., a homeless man watching fireworks), but their mission is clear: to capture truthfully the spirit of their community on this holiday.

Students are then required to bring their photos to class on the first day of their sophomore year. The photographs are always quite varied—some students spend a quiet holiday with their immediate family; others travel to participate in grand celebrations elsewhere. Upon returning to school, students spread out their photos and the class shares them through a gallery walk. Once the sharing is complete, I ask students to pick the one photograph of theirs that best captures the spirit of their holiday. It this photograph that will drive a piece of "small" writing. When all the pieces are complete, we create a booklet entitled *Our Community on the 4th of July*, complete with scanned photographs.

This assignment does not need to be tied to the 4th of July. It works well over winter break or around any other holiday. In the past I have also chosen a day randomly and created a booklet around it (e.g., *A Day in the Life of Our Community: October 15, 2006*).

Limited Choice Assignments for Responding to Literature

The Writing Fountain   Early one year my freshman students were reading Sandra Cisneros's *The House on Mango Street*. They had just finished the vignette, "Hairs," in which Esperanza describes how the hair of her family members differs from person to person. I asked my students to use her essay as a model by writing about the various kinds of hair found in their own families. That night, I was surprised by how quickly I tired of reading their drafts. Frankly, there was a sameness about them that made them boring to read. My father has thick hair. My sister has pretty hair. I do not like my hair. Blah, blah, blah. Reading these, I soon found myself wishing I were doing something more fun, like undergoing root canal surgery.

I took the papers back to class the next day and told my students we would revisit the idea of hair by creating a Writing Fountain (a variation of the Topic Blast). I told them that I had read their papers and for the most part, found them boring. I added that it was probably my fault in that, I, as their teacher, had narrowed their topic too much. I then placed a graphic organizer of a fountain on the overhead with "hair" written on its base and asked the students to consider all the interesting stories that might spring from the topic of hair. I started by writing "my hair history" on one of the streams emanating from the fountain, and went beyond all calls for bravery by showing them photographs of the various stages of the history of my hair. (They howled when I showed them my senior photo, which captures me with long hair.) I then asked the students to create their own hair fountains. In Figure 5.7, you'll see Daniel's fountain.

Students then chose which hair angle they wanted to write from. Unlike their first attempts, these new drafts were a pleasure to read—no two essays were the same, and they contained a liveliness that had been missing in their first attempts.

Words of Wisdom Project   This project, adapted from Joan Hoffman's article in the March 1998 issue of *Classroom Notes Plus*, works well with any literary work that contains pearls of wisdom. As students begin reading the literary work, they are asked to make note of any words of wisdom they encounter. Upon completing *To Kill a Mockingbird*, for example, students might list the following:

> *You never really understand a person until you consider things from his point of view—until you climb into his skin and walk around in it. (p. 34)*
>
> Atticus

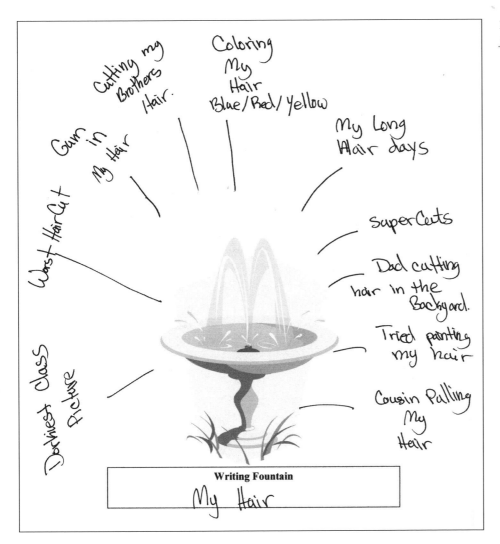

Figure 5.7 *Writing Fountain for hair*

The handwritten labels around the fountain read:

- Cutting my Brothers Hair.
- Coloring My Hair Blue/Red/Yellow
- Gum in My Hair
- My Long Hair days
- Worst HairCut
- SuperCuts
- Dorkiest Class Picture
- Dad cutting hair in the Backyard.
- Tried painting my hair
- Cousin Pulling My Hair

Writing Fountain

My Hair

You oughta let your mother know where you are. (p. 143)

Jem

Courage is when you know you're licked before you begin but you begin anyway and you see it through no matter what. (p. 80)

Atticus

I ask students to chart the wisdom as they work their way through the novel. When their reading is completed, students are asked to complete a three-part writing assignment.

Part One

Choose the wisest thing said in To Kill a Mockingbird. *Explain how Harper Lee develops this idea in the novel through the use of literary devices (e.g., plot, setting, characters).*

When students have written their analyses, we move on to Part Two of the assignment. I bring in copies of H. Jackson Brown's *Life's Little Instruction Book.* Brown wrote this book for his son and gave it to him the day his son left home. In it, Brown has collected all the snippets of wisdom he knows. After students have had a chance to examine the wisdom in Brown's book, they are ready to move to Part Two.

Part Two

Your assignment is to create your own Life's Little Instruction Book. *Your booklet must contain the following:*

- *Five (or more) pearls of wisdom from* To Kill a Mockingbird.
- *Ten (or more) pearls of wisdom from wise people in your world. Consider asking your parents, grandparents, aunts, uncles, neighbors, teachers, coaches, advisors, ministers, your dentist, your mail carrier, your plumber, and the guy working behind the counter at 7/11.*
- *Ten (or more) pearls of wisdom from research sources, including other novels, books, newspapers, websites, television shows, movies, song lyrics, and speeches.*
- *Five (or more) pearls of your own. Consider what you have learned thus far in your life. What advice can you offer?*

I remind the students that their quotes can be philosophical ("Never cut what can be untied"), practical ("Always own a good dictionary"), or humorous ("Boys, always flush the urinal with your elbow"). I bring in some resources of wisdom (*Bartlett's Familiar Quotations;* toastmaster books), but for the most part the creation of their booklets is done almost exclusively at home. I do not spend much class time on it.

Here are the directions for Part Three, which I give to my students the day they bring their finished booklets to class:

Part Three

1. *Revisit the wise things you found from the people whom you talked to directly. Choose one pearl of wisdom that you believe to be particularly wise.*
2. *Interview this person for a second time, asking how he or she came to believe this piece of wisdom. For example, if your grandfather told you, "Slow and easy wins the race," ask him how he learned that lesson in his life. Ask your source to describe an experience that he or she had that made that pearl of wisdom a truism. Through this second interview, find the story behind the wisdom.*
3. *Write the story.*

I like this assignment because it gives students some say in the direction of their papers. They are given choice in whom to interview and choice again when they decide which pearl of wisdom they will research and write about. The best part of this assignment is that it spawns interesting discussions between my students and wise people.

Limited Choice Assignments for Expository Compositions:
The Half-and-Half Research Paper

The senior curriculum in my school district requires that my students write an historical investigation report. For the past ten years, I have led my seniors through an extensive unit on the Kennedy assassination. Through a number of films, lectures, photographs, eyewitness accounts, and other artifacts, my students carefully examine the events of November 22, 1963. I chose the Kennedy assassination for two reasons: (1) it is the most fascinating eight seconds in American history, and (2) it fit into that year's senior theme, "Overcoming the Wasteland" (many people believe that America's modern wasteland began when those shots rang out in Dealey Plaza). Upon completion of this unit, students write a traditional research paper outlining the events of the assassination.

After reading these papers over a number of years, I began getting tired of them. The sameness of the papers began to numb me as I repeatedly read the same account. I realized the assignment needed life infused into it. Four years ago, I changed the assignment from a straightforward research paper to what I call the half-and-half research paper.

In the half-and-half research paper, the students share traditional research in the first half of the paper. For the Kennedy assignment, for example, students must demonstrate they understand the basics—the who, what, when, where, and why of the event. They must understand the government's findings and should be able to demonstrate that they have a grasp of the key conspiracy theories.

It is in the second half of the paper that the assignment opens up so that students can choose their avenues of exploration. In the second half, students are asked to find the one element they are most intrigued by and to research it in depth. I have one caveat: their research must be driven by a student-generated question. Here are some of the questions my seniors have explored:

- Did Oswald act alone?
- Was there a second gunman on the grassy knoll?
- Who is the "Babushka Lady"? Why has she never been found?
- Is there a connection between Kennedy and the mob?
- How likely is it that Cuba played a role in the assassination?
- Were the Russians involved in the killing?
- What is the "magic bullet"? Can it be explained?
- What happened behind the closed doors of the emergency room at Parkland Hospital?

Because they had some say in their avenues of research (and because it's an interesting topic), my students worked very hard on their papers. Again, one benefit as a teacher is that I am not stuck repeatedly reading the same paper.

The Kennedy paper has become a senior tradition at my school, but this year those of us who teach the twelfth grade decided it was time for change.

As I am writing this, my students are investigating the events of 9/11, and when their research is completed I will assign the half-and-half format. In the first half of their papers students will outline the events of that fateful day; in the second half they will each pick a hot spot to research. Some of them have already chosen topics:

- What happened on Flight 93?
- What happened inside the Pentagon that day? What was the extent of the damage (lives/national security)?
- Structurally, why did the towers collapse?
- What happened inside the towers prior to the collapse?
- Who were the attackers, and why did they attack us?
- Is it fair to say the U.S. ignored crucial intelligence prior to 9/11?
- As a result of 9/11, are we now safer?
- What are the criticisms from the 9/11 Commission Report?
- What effects (short-term/long-term) did that day have on our economy?
- What are the pros and cons of arming air marshals and airline pilots?
- What are the pros and cons of the color-coded warning system?
- What art (music, film, paintings, sculptures) has been inspired by the events of 9/11?
- Was 9/11 exploited to justify invading Iraq?
- Why do so many Americans believe that Iraq was involved in 9/11?
- What will be built at Ground Zero? How was this decision made?
- What are some of the conspiracy theories? Do any of them hold water?
- Is it too early for Hollywood to make 9/11 films?

Unlike reading lockstep research papers, reading these papers will be interesting because no two will be alike.

Limited Choice Assignments for Persuasive Compositions: The Four-Sided Argument

One of the dangers in writing persuasive papers is that my students frequently see complex issues in black and white, often without much consideration to the point of view of others. To shake them from their tunnel vision I assign the four-sided argument.

I first introduced the four-sided argument years ago in the shadow of the O. J. Simpson trial. My students were worked up over it, so much so that when the verdict was read they had a hard time even considering any viewpoints contrary to their own. To get them past this, I had the class brainstorm a list of the stakeholders in the trial. They started with the obvious names:

O. J. Simpson	Kato Kaelin	Mark Furman
The jury foreman	Judge Ito	Johnny Cochran
Marcia Clark	Nicole Brown's sister	Ron Goldman's father
Alan Park (O. J.'s limo driver)	O. J.'s daughter	TV newsperson

When they finished we had a list of over thirty stakeholders. Students were asked to choose four stakeholders, making sure that the four chosen possessed differing views. Students were then assigned to write four one-page responses to the verdict, each from the point of view of a different stakeholder.

I have used this strategy a number of times since, most recently when the citizens of Orange County (where I live and teach) were fighting over the issue of building a new airport in the middle of the county. The debate was heated, but like most debates, it wasn't simply black and white; there were many valid arguments. Having students consider the issue from various points of view (e.g., a land developer, a homeowner, a pilot, or the mayor) broadened their thinking on the issue. After students carefully considered the viewpoints of various stakeholders, they were much better prepared to write compelling persuasive essays on the issue.

These four examples—(1) the Introduce Yourself Booklet, (2) the Capture Your Community Paper, (3) the Words of Wisdom Project, and (4) the Four-Sided Argument—are appealing to students because they all have an element of choice in them. Once students are up and running as writers, I work toward opening up broader student choice. Here are two assignments my students enjoy that allow them wide-open choice.

Ever Wonder Why?
The comedian Gallagher (no relation—he has more money; I have more hair) once asked a truly puzzling question: "Did you ever wonder what a chair would look like if your knees bent the other way?" Okay, so maybe that one is a little too deep. But surely there are questions out there worth careful consideration, questions that burn inside your brain (Ralph Fletcher calls these "Fierce Wonderings" [1996]). To get my students to start thinking about questions that pique their curiosity, I give them a quiz pulled from Douglas B. Smith's *Ever Wonder Why?* (1991). Here are the questions I gave to my students:

1. Why are wedding bands worn on the fourth finger of the left hand?
2. Why are tennis balls fuzzy?
3. Why is blue considered a boys' color?
4. Why do worms come out on the sidewalk when it rains?
5. Why is someone who is feeling great said to be "on cloud nine"?
6. Why do we nod our heads yes and shake our heads no?
7. Why do ostriches stick their heads in the ground?
8. Why do bats sleep upside down?

I assure them that there are answers to each of these questions and give each group a few minutes to hypothesize. We then share out, and this discussion is always rich and full of laughter. (See Figure 5.8 for the answers to the eight questions.) This exercise prepares students to develop awareness about those things they truly wonder about. To further nudge them in this direction, I share my list of things I truly wonder about.

Figure 5.8 *Answers to Ever Wonder Why*

"Ever Wonder Why?" Answers

1. Wedding bands are always worn on the third finger because it was once thought to be the site of the vein of love.

2. The fuzz slows the ball down in flight so it won't bounce too high.

3. It was once believed that blue (the color of the heavens) held off evil spirits who tried to invade infant boys.

4. Worms come out on the sidewalk when it rains because their bodies are full of water and they are seeking higher ground.

5. Types of clouds are numbered according to the altitude they obtain. Nine is the highest, symbolizing the idea of floating above all your problems.

6. Charles Darwin related these head gestures to a baby's nursing habits. Babies who want to eat move their heads up and down. Babies who don't move their heads side to side.

7. Ostriches rarely stick their heads in the ground, but when they do they are looking for water.

8. Bats sleep upside down so they can hang from the ceiling and avoid predators.

Ten Things Mr. Gallagher Wonders About

1. I wonder how my IPod can hold 5,000 songs.
2. I wonder what happens to a lost email. Where does it go?
3. I wonder where our moon came from.
4. I wonder how it is possible to play a video game with another person who is sitting somewhere else in the world.
5. The Queen Mary weighs 81,000 tons. How does it float? A 747 weighs 1,200 tons. How does it fly?
6. I wonder who had the courage to drink the first glass of milk.
7. I wonder where the idea of wearing neckties originated.
8. I wonder how astronomers know that planets exist outside our solar system if they can't see them.
9. I wonder how GPS systems in cars work.
10. I wonder how a DVD actually produces visuals and sound.

After our initial discussions of "I wonder why" questions, students are now ready to develop their own "I wonder . . ." lists. Because the lists are generated from their own interests, students are much more motivated when it comes time to write.

I Am an Expert

Everyone has expertise in one area or another. Here, for example, are ten things I could write about with a reasonable degree of expertise:

bodysurfing
scuba diving

Disneyland
baseball
negotiating airports
driving the southern California freeway system
reading
seventies rock music
the Kennedy assassination
waiting tables

After sharing my list with my students, I ask them to generate lists of their own. Here are three of them:

Adrian	**Linda**	**Jimena**
making quesadillas	dancing	Texas Hold 'Em
Anaheim fast food	cross-country running	making eggs
building Legos	debating	the Holocaust
rock climbing	making my parents mad	Johnny Depp
water polo	cleaning the house	anemia
TV show *Lost*	TV show *South Park*	TV show *Full House*
wakeboarding	finding out secrets	chess
Kobe	getting out of trouble	drawing

Once their lists are complete, students choose topics from their lists and then share their expertise in writing.

A variation of this assignment: Have students brainstorm a list of areas where they *wish* they had expertise (e.g., how to fly a plane, the Vietnam War, raising chinchillas). Have them conduct research and share their research in writing. Upon the completion of the writing, each student orally shares something he or she learned. (For tips on how to facilitate the research process, I recommend Ken Macrorie's *The I-Search Paper: Revised Edition of Searching Writing*).

This chapter began with Todd's complaint that student writing is forced upon students only as a means of making teachers look good. One way of moving students beyond this mind-set and to help them develop as writers is by infusing choice into the writing process. As Laura Robb, a teacher of forty-three years and author of fifteen books, once told me, "We have a nation of students who can't write very well. We will not have a nation of students who can write well until they are allowed to write about the things they care about."

Creating opportunities for students to have choice while writing doesn't mean that teachers must give up control of their classrooms. Rather, as Anderman and Midgely (1998) have found, "Even small opportunities for choice . . . gives students a greater sense of autonomy" (p. 3). Likewise, Paula Denton (2005), after examining thirty-two studies on the effect that choice has on learning, found that "most of the research demonstrated that when students had choices in their learning, they became highly engaged and productive. They were excited about learning and shared their knowledge. They were likely to think more deeply and creatively, work with more persistence, and willingly use a range of academic skills and strategies" (p. 2). Rather than forcing students to write about things they don't care about, creating student choice within our writing assignments helps students like Todd realize that learning to write holds way more value than simply making the teacher look good.

The Importance of Purpose and Audience

In this chapter we turn our attention to the importance that both purpose and audience play in building writers. Though purpose and audience go hand-in-hand, I will begin by discussing them separately. This creates a paradox: by discussing them independently, it is my hope that by the end of the chapter you will come to see why one cannot be considered without the other.

Let's start with the importance of teaching our students to recognize the author's purpose.

A Crash Course in Understanding Author's Purpose

One year, Vice President Dick Cheney was in the news for over a week due to a near-tragic hunting accident. While hunting for quail, the vice president accidentally shot a friend. Consider the following excerpts from three written accounts of the incident:

> *Vice President Dick Cheney accidentally shot and wounded a campaign contributor during a weekend quail hunt on a friend's South Texas ranch, local authorities and the vice president's office said Sunday.*
>
> *The wounded man, 78-year-old Harry Whittington, was in intensive care at a Corpus Christi hospital after being hit by several pellets of birdshot Saturday afternoon, hospital spokesman Peter Banko told CNN. (Bash 2006)*

> *At a brief news conference prior to his release from the hospital today, vice-presidential shooting victim Harry Whittington thanked the hospital staff and the media, and had this to say about Dick Cheney: "My family and I are deeply sorry for all Vice President Cheney and his family had to go through this past week."*
>
> *It says everything you need to know about this administration that the deepest regret and most heartfelt expression of contrition about the incident came from . . . the guy who had been shot in the face.*
>
> *Check the transcript: in his 30-minute chat with Brit Hume, Cheney's lamentations were all directed at himself: "The image of him falling is something I'll never be able to get out of my mind . . . It was, I'd have to say, one of the worst days of my life."*
>
> *I'm sure it wasn't too swell a day for Harry Whittington, either. (Huffington 2006)*

> *Vice President Dick Cheney accidentally shot a man during a quail hunt . . . making 78-year-old Harry Whittington the first person shot by a sitting vice president since Alexander Hamilton. Hamilton, of course, was shot in a duel with Aaron Burr over issues of honor, integrity and political maneuvering. Whittington? Mistaken for a bird. (Stewart 2006)*

These three pieces discuss the same subject, the Cheney accident. That said, these three accounts differ considerably. These differences are driven by the purpose of each author. The first example was written to inform, the second to criticize, the third to entertain. Same subject, but what was written in each case rose from the purpose each writer had in mind when sitting down to write.

One does not need a splashy national story like the Cheney incident to introduce students to the importance of author's purpose. Consider the following story that recently ran in a local newspaper:

8 Hurt After Car Crashes into an El Pollo Loco

A suspected drunk driver crashed into a restaurant south of downtown Los Angeles late Friday night, injuring himself and seven other people, authorities said.

About 9:30 p.m., a 25-year-old man driving a black Chrysler 300 made "an unsafe turn" at the intersection of Washington Boulevard and Maple Avenue, according to Los Angeles Police Department spokesman Mike Lopez.

The man's injuries were severe and he remained hospitalized Saturday, Lopez said.

Crews used the Jaws of Life to pull the driver from the crash, said Brian Humphrey, a Fire Department spokesman.

The other seven people had minor injuries, authorities said. (L.A. Times 2006)

I shared this piece with my students and asked them, "What was the purpose of this article? Why did the newspaper run this story?" After a bit of discussion, they came to the notion that this article was run to inform readers of the details of an unusual automobile accident.

I then ask my students to consider three alternative versions of the automobile accident piece:

Rewrite #1

A suspected drunk driver crashed into a restaurant south of downtown Los Angeles late Friday night, injuring himself and seven other people, authorities said.

This accident, the latest in many, serves as one more example as to why our drunk driving laws need to be revisited. Clearly they are not working, and this incident leads to an inescapable conclusion: it's past time to strengthen the penalties for drunk driving.

Rewrite #2

I was walking home on a cold, quiet night last week when a driver slamming his sports car into a restaurant south of downtown Los Angeles shattered the evening's solitude. The crash created an explosion, spraying shards of glass, while screaming customers dove for cover. When the dust settled, injured people were left strewn like overturned mannequins throughout the shattered restaurant.

Just before the collision, I heard tires screeching, and turned just in time to catch sight of a yellow blur jump the curb and zero in on the restaurant. I cringed as it slammed through the front of the restaurant; it sounded like a bomb set off in a glass factory. When the 2004 Ferrari came to halt inside the restaurant, it had smashed into the soda dispenser, spraying everyone and everything in the dining area with a continuous geyser of Mountain Dew.

Rewrite #3

They say fast food is not healthy. Too much fat. Too many calories. Not enough nutrients. But that's nothing compared to the newest danger facing the fast food eater: getting run over by a $300,000 sports car while peacefully eating your chicken nuggets.

It's bad enough that I have to watch my carbs. Now I have to watch my cars? Do I now have to keep my eyes peeled for Mario Andretti wannabes, long on testosterone and short on brain cells, crashing through the front of the restaurant? Makes me wonder what I should order on my next visit: "I'll have the number two, please. Super-size it, and throw in a road block, a crash helmet and body armor." I've heard of crash diets before, but this is taking the concept a bit too far.

The original article about the automobile accident was written to inform, but in examining the rewrites, students begin to see that purposes can vary. In rewrite #1, for example, the purpose was to persuade; in rewrite #2, the purpose was to describe; and in rewrite #3, the purpose was to entertain. Unfortunately, many of my students come to me every year unaware that writers often sit down to write with specific purposes in mind. Through the introduction of this automobile crash article and the three divergent rewrites, my students begin to see the importance of recognizing purpose—that *what* a writer writes is driven by *why* he is writing.

Why Do Writers Write?

Most of the state-level standards that I have seen require students to approach writing through the lenses of the traditional discourses, usually one at a time. Younger writers, for example, often begin writing autobiographically, before "graduating" on to more difficult domains: literary analysis, persuasive writing, and expository writing. This approach lends a narrow, school-induced artificiality to the writing process. Writers in the real world do not limit themselves to staying strictly within the boundaries of a given discourse. Real writers in real writing situations stretch and cross these boundaries, often blending discourses for effect. A strong persuasive essay, for example, might begin by connecting an argument to an autobiographical experience.

If we want our students to understand the value that writing can play in their lives, maybe we should consider shifting instruction away from strict adherence to the traditional discourses and begin having our students explore the *reasons* real writers write. When students understand the real-world purposes for writing (instead of simply writing to meet the next school requirement) they begin to internalize the relevance of writing, and more important, they develop an understanding that writing is an important skill to carry into adulthood. When students begin to understand this relevance, their writing improves.

If we are going to teach students why writers write, where should we begin? What are the purposes behind meaningful writing? There are many different models explaining why writers write, but the one that makes the most sense to me and to my students is proposed by Bean, Chappell, and Gillam in *Reading Rhetorically* (2003). The authors outline eight major purposes for writing:

We Write to
express and reflect
inquire and explore
inform and explain
analyze and interpret
take a stand
evaluate and judge
propose a solution
seek common ground

To help my students understand how writers compose with these eight purposes in mind, I provide them with the following chart, which is also found in Appendix 9:

Purpose	Explanation	Examples
Express and reflect	The writer • expresses or reflects on his or her own life and experiences. • often looks backward in order to look forward.	• Attending my first Lakers game with my dad and what it means to me as I raise my own children • Telling the story of my grandmother's journey to America and what it taught me • Discussing the pain of my parents' divorce • Attending my first concert and reflecting on my musical journey since then
Inquire and explore	The writer • wrestles with a question or problem. • hooks with the problem and lets the reader watch him or her wrestle with it.	• What are the things I need to do if I want to prepare myself to have a chance at making the NBA? • How did my grandmother find the strength to overcome all her obstacles? • What are possible reasons my parents got a divorce? • Why is live music so important to me?
Inform and explain	The writer • states a main point and purpose. • tries to present the information in a surprising way.	• Explain the most important trades the Lakers made to help them win a championship • Discuss my grandmother's philosophy of life • Explore the history of divorce in America • Inform the reader of the history of a rock band
Analyze and interpret	The writer • seeks to analyze and interpret phenomena that are difficult to understand or explain.	• Analyze the reasons why the NBA stars lost in the Olympics • Analyze a choice my grandmother made and reflect whether it was wise or not • List in order the top factors that led to my parents' divorce • Interpret song lyrics from my favorite band
Take a stand	The writer • seeks to persuade audiences to accept a particular position on a controversial issue.	• Instant replay should be allowed in the NBA • My grandmother fits the definition of a hero • Divorce should be illegal • Musical groups should get involved in political campaigns

continued

Purpose	Explanation	Examples
Evaluate and judge	The writer • focuses on the worth of person, object, idea, or other phenomenon. • usually specifies the criteria for the object to be seen as "good" or "bad."	• How to determine the best player in the NBA • My grandmother received the most effective medical treatment • My parents' divorce was best for all in the long run. Who benefited most? Who suffered most? • The greatest all-time song by this band is?
Propose a solution	The writer • is calling for action. • describes the problem, proposes a solution, and provides justification.	• How the Lakers can improve their defense • How I can make sure my own children understand their great-grandmother's legacy • Suggestions for how the divorce rate can be lowered • How the band could rediscover its artistic integrity
Seek common ground	The writer • aims to calm the intensity. • respects the values of all readers.	• Instead of arguing which one is better, write about the strengths of both college and pro basketball • Discuss why my grandmother's decision to leave her native country was both a good and bad idea • Balance the ill effects divorce has on children with the benefits some children receive via divorce • Compare two great songs from a band and explain why an argument could be made for each one being the best song.

Adapted from Bean, Chappell, and Gillam 2003.

I contend in Chapter 1 that our students are not writing enough. I also mention that one way I pump up the volume of writing is by requiring my students to write five pages a week in their writer's notebooks. Though my students start the year by writing with the purpose of expressing and reflecting, I quickly move the focus of their writer's notebooks toward the other seven author's purposes for writing. It is important for my students to know, however, that a writer's notebook is not a diary. It is not a place simply to record a yearlong reflection on whether your true love is going to ask you to prom. To give them the kind of practice in their writer's notebooks that they may come to find useful as adults, I have set up a timetable for them to rehearse the different purposes for writing:

Writer's Notebooks Schedule

Month	*Purpose*
September	express and reflect
October	inquire and explore
November–December	evaluate and judge
January	inform and explain
February–March	analyze and interpret
April	propose a solution
May	take a stand
June	seek common ground

When we transition to writing with a different purpose in mind, I bring in real-world examples that I have downloaded or clipped from periodicals. I keep a file for each of the eight purposes at home and whenever I come across a strong model I drop it in the file. Much like the restaurant review assignment found in Chapter 3, these models enable my students to understand how real writers construct.

My approach to teaching these eight purposes for writing is driven by two underlying principles.

Principle #1: I Do Not Get Hung Up on Strict Boundaries When My Students Are Writing in a Specific Domain

I want my students to understand that professional writers often blend purposes. For example, an editorial might first analyze a policy before passing judgment on a senator's vote, or a politician might write a speech in which he explores all the sides of a ballot proposition before taking a stand. When my students begin to blend domains, I do not become alarmed; I see it as a sign of writing maturity. See Figure 6.1 for the first page of an argumentative essay written by Ines, a ninth grader. Notice how she enters her persuasive argument through an autobiographical incident, thus strengthening her argument (Note: this is an unedited draft).

Ines
P. 3

The Costa Mesa Policy

"I'll call you back later ok. I have to pull over because there is a cop behind me," my cousin, Eduardo Chairez replied to me on the phone. As I hung up the phone, I was so nervous. Eduardo was an illegal immigrant. What if they sent him back to Mexico? What is going to happen to him if he is asked for his paper? All these questions were going through my mind.

"I'm alright. I gust got a ticket for not coming to a complete stop on the intersection," my cousin said. He called me, after the police officer left. I was so relieved after I found out nothing happen to him. I still think what would've happened if he was pulled over at Costa Mesa, and the Costs Mesa policy was approve?

The mayor of Costa Mesa, Allan Mansoor, has purpose a new policy for Costa Mesa. The policy states that police officers in Costa Mesa are allowed to begin checking the immigration status of people suspected of serious crimes. This policy is causing a lot of conterversery, not just in Costa Mesa, but also in Southern California.

Mayor Allan Mansor says, " There has been a demand from the public for this type of enforcement." Mansoor estimates that ten percent to fifteen percent of the four hundred people taken to jail on an average month are illegal immigrants. Many people think that this policy will help make the city a lot safer. The mayor has stated," This will not solve all our immigration problems, but it will make the community safer."

However, other people believe that the crime rate will rise. People will hesitate to call the police to report a crime. Critics have already warn that people will hesitate to call police for help if it could get someone booted from the country. The policy will end up

Figure 6.1 *Mixing discourses to strengthen argument*

Principal #2: To Ensure I Move Beyond the Grecian Urn Approach, I Write Alongside the Students in Each of the Domains

I want to make sure my students see my trials and tribulations as I, too, wrestle with the different authentic purposes for writing. I want to reemphasize the notion that good essays do not just magically appear; rather, they are the end product of a lot of hard work and experimentation.

Practice Makes Purpose

Here are four additional activities I have found useful in helping students recognize the importance of author's purpose.

Revise the Purpose

Have students choose a paper they have already written and have them revise it with a different purpose in mind. For example, Leticia wrote a reflective essay about the sadness she felt while sitting at our school's International Week assembly and feeling that her culture was under-represented in the activity. When she revisited the essay, she rewrote with the expressed purpose of proposing a solution. She outlined the reasons she would run for the student office in charge of planning assemblies. Kenny, a water polo player, wrote a descriptive piece about what it was like to play in the big game against our cross-town rivals. In his revision, he shifted his purpose to analyzing the reasons why they lost the game in the last minute.

Students can also benefit by revising the purpose of others' writing. Much like I did with the automobile accident story at the beginning of this chapter, students can cut out newspaper articles and revise them with a different purpose in mind.

Purpose Packets

Put students in small groups and hand each group an oversized envelope that contains a number of different clippings from newspapers and magazines. Make sure that each envelope has a good mix of writing in it (for example, an editorial, a news story, an ad, a horoscope, Dear Abby, and gardening tips). Have students determine the *primary* purpose for each piece in the envelope. This activity will generate interesting discussions about authors' purposes. At the end of the discussion period, choose one person randomly from each group to share the group's findings—this ensures all group members participate. Sometimes the purpose they find is obvious; other times it is not. I actually like it better when the purpose is debatable, for the richest discussions occur when my students challenge one another.

Purpose Hunt

Instead of providing students with a mixture of articles, have students find them. Give each group an entire newspaper and have them hunt and clip examples of the eight purposes. Again, this is guaranteed to generate interesting discussion, both within the groups and when each group shares its findings via whole-class sharing.

Identify Purpose in Core Works

Each year, my freshman read Elie Wiesel's searing Holocaust memoir, *Night*. One year, I asked them to consider why he wrote the book. To help them record their thinking they completed a purpose t-chart. On the left-hand side they considered the reasons the author felt compelled to tell such a painful story; on the right side they listed passages that supported the stated purpose. Here is Stephanie's chart:

Author's Purpose in Writing *Night*	Textual Support
To inform so as to prevent it from happening again	"To hang the boy in front of thousands of spectators was no light matter." p. 61
	"I did not know that in that place at that moment, I was parting from my mother and Tzipara forever." p. 27
	"...thousands of children were burned ...he kept six crematories working day and night." p. 64

Students (and adults) who cannot identify an author's purpose will go through life susceptible. It is imperative that our students, as readers, be able to discern the fine line between someone trying to inform them versus someone trying to sell them something. We should cultivate in our students the ability, for example, to understand the difference between straight news and veiled persuasion (though that distinction is getting very blurry). Students who cannot determine when analysis crosses the line into persuasion are vulnerable when they leave our schools. I chip away at this vulnerability daily. Every time my students read anything, I ask them why the writer wrote it. Any time my students write an essay, I have them complete the following sentence stem at the top of their papers: "The purpose of this essay is _____."

Exploring Thinking Before Determining Purpose

Having just spent a few pages trying to convince you that it is crucial our students be able to recognize the purpose behind the texts they read and write, let me add one brief disclaimer: sometimes when I sit down to write I do not know my purpose. Often I will use writing as a vehicle to explore my thinking, and as I do so, I begin writing without any expressed purpose in mind.

To demonstrate to students that writers explore thinking through experimental writing, I sometimes have them "cube" a topic. Cubing (Cowan and Cowan 1980) is a strategy that enables students to explore a topic from different angles (the name originates from the fact that a cube has six different sides). Here are the six perspectives students are asked to consider:

Describe It
How would you describe this topic/issue/event/person?
What characteristics does it have?
What does it look like?

Compare It
What is it similar to?
What is it analogous to?

Associate It

What does it remind you of?

How does it connect to other topics/issues/events/people?

Analyze It

How did it happen?

Why did it happen?

What are the contributing pieces/factors?

Apply It

What can you do with it?

How can you use it?

What lesson(s) did it teach?

What understanding did it generate?

Argue for or Against It

I support this because . . .

I oppose this because . . .

This is a good because . . .

This is bad because . . .

Upon finishing *Night* and our unit on genocide, Jimena, a ninth-grade student, cubed "The Holocaust." Here are her four-minute quickwrites:

Describe It

The Holocaust was the systematic persecution and murder of Jews living in Europe during the 1930s to the 1940s. It all began as Adolf Hitler became chancellor of Germany, he had a pathological hatred of Jews. Hitler wanted Europe to be free of Jews, and to do so he developed, with the help of millions, ways to kill six million Jews. The system that was developed involved rounding up Jews, deportation to ghettos and concentration camps, torturing, and killing Jews in ways unimaginable.

Compare It

After the Holocaust, a series of genocides have occurred, some still do this day, that are very similar to the Jewish genocide. One genocide that can be compared to the Holocaust is the Bosnia genocide. Slobodan Milosevic, a former Communist, turned to nationalism and religious hatred to gain power in Yugoslavia. He encouraged Serbs to murder Muslims, which resulted in 200,000 deaths. And just like the Nazi system, Muslim men were sent to concentration camps and women were tortured.

Associate It

The Holocaust can be associated with many events, but the one that comes to my mind is the act of racism towards African-Americans. These innocent humans were torn apart from their homes and were sent to colonies that we now know as the U.S. There they were forced to work as slaves for white families. Slaves were flogged, tortured, discriminated, and killed and all because of the color of their skin.

Analyze It

Most people accuse Hitler of being responsible for the Holocaust. But the truth is, one man cannot kill millions without the support of millions. Thousands of Germans and other races were involved in building camps, persecuting Jews, guarding Jews, and above all killing Jews.

Apply It

I have learned from the Holocaust that the thoughts and actions of a man and the silence of many can cause suffering in the lives of millions. It is important not to keep silent when seeing something that is morally wrong, or just wrong for that matter, is occurring or about to. One must stand up for one's rights and beliefs.

Argue for or Against It

Hatred is but a mere disguise for fear, fear of things not accustomed to. I believe Germans or anyone who "hated" Jews were afraid that Jewish culture would overwhelm their sacred country. And by disguising their fear with hatred were capable to free themselves from the chances of this happening by getting rid of the Jews.

Much like a novice painter experimenting with paints, young writers must be given opportunities to explore ideas via writing. Jimena's cubing gave her an opportunity to explore some of her thinking on the Holocaust before tackling a larger piece. After finishing her cube, Jimena wrote a longer piece analyzing in greater detail who, besides Hitler, was responsible for the Holocaust.

The Influence of Audience on the Writer

Once students have shown they can accurately assess an author's purpose, it's time to move on by asking them to consider another essential element, the audience.

When you write, what makes it onto the paper (or computer screen) is not only driven by the *reason* you feel compelled to write (your purpose), it is also influenced by who you expect to read your piece. When I write thank-you notes, for example, I know my purpose (to give thanks), but I also know that what I write will be shaped by knowing who the recipient of the writing will be. What I write to my grandmother will look very different than what I write to a buddy of mine. Considering who my audience is before I write shapes what I write.

To help my students understand how audience shapes communication, I write the following expression on the board: "Hello. How are you?" I then ask students to consider the idea that *how* they say this may be dictated by *who* is receiving the greeting. I ask them to generate a list of five people and ask them how they would greet each person on the list. Anthony, seventeen, wrote the following:

> To his grandmother: "Hi, Grammy. How are you today?"
> To his best friend: "What's up, Dawg?"
> To his coach: "Hey Coach, what's goin' on?
> To his teacher: "Morning, Mr. G."
> To his girlfriend: "Hey, Baby-girl."

Each greeting, shaped by its intended audience, is different.

It has been my experience that even when students understand the purpose behind their writing, they often give little thought to who their audience might be. They might know *why* they are writing, but they don't give much thought to *who* will read their writing. Many of my students have come to think that there is only one audience—the teacher—and that writing is just another laborious school hoop to jump through. By the time they become seniors in high school the notion that audience might be someone other than their teacher has long since drowned in a decade-long flood of "fake" writing—writing they will never use outside of school. Or, as Carol Jago states in *Papers, Papers, Papers* (2005), by the time students finish high school, they finally tire of "practicing, practicing, practicing for a day that never comes" (p. 80).

To move students into an understanding of the importance audience has on real-world writing, I get outside the textbook and use as much contemporary writing as possible. One year, for example, a debate filled the news regarding the Bush administration's domestic spying program. Below you will find an excerpt on the topic from the *Los Angeles Times:*

> *"I did say to the National Security Agency that they should protect America by taking the phone numbers of known Al Qaeda and/or affiliates and find out why they are making phone calls into the United States and vice versa. And I did so because the enemy wants to hurt us. If somebody is talking to Al Qaeda, we want to know why . . . I meant it when I said I'm going to uphold the Constitution. I have the right as commander in chief in a time of war to take action necessary to protect the American people." (A statement from President George W. Bush as quoted in Gerstenzang 2006)*

I shared this excerpt with my twelfth-grade students and asked them two questions: (1) Why did the president (or his speechwriter) write it? (2) Who was his intended audience? Through both small-group and whole-class discussion, they suggested the following:

Why Was It Written?	Who Was the Intended Audience?
• To explain and justify his actions • To build public support for his decision • To slow down or stop criticism	• The American public (voters) • Democrats who are out to criticize his actions • Republicans who may be wavering in their support • The media—in the hope that they would carry his rationale across television, radio, and newspapers

After they wrestled with that one, I gave them a different excerpt, this one from *The New York Times*:

> *Let's be clear about this: illegal government spying on Americans is a clear violation of individual liberties, whether times are troubled or not. Nobody with a real regard for the rule of law and the Constitution would have trouble seeing that. The law governing the National Security Agency was written after the Vietnam War because the government had made lists of people it considered a national security threat and spied on them. . . . This particular end run around civil liberties is unnecessary.* (The New York Times [editorial] 2005)

Students were asked the same questions. As a class they brainstormed the following:

Why Was It Written?	Who Was the Intended Audience?
• To criticize the president's actions • To build public support against domestic spying • To step up criticism in an effort to get the practice stopped	• The citizens of New York and other regions where the paper is read • Lawmakers • Voters • Democrats who are out to criticize his actions • Republicans who may be wavering in their support

In addition to identifying the intended audience in contemporary writing, we also have this discussion when reading core works. Earlier in the chapter you saw Stephanie's purpose chart for *Night*, in which she brainstormed the purposes behind Elie Wiesel's memoir. Below she adds a layer to it by considering who Wiesel's intended audience might be:

Author's Purpose in Writing *Night*	Textual Support	Intended Audience
To inform so as to prevent it from happening again	"To hang the boy in front of thousands of spectators was no light matter." p. 61 "I did not know that in that place at that moment, I was parting from my mother and Tzipara forever." p. 27 "...thousands of children were burned...he kept six crematories working day and night." p. 64	• Jewish people (to honor and to teach) • Germans • Racists from any country • Younger generations who were not alive when the Holocaust happened • Teachers • Lawmakers and politicians • Everyone (to help prevent it from happening again)

Putting these three columns together enables Stephanie to consider both the author's purpose and his intended audience. It is my hope than when my students begin considering both purpose and audience in others' writing that they will develop a similar awareness of these elements in their own writing.

Writing to Authentic Audiences

Even though you've never met him, many of you already know my student Nela. He is a big, strong seventeen-year-old who has his priorities backward. In Nela's world, football comes first and academics are a distant second. Nela, though not dumb, is often listless in English class and rarely seems to take much more than superficial ownership of his learning. But when I talk to the football coach, I am told that Nela is a very hard worker who often leads by example. Apparently, Nela's strong work ethic surfaces the moment he walks out of English class and walks onto the football field. This stoked my curiosity so I pulled Nela aside for a little talk.

"Nela, your coach tells me you work very hard in football practice," I said. "This makes me wonder why you don't work hard in English. Tell me, why do you work so hard on the football field?"

"Friday night lights," he answered.

"What does that mean?" I asked.

"I love Friday night."

"What about Friday night do you love?"

"Everything. The game. The band. The crowd. Everything."

The game. The band. The crowd. Everything. Nela's answer struck home. It dawned on me that Nela's football work ethic is partially driven by knowing he will have an audience. He performs in front of a crowd that includes friends, family, and, of course, girls. The game will be written up in the newspaper. A recap of the contest will be broadcast Monday morning over the school's PA system. I am sure Nela likes the game itself, but certainly part of his motivation to work really hard at practice stems largely from knowing his efforts will have an audience.

In building young writers we can learn from Nela. Students are much more likely to take their writing seriously if they know there will be an audience waiting to read their work. By *audience* I mean more than the classroom teacher. Young writers also need "Friday night lights"—a place where they can show off their hard work. Below you will find ten strategies, five inside the classroom and five outside the classroom, useful in providing young writers with an audience beyond the teacher.

Five Strategies to Create "Friday Night Lights" Inside the Classroom

1. Author's Chair

A staple of many writing project sites is the author's chair, a place where any student (or teacher) can sit and share writing with the class. In some classrooms I have visited, the chair is placed in a prominent position and can only be used by an author who wishes to share his or her writing—at all other times it remains empty. In a classroom with limited space, like mine, I simply pull a regular chair to the front of the classroom.

What kind of writing is shared from the chair? A student may share a piece he or she is particularly proud of, or bring a draft with which he or she is struggling. If the paper is in draft form, the author may ask for feedback or may indicate that he or she only feels like sharing.

When I read student writing at home, I will often pull out stellar examples and privately suggest to students that they should share their writing next time we have the author's chair.

2. RAG Competitions

In Chapter 4, I discuss read-around-groups (RAGs), a process by which students read each other's papers and discuss the strengths of each paper (see page 86). I have found that students will spend extra time on their papers at home when they know everyone else in the classroom will be reading their work in class the next day. Struggling writers try harder if they know an audience of their peers awaits; the strongest writers take their papers more seriously if they know their peers will identify the best work.

3. Golden Lines

Often, when assigning a draft, I tell students this will be a "golden lines draft." When students walk into class the next day, they hand me their drafts. While they begin working on a sponge activity, I quickly skim their papers looking for strong ("golden") lines. When I find a strong line, I highlight it with a yellow marker and quickly move to the next paper. In less than five minutes I have a number of sentences selected from various papers, and I then read aloud the best lines.

What is nice about this strategy is that enables me to recognize all my writers at one point or another. Even the most reluctant writer will occasionally produce one great image or sentence (even if the rest of the paper is lacking). This not only allows everyone to be recognized, but also enables students to hear examples of strong writing models, an important added benefit.

4. Targeted Bulletin Boards

Rather than simply post the "best" student essays on the bulletin board, I target one specific criterion to determine which papers will be displayed. Usually, I will choose papers that demonstrate competency in the skill taught through the most recent mini-lesson. For example, after teaching a mini-lesson on hooking the reader, I may post essays that have the most interesting introductions. Other bulletin boards I have had in the past include the following targets:

> Gripping conclusions
> Smooth transitions
> Strong research citations
> Sentence variety
> Strong verbs
> Show, don't tell
> Mature vocabulary
> Writing "small"

5. Classroom Anthologies as Part of the Classroom Library

As part of my classroom library a shelf contains writings from my students, usually in the form of classroom anthologies they have created. Here are three student anthologies currently found on my classroom bookshelves:

Bloodlines Every year I do a unit with my students in which they recall their favorite family story. I ask them to consider one story that is told every time there is a large family gathering. Some of the entries I receive are humorous, such as the time Carina thought she was helping her dad wash his prized '63 Chevy. Unfortunately, she helped dry the car by using sandpaper instead of a chamois (okay, maybe that's not so humorous). Other entries are serious, such as the story Jonathan told about his grandparents paying a "coyote" to lead them on a harrowing crossing of the desert as they immigrated to the United States.

Before we begin writing I pass out previous issues. The first group of students to compile the anthology titled it "Bloodlines." I give students some time to read through them randomly. This serves two purposes: (1) It primes the pump by sparking writing ideas in this year's writers, and (2) It motivates them by allowing them to see that their writing will soon become part of this classroom's tradition, and that next year other students will be reading their writing.

"Ever Wonder Why?" Revisited   In Chapter 5 I introduced the "Ever Wonder Why?" writing assignment (see page 115). This assignment is a natural for creating a classroom anthology. Each entry is titled with the following sentence stem: "Did you ever wonder why _____?" Students then answer the question, often dropping photographs, charts, or graphs into their pieces to assist in their explanations. Once finished, the pieces are collated and placed in a classroom anthology.

"The Myth of the Boring Topic" Revisited   Also introduced in Chapter 5 (page 98), "The Myth of the Boring Topic" assignment can easily be collated into a high-interest reading anthology. In this assignment, students take a topic that might appear to be boring on the surface and dispel that notion through research. Students write their myths of the top of their papers (e.g., "Water is boring") and follow with their written refutations (e.g., "Did you know there are more living organisms in a single drop of water than there are people living in Idaho? This is one of many interesting facts about water . . ."). These pieces are bound together to create a classroom anthology that students look forward to reading.

Creating classroom anthologies of student writing produce a number of immediate benefits. Among them are the following:

- Students take their writing more seriously when they know their work is headed for public display.
- Students read the writing of their peers, giving them valuable exposure to additional writing models.
- Showcasing student writing in the classroom sends the message to our young writers that the teacher values their work.
- Students, even those who are reluctant readers, enjoy reading the finished anthologies.
- The anthologies serve as emergency back-up on those days a student forgets to bring a book for sustained silent reading time.

Five Strategies to Create "Friday Night Lights" Outside the Classroom

1. Apply a Required Writing Standard to the Real World

The writing standards in my state require my freshmen to write persuasive essays. When I teach the persuasive essay, I often try to tie the writing into something both real-world and timely. The following paragraphs describe two such examples.

One of my classes is a Puente Project class; the Puente Project is an outreach program supported by the University of California with one focused goal: to help under-represented students make it into four-year universities. The program at my site has been very successful; for example, we recently sent two of our Puente students to Stanford, the first two students in the forty-three-year-history of my high school to make it into that prestigious university. But despite this and other successes, we learned one year that due to serious shortfalls in the state budget, the Puente Project was in danger of being eliminated. Though the budget had not yet been finalized, the outlook was bleak.

My Puente students, many of whom have had older siblings succeed in this program, were incensed by this news. Seeing this, I immediately halted the unit we were working on and asked my students how we, as writers, could sway opinion on this crucial matter. They quickly came to the conclusion that they could write letters to the governor. Good idea, I told them, but when you write a letter attempting to persuade someone to see an issue your way, you had better know what you are talking about. I presented them with the following question for homework: "Why is the Puente Project worth fighting for?" I also had them look at www.Puente.net to find some ammunition for their arguments. They came back the next day with some interesting information, including:

- Puente students are over three times more likely than non-Puente students at the same high schools to be eligible for admission to the University of California (UC) (19 percent versus 6 percent).
- Puente students enter college (two-year and four-year) at a rate of 83 percent, compared with 49 percent of all California graduating high school seniors.
- Puente high school students are almost twice as likely to enroll in a four-year college as their peers (43 percent versus 24 percent), even though they are recruited from all achievement levels.
- Puente students in northern California passed the California High School Exit Exam at a significantly higher rate than other students in the same school districts (96 percent versus 69 percent for the English section; 81 percent versus 56 percent for the math section).
- The number of Puente students who applied to UC increased 198 percent between 2001 and 2003. (Puente Project 2006)

Armed with this information, students began drafting letters. They believed strongly in their purpose for writing (taking a stand to save the program), and they were motivated by knowing they must attempt to influence their intended audience (in this case, the governor). Applying the writing standard (persuasion) to a real-world situation—a situation my students found highly relevant—served as a motivation to my students. (Postscript: as it turned out, the Puente Program was spared at the last minute and continues its strong work. I do not know if the letters helped; as of this writing, we have not received a response from the Governator).

Another year, a new opportunity arose which enabled me to teach persuasion again. A local city, Costa Mesa, is considering becoming the first city in the nation to give its police officers the power to check the immigration status of anyone they arrest (a task, up to now, which had been reserved for the Immigration and Naturalization Service). The issue has touched off a firestorm of controversy. Some of my students are recent immigrants and much like when they argued to save the Puente Project, they have strong reactions to the city's proposal. Unlike the previous assignment, in which students were united in trying to save a program, my students' opinions on this immigration issue are decidedly mixed. Some favor it; others oppose it.

After providing my students with a number of news stories, editorials, and letters-to-the-editor on this issue (how did we manage before Google?), my students t-charted the arguments on both sides of the issue. After seeing the issue from all sides, they started drafting. My students mailed their letters, pro and con, to the mayor and the members of the city council.

2. Another Set of Eyes

I have found that my students will take their writing more seriously if they know ahead of time that I will not be the only person who will assess their work. For that reason, I try to get other sets of eyes on their papers. Below are three examples of how this might be done:

1. In my Puente Project classes my students are motivated by knowing their portfolios will be read and scored not only by me, but also by a committee of teachers from other sites (we meet every year to exchange and score portfolios). My students try harder when they know "outsiders" will be assessing their writing.
2. In my senior classes, my students know that the senior teachers have grading sessions after school, during which we trade and grade each other's papers. As my seniors begin their final drafts, I find it helpful to remind them that the other senior English teachers will read their papers.
3. Many schools require all students to complete a "Senior Project" in order to graduate. It is a yearlong research project which culminates not only in written research, but also in student presentations that share what students have learned. Both the papers and presentations are assessed by panel of adults, most of them from outside the school. As a recent judge myself, I can say with complete certainty that these students elevated their work knowing an audience other than their teacher awaited them.

3. Campus Displays

One year, every senior at my high school wrote an intensive historical research paper on the events of September 11. Working individually, students spent an entire month researching and writing their papers. The typed final drafts, without graphics, averaged eighteen pages in length. It is safe to say that for my students this was easily the most ambitious writing project they had ever undertaken.

Upon completion, the projects deserved some recognition. My school has a display case that is usually reserved for photographs of the most recent dance or athletic contest. We cleared out the case and created the "Senior Writing Awards," giving recognition to a number of students in the following categories: Grand Finalists, Most Intriguing Research, Most Improved Writer, and Best Use of Graphics/Visuals. After displaying the exemplary work, we made the winning entries available for checkout in the school library. The faces of the young writers whose papers were actually being put on the library shelves were priceless.

The precedent being set, students in subsequent years began the historical research paper knowing there would be some "Friday night lights" waiting at the end of the project.

4. Promote Writing Contests

On our campus we have a student writing anthology, *Released,* which publishes student fiction and poetry. Every year I am surprised when some of my reluctant writers submit entries. This year's biggest surprise came from Daniel, who rarely speaks up in class and who is obsessed with baseball. When Daniel submitted his poem, I had no idea he had been working on it at home for a week. A few days ago, Daniel received good news: his poem had been selected for publication. His face lit up when I congratulated him on submitting his poem. It lit up again when I told him his poem would be published in *Released.*

I encourage my students to enter writing contests outside of school as well. Here are my three favorite sites that sponsor contests:

* **NCTE.org** sponsors writing contests for students and suggests places where students can get their writing published.
* **TeenInk.com** sponsors annual writing contests in poetry, narration, and exposition for elementary, middle, and high school students.
* **Writing.com** has links to writing contests as well as guidelines for those students who want to set up blogs.

5. Create Public Readings

Every year at our school's open house, we provide an opportunity for students to read their work. We invite parents and visitors into our theater, and students take turns reading their poems and short stories. It is rewarding to see how proud students can be when they receive public recognition for their writing.

My colleague Robin Turner provides another public forum for his young writers. After his students finish creating poems, he invites them to read their poems publicly at the local coffee shop. The shop sponsors an open mike on Friday nights and Robin has had a number of students read their poems to the public.

Of course, any discussion of sharing writing publicly would be incomplete without talking about the largest public forum known to our students: the blogosphere. I began noticing this phenomenon last year in my own house when my daughter was constantly writing on her computer. It turns out she was posting a daily blog on Livejournal.com. On this site, students post under pseudonyms, and then determine which of their friends will have access to their blogs.

Last year I polled my students to see how many of them write regularly on a blog. My unscientific estimate came in at approximately 10 percent. This year, I asked again and found that the number had doubled. Clearly, for many students, writing to an audience is becoming a part of everyday life. This is interesting when one considers that many of these students who are writing on blogs every day are the very same students who don't like writing in school. What motivates them to write daily in their blogs? Having an audience they value and a real-world purpose to write.

Know Your Purpose and Audience

When we teach our students to recognize purpose and audience, we give them skills they will use long after graduation. Sure, I want my students to be able to recognize the theme in a novel or to identify foreshadowing in a short story, but ten years from now it will be even more important that they have developed the ability to recognize the difference between information and persuasion. Understanding how an author uses flashback is one thing; understanding the purpose behind a politician's speech and recognizing his or her intended audience is another.

How can we teach our students to recognize purpose and audience? It starts with giving them lots of real-world text to analyze. Studying purpose and audience in the writings of others is the first step to helping them gain the ability to consider purpose and audience in their own writings. Students who develop the ability to recognize purpose and audience reap two benefits: (1) they read the world more critically, and in doing so, (2) they sharpen their own writing skills.

Using Assessment to Drive Better Student Writing

One of my favorite books of late is *True Notebooks*, a nonfictional account of life inside L.A.'s Central Juvenile Hall. Mark Salzman, the author, spent a year in the lock-up teaching a writing class to violent teenage offenders, many incarcerated for murder. These were hardened, tough young men—often the "survivors" of gangs.

Early in the book Salzman describes bringing a small group of inmates together in a circle so they would be able to share their writing with one another:

> *The young men opened their folders and pulled out examples of their writing, but then everything in the room seemed to stop. It was like seeing a group of people in bathing suits run up to a swimming pool on a hot day, then halt right at the edge and look everywhere but the water; no one wanted to be the first to jump in. (2003, p. 18)*

After the students hemmed and hawed a bit, a young man by the name of Ruben built up enough courage to be the first to share his piece. He cleared his throat and began shifting his body uncomfortably in his chair. Salzman recalls Ruben's nervousness:

> With my gaze lowered prudently, I could not help noticing that the squirming and throat-clearing were mere diversionary tactics. The real battle was taking place in Ruben's hands: they trembled so badly from stage fright he could barely hold on to the page. When he began reading his voice sounded the way his hands looked. (p. 19)

I am floored by this recollection. Here is a young man, Ruben, who has been hardened in the mean streets of Los Angeles. A young man who has been conditioned in jail to mask any weakness. A young man in jail for *murder*. Yet when it came time to share his writing, he shook like a leaf.

Salzman's anecdote reminds me of the risks involved when we share our writing with one another. This risk is not limited to adolescents; it is a natural response among adult writers as well. Next time you are in a workshop where adults are asked to share their writing, listen to the dialogue that takes place as the papers are being exchanged. You'll hear phrases like, "Well, this isn't my best work," or "I was up late last night so I had a hard time writing." I, too, plead guilty to being defensive about my writing—when I sent rough drafts of chapters of this book to my editor, Bill Varner, I was always quick to remind him that these were *rough* drafts. My friend, Mary K. Healy, calls these exchanges "ritual apologies"—defense mechanisms that spill out of us when it comes time to opening ourselves up to feedback.

The ritual apologies that pour from my adolescents serve as a continual reminder of the risk my students take when they entrust me with their writing. As their teacher and primary responder, two central questions come to mind every time I collect a set of student papers: (1) How can I respond to these papers in a way that nurtures the trust my students have placed in me? and (2) How can I provide feedback that is not only meaningful, but that also drives my students to improve their writing?

One Central Goal: Everyone Improves

The challenges I face in responding to my students' writing is exacerbated by the wide range of writing abilities found in each of my classes. If you were to chart my fifth-period class, it would resemble the graph in Figure 7.1.

Each dot on the line represents one of my students. Some have advanced skills; others are in need of extensive remediation. But strong or weak, fluent or hesitant, the goal for each student is the same: everyone improves. With the wide range of ability and overwhelming class sizes, it is unrealistic to think I am going to make every one of my 165 students a strong writer. It *is* realistic, however, to begin each year with the goal that every student of mine, regardless of ability, is going to get better. Weak writers will transition into being average

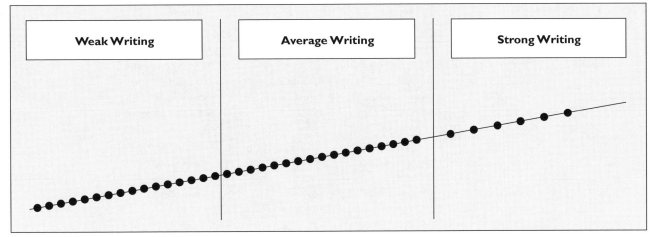

Figure 7.1 *Week/strong diagram*

writers. Average writers will begin producing strong writing. Strong writers will become special writers. Everyone, regardless of ability, works toward the same goal: improvement. Charted, it might look like the graph in Figure 7.2.

When "everyone improves" became my mantra, my focus shifted away from ranking students into winners and losers and moved toward helping them. To gather and maintain the necessary trust of all my students, I now emphasize grading less and focus more on providing them with meaningful feedback—feedback that I hope will help them to improve. In short, I have become less of a grader and more of a responder. Rather than focusing my students, via grading, on what they can't do, I want to focus them on what they can do by providing helpful response. It has been my experience that for this to happen, my students, particularly the reluctant writers, need to get out from under the shadow of the red pen.

In deciding what kind of feedback might drive writing improvement, I respond to my students' papers in two areas: (1) craft and (2) editing. *Craft* is defined as those things that good writers do. *Editing* is defined as fixing mistakes writers make. See Figure 7.3 for a listing of both craft and editing elements.

Figure 7.2 *Week/strong diagram with arrows showing movement*

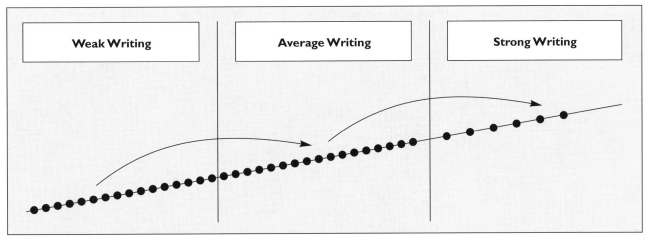

Figure 7.3 *List of craft and editing elements*

Elements of Craft	Elements of Editing
• Strong voice	• Sentence boundaries
• Sentence sense/variety	• Run-on sentences
• Word power (mature vocabulary/use of metaphorical language/show, don't tell)	• Fragments
	• Comma errors
• Strong verbs	• Subject/verb agreement
• Paragraphing for effect	• Quotation marks
• Effective introductions/conclusions	• Pronoun agreement
• Clear thesis	• Pronoun vagueness
• Flow (sequence/coherence)	• Capitalization
• Development/complexity of ideas	• Apostrophes
• Effective transitions	• Semicolons
• Special narrative strategies (e.g., flashback, time shifts)	• Colons
	• Italics
• Strong dialogue	• Numbers
	• Parenthesis
	• Word choice
	• Spelling

Let's look at craft and editing issues separately before concluding the chapter with ideas on how meaningful feedback can improve both areas.

Focus First on Craft: What Good Writers Do

In many classes I have visited, there is often a heavy emphasis on responding to students' errors (which, to some degree, is of course necessary). Often, however, I have found that there is little or no focus on the craft of student writing. Always telling students what is wrong with their papers is a recipe for killing off young writers. When responding to student papers, I start by examining what good writers do. The following sections give five approaches that not only recognize my students' craft, but also help them to improve it.

Adopt the Stance of a Reader, Not a Grader

When responding to students' writing, either via written commentary or conferencing, I am careful to take a stance as the reader rather than as the grader. I will often use the following phrases:

> As a reader, I wonder . . .
> As a reader, I am confused about . . .
> Will the reader understand . . . ?
> What about this passage might confuse the reader?
> Is this enough context for the reader?
> What might still be missing for the reader?
> What do you want the reader to take from this sentence/passage/piece?

Couching response through the lens of the reader rather than through the lens of the grader lowers the anxiety of my students. This, in turn, makes them receptive to commentary that will help them become better writers.

Read the Paper Through a Craft Lens

Traditionally, teachers collect their students' papers at the end of the writing process and it is only at that point that students receive feedback. Often, I will collect student papers midprocess—after an initial draft—and I will read them with a focus on craft issues. Midprocess is where the real growth potential lies; feedback at this stage almost always drives writing improvement better than feedback after the paper is completed (more on this will be discussed later in this chapter).

Providing feedback midprocess does not add another layer of work for the teacher—it moves the bulk of the end-of-paper response to the middle of the process. It is where I choose to give most of my attention to the papers, especially to craft issues. As a result, I respond as much as I can in the middle of the process, and end up responding much less to final draft papers.

Color Coding Summary Versus Commentary

When writing expository essays, particularly literary analysis pieces, my students have a tendency to summarize instead of analyze. Telling them I have already read the novel fifty times does not register with them. They remain intent on summarizing the book to me. To help them see the difference between summarizing and analyzing, I show them a thirty-second clip of *Monday Night Football.* The students listen to the two announcers in the clip, Al Michaels (AM) and John Madden (JM):

AM: It is third down and three. Farve drops back to pass . . . looking . . . throws over the middle . . . incomplete. Intended for Driver. The Broncos have held. This brings up fourth down and the Packers will have to punt.

JM: That play was doomed from the start. The Packers did not pick up the blitz. Notice how they did not read the blitz (*replay is being shown*), and Wilson has a direct line to Favre. Favre had to throw that ball sooner than he wanted to.

I tell the students that although Michaels and Madden are both announcers, their jobs are actually quite different. Students are then asked to consider what each announcer brings to the telecast. I want them to understand that Michaels, the play-by-play announcer, is primarily responsible for telling the viewers what happens. Madden, the color commentator, is there to break the action down and to tell the viewer *why* each play turns out the way it does. In short, Michaels summarizes; Madden analyzes. Using the football analogy helps my students to see the difference.

Once the distinction between summary and analysis is understood, I hand students their drafts and give each of them two highlighters of different colors. I ask them to highlight every sentence—one color for where they summarized and the second color for where they analyzed. Below you will see a paragraph from a first-draft essay written by Crystal, a ninth grader. The bold text is what she color-coded as commentary; the plain text is what she color-coded as summary.

> **When deciding who should be punished, Paris certainly comes to mind.** *"But what now, my Lord, what say you to my suit? Younger than she are good mothers made," said Paris when he talked to Old Man Capulet. This is the match that started the reason for Capulet to throw the party intended for Paris to seek Juliet's love. This party did not go as Paris intended because Romeo and Juliet met. Paris did not recognize that Juliet loved someone else and he kept pushing for the marriage.* **If he hadn't push so hard to marry Juliet she wouldn't have pretended to be dead and none of them would have killed each other.**

Crystal's paragraph is primarily summary. Her color coding helped her to recognize the imbalance. I then chose a summary-laden student draft to share with the class and together we worked on revising it to include more analyzing. When the mini-lesson was over, I handed their papers back and asked them to revise. Here is Crystal's revision of her first draft:

> **When deciding who should be punished, Paris certainly comes to mind.** *Paris, the young and handsome bachlor who craves Juliet's love, commits* **selfish** *acts that affect the lives of others.* **His decision to ask Old Man Capulet for Juliet's hand in marriage was what ignited the first domino to fall.** *He asks for her hand knowing that she doesn't love him.* **This causes Juliet to drink the potion, which creates the tragedy. Paris is at fault for pushing the marriage when he should have backed off. He was only thinking of himself. For this, he shares responsibility and deserves to be punished.**

Though still in draft form, color coding helped Crystal see that she needed to add more analysis in her revision. Her second draft is primarily commentary (in bold).

"I Like . . ." Conversations

Often I will place a rough draft on the projector for the entire class to consider. (I cover the name to keep the paper anonymous.) We then have an "I like . . ." conversation. I ask the students to look at the paper and share what they like about it. I chart their responses on the projector (before I had the projector, I would make an overhead transparency of the essay). In Figure 7.4 you will see

Figure 7.4 *"I like . . . "
student sample*

Angel Torres
Period 3

The morning started off as a normal monotonous school day at the insignificant

INTERESTING DICTION

speck of land known as Francis Scott Key Elementary School in Anaheim, CA. This was

during the best year of my life, which was 2002, and little did I know that I was about to

SETS ANTICIPATION

learn a very important life lesson. My closest acquaintances George, Rolando, and I

started heading down the aged blacktop to our usual destination, which happened to be a

VIVID DESCRIPTION

rusted old swing set worn down from years of misuse.

APPEALS to SENSES I could smell the freshly cutgrass as the swing set came into view, and I saw the

NICE DETAIL

one person I truly disliked, Mason, whose last name I never bothered to learn. I had

several altercations with Mason prior to that day. I started to quicken the pace of my

footsteps, and as if my two friends could read my mind they both looked at me at the

same time shook their heads, and murmured the two words we were all thinking, "not *MORE ANTICIPA-TION*

again."

"Not again" is right, Mason seemed to crave confrontation, and I of course, never

let him down. My two acquaintances took their usual seats on the two swings next to the

one at the end. I stepped in front of my usual swing and not particularly being in the

mood for confrontation at the time I began to count to 60, which was the usual ritual on

the playground when you wanted someone off the swing. When I reached the number 13

TENSE DIALOGUE Mason said confidently, "I'm not getting off."

I simply replied, "We'll see about that," and continued to count.

When I had finally reached 60 after what seemed like an eternity of counting I

told him to get of and once again he replied confidently, "no."

As if that word were an alarm both of my acquaintances stood up in unison, so I *READER CAN SEE IT*

motioned for them to sit back down, and they did so a little hesitantly. He continued to

a freshman paper (rough draft) that recently went through an "I like . . ." conversation. The marginalia is mine, a charting of the comments my students made during the whole-class conversation.

Golden Line Exchange

A smaller-scale version of the "I like . . ." assignment can be achieved by simply having students exchange papers and read them for "golden lines." When they find something in the paper that they see as exhibiting craft, they highlight it in yellow. In the margin they write brief notes explaining why they recognize these highlighted lines as having a high degree of craft. I collect the highlighted papers and share golden lines by reading them to the entire class.

Moving Away from "Sucker Punch Grading"

The strategies discussed thus far in this chapter are used while the students are still drafting. It has been my experience that if you want to see a student's writing improve, you have to provide the student with meaningful feedback *before* the paper is finished. What benefit is there for students when we suggest changes after their papers are completed?

Doug Reeves, in *The Learning Leader* (2006), calls end-of-paper grading "sucker punch grading" because it resembles "the blow delivered to the unsuspecting boxer who does not see the devastating punch until it is too late to offer a defense" (p. 115). The metaphor is apt and can be extended when you consider that a boxer returns to the corner for advice between each round. To maximize performance, the boxer is continually coached. To be successful, the boxer makes adjustments *as the fight unfolds.* You would not last a day as a boxing trainer if you told your fighter before the match, "Fight your best. Good luck. I'll see you after the twelfth round."

Unfortunately, that is precisely what happens to young writers. After some prematch instruction, they are thrown into the ring and advised to hold their own. The teacher has in essence told them, "Fight your best fight. I'll see you when the fight is over." This, of course, is not a very productive approach. If we want to improve the performance of our students, we have to offer them suggestions while the fight is still unfolding. As Tomlinson and McTighe (2006) note, "The most successful coaches and sponsors of extracurricular activities such as yearbook, orchestra, theater, and athletics recognize the importance of *ongoing* assessments" (p. 71). With this in mind we need to be in our students' corners *during* their writing bouts. It does adolescent writers little good for the teacher to show up after the final bell has rung.

Later in this chapter I will discuss how I coach my students to improve their craft while their papers are in process. But before we look at how that works in a real-world classroom, let's shift our attention to another key element: the teaching of editing skills.

Ten Tenets of Teaching Editing Skills

To help my students refine their editing skills, I adhere to the Ten Tenets of Teaching Editing Skills.

Tenet #1: Determine Editing Needs and Address Them as They Arise

I do not teach out of a grammar book page-by-page, unit-by-unit. Instead, I take notes as I read my students' papers to determine what grammar issues need addressing. The few whole-class mini-lessons I end up teaching are generated from my reading of their papers. Grammar issues arise organically and do not follow the chapter-by-chapter outline of any grammar book I have ever read.

Tenet #2: Teach Less to the Whole Class; Teach More in Conferences

Though I still teach some whole-class grammar mini-lessons, these are reserved for a few key issues that seem to be problematic for most of my class (e.g., subject-verb agreement, fragments, run-ons). The problem with whole-class demonstrations is that I am wasting the time of the students who have already acquired the skill. I have found it to be a much more productive approach to have two-minute conferences with individuals or small groups of students to help them identify their specific editing shortcomings. Later in this chapter I will outline how I set up conferences in my classroom.

Tenet #3: Instead of Using Grammar Books, Make Them

My students construct their own grammar guides as part of their writer's notebooks. Each grammar guide is divided into two sections: craft and editing. When I conduct an editing mini-lesson, students record the lesson in their notebooks. I explain the rule, show a few examples, and then give them some practice sentences. When I conduct small group conferences, I have each member of the group add the rule specific to addressing their problem into the grammar section of their writer's notebook.

Tenet #4: Keep the Focus Narrow

When teaching mini-lessons to the entire class, I keep the focus on one issue. If I see the class is having trouble with run-on sentences, for example, we will work on that skill repeatedly before we shift our focus to any other problem. They also might be having problems with both subject-verb agreement and lack of sentence variety, but I will ignore those issues until I feel the run-on sentence issue is resolved. (This is difficult because the English teacher in me wants to point out everything that needs improvement in their papers.)

Maintaining a narrow focus makes sense, doesn't it? Imagine learning to play the piano from a teacher who points out twenty-seven things you did wrong after your first lesson. Certainly, that would be counterproductive. The best piano teacher is one who starts by teaching the pupil one skill and does not move to the next skill until her student demonstrates improvement. The teacher is aware of the young musician's other deficiencies, but those are momentarily set aside so that progress can be made.

Once most of my students have demonstrated improvement, it is time to move on to a new whole-class focus.

Tenet #5: Teach the Big Eight

Don't worry about complex rules for struggling writers. Ron Strahl, the director of the South Basin Writing Project, advocates that before we assume anything, we must start by making sure our students can recognize the subject and the verb in any sentence. It may sound funny discussing this in a high school context, but it has been my experience that many incoming ninth-grade students, both native speakers and English language learners, have trouble consistently identifying the subject and the verb. This deficiency must be cleared up before any understanding of grammar will occur. Once students are clear about subjects and verbs, we must teach them to recognize what Strahl calls the "little words"—prepositions, coordinating conjunctions, subordinating conjunctions, and simple transitions.

When students can recognize the subject, the verb, and the "little words," the rest of the year is spent focusing on eight rules. Here are the Big Eight:

1. Identifying the difference between a fragment and a complete sentence
2. Understanding comma splices, semicolons, and colons
3. Understanding subject and verb with no intervening phrases
4. Understanding subject and verb with intervening phrases
5. Using pronoun case correctly, which again ties to subjects (and objects) of sentences
6. Using commas inside the independent clause
7. Understanding irregular verbs (and their three stems for the six tenses)
8. Correctly aligning the pronoun with its antecedent

If we direct our attention to these eight issues, Strahl argues, most of the editing issues will go away. We should be giving extended focus to these issues before we give any thought to teaching students more sophisticated rules (e.g., the correct usage of the infinitive phrase).

Tenet #6: Don't Drown the Paper in Corrections

One way to kill off young writers, especially those who are reluctant or struggling, is to mark a ton of errors on their papers. Developing writers are fragile, and overdoing error correction can break them.

When marking a student's paper, I point out no more than six errors. As I read the paper, I highlight sentences that have problems in them. If a particular sentence has two problems, I highlight it, and at the end of the sentence I write "2" (or "3" if there are three problems, and so on). I do not comment on the problem; I simply highlight it. When I have highlighted six sentences, I stop. I have found that my students, upon getting their papers back, do not have the capacity to focus on twenty-two errors. Marking that many errors is a waste of my time and theirs.

When reading a student's paper, I will often see one major problem resurface throughout the paper. When that occurs, I try to highlight that problem

Independent Correction Sheet

Use this sheet to keep track of areas where you can improve your writing. The various selections enable you to track areas where you can strengthen your writing.

Write the sentence where the problem occurs here:	Write a corrected view of the sentence here:	Identify the particular problem and the problem area here:
It was Mr. Gonzales, the Puente Counseler at Magnolia High School.	It was Mr. Gonzales, the Puente Counseler at Magnolia High School.	grammar, word choice, run-on, (commas), clarity, spelling / punctuation, sentence structure, verb tense, documentation, active voice, dead words ·
I was both nervous as well as excited.	I was both nervous, as well as excited. (see me)	grammar, word choice, run-on, (commas), clarity, spelling / punctuation, sentence structure, verb tense, documentation, active voice, dead words
Then I looked down at the form and saw a question that asked "who told you about the Puente Program?"	Then I looked down at the form and saw a question that asked, "who told you about the Puente Program?"	grammar, word choice, run-on, (commas), clarity, spelling / punctuation, sentence structure, verb tense, documentation, active voice, dead words
I also heard about the Program from Mr. Laningham my 8th grade English teacher at Dale Junior High School.	I also heard about the program from Mr. Laningham, my 8th grade English teacher at Dale Junior High School.	grammar, word choice, run-on, (commas), clarity, spelling / punctuation, sentence structure, verb tense, documentation, active voice, dead words
Mr. Gonzales was asking me questions about how I felt about the Puente Program, what I planned on doing after high school, and what goals I have in mind. (see him)	Mr. Gonzales asked me question about my thoughts toward the Puente Program, what I planned on doing after high school, and what goals I had in mind. (See me)	grammar, word choice, run-on, commas, clarity, spelling / punctuation, sentence structure, (verb tense), documentation, active voice, dead words
		grammar, word choice, run-on, commas, clarity, spelling / punctuation, sentence structure, verb tense, documentation, active voice, dead words

Figure 7.5 *Independent Correction Sheet*

repeatedly. If Greg, for example, has serious fragment problems, I will highlight mostly fragment errors. To do this I may have to ignore, for the time being, the capitalization error he made in the second paragraph or his incorrect use of quotation marks in his conclusion. I will address these eventually (more on that later in this chapter), but for today, I want him to have a laser-like focus on his most serious issue—in this case his fragment problems.

When students receive their drafts with six highlighted sentences, I hand them their essays and Independent Correct Sheets (see Figure 7.5) and ask them to do the following:

1. Read the highlighted sentence a couple of times. If you know what the error is, fix it on the Independent Correction Sheet.
2. If, after reading the highlighted sentence, you are unable to figure out the error, then meet with the other three students at your table and elicit their opinion. Between the four of you, try to figure out the problem.

3. If the four of you are unable to figure out the error, then all four of you will have a conference with the teacher. Bring your notebooks to record the rule and mini-lesson.

Notice that in the example depicted in Figure 7.5, I have focused on Beatriz's most pressing issue, comma usage.

When I first started teaching, I told the students what the errors were. I wrote "frag" or "run-on" in the margins, but far too frequently, the students ignored my comments. Even if the students did read my comments, very rarely did the reading of the comments drive any long-lasting improvement. It did not take me long to realize that a system in which the teacher does all the work while the students learn very little is probably not a very good system. Now, through the process described above, the students do the work to determine their own shortcomings. (See Appendix 10 for a reproducible copy of the Independent Correction Sheet.) I want them to recognize and to take ownership of their grammar issues. Once they have done so, they are less likely to repeat the errors.

When I collect the completed Independent Correction Sheets early in the school year, I read them carefully to make sure the corrections have been remedied properly. I do not give any points or credit for finishing this assignment. Students should not be rewarded for taking ownership of their own progress. That is *expected* behavior. However, if a student fails to make the corrections or makes new errors in doing so, I will *deduct* one letter grade from the final essay score. Students are not rewarded for completing their corrections; they are penalized if they fail to do so. If a student has "corrected" an error incorrectly early in the year, I will return it for a second try. In Figure 7.5, for example, you will notice that I have asked Beatriz to see me in conference to discuss two of her corrections. Though she almost has the skill down, she still needs a bit of fine-tuning. As the year progresses, however, each student is expected to turn in error-free correction sheets. Failure to do so results in a lower grade. This policy generates meaningful grammar discussions amongst my students and encourages them to conference with me when they cannot figure out how to repair their editing shortcomings.

Tenet #7: Whole-Class Peer Editing Is an Ineffective Strategy

Every time I have asked an entire class of students to trade papers with one another to edit each other's papers, something unintended occurs: they often make each other's papers *worse*. Invariably, students will take sentences that are correct and "edit" them so that they are completely wrong. This does not happen once in a while. It happens to someone's paper *every time* I try this strategy. I am embarrassed to admit how long it took me to figure this out, but the whole-class peer editing approach is not a good idea. Instead, I now designate the top three or four student grammarians in each of my classes as

Student-Editors. If a student wants some peer editing, it must come from one of these designated students, or the student must find time to conference with me.

Tenet #8: Make Students Track Their Spelling Demons

We all have spelling demons. I want my students to be aware of theirs. When I come across a spelling error in a paper, I highlight it in a different color than the color used for illuminating editing errors. (I use blue because I tell my students that it makes me blue that in the age of spell checkers they are still turning in papers that contain spelling errors). I have students chart their errors on Spelling Demon Charts (see Appendix 11). As their list of spelling demons grows, they consult the list before turning in future final drafts.

Tenet #9: I Can Effect More Improvement in a Student's Writing via a Two-Minute Discussion Than I Can by Taking Five Minutes to Write Comments on the Paper

In my twenty-one years as an English teacher, this is probably the most valuable lesson I have learned when it comes to the teaching of writing. I need to structure my class so that each of my students gets some conference time with the most experienced writer in that class—me. Granted, this is easier said than done, especially considering the fact that I have 165 students, but in the next section of this chapter you'll see how I build in essential conference time with my students.

Tenet #10: Repeat After Me: "I Am Not Superman. I Am Not Superman. I Am Not . . ."

Confession time: I do not expertly implement all of the previous principles in my classes every day. Some days go better than others. Just typing these ten tenets is stressful! Therefore, in order to maintain a reasonable degree of sanity, I have granted myself permission to occasionally fail. I remind myself that learning how to teach writing is a process itself, and failure provides me with the opportunity to improve my craft. It also helps me to think about the challenges of teaching writing to adolescents in these terms: If you mixed the DNA of Donald Graves, Donald Murray, Nancie Atwell, Barry Lane, and Peter Elbow to clone the perfect English teacher, I would still doubt that teacher's ability to expertly implement every one of these principles every day to 165 divergent students. I take consolation in recognizing that my job is ridiculously *hard*.

Implementing the Ten Tenets into a Real-World Classroom

If these, again, are the ten tenets that guide the teaching of editing skills . . .

Tenet #1: Determine Editing Needs and Address Them as They Arise

Tenet #2: Teach Less to the Whole Class; Teach More in Conferences

Tenet #3: Instead of Using Grammar Books, Make Them

Tenet #4: Keep the Focus Narrow

Tenet #5: Teach the Big Eight

Tenet #6: Don't Drown the Paper in Corrections

Tenet #7: Whole-Class Peer Editing Is an Ineffective Strategy

Tenet #8: Make Students Track Their Spelling Demons

Tenet #9: I Can Effect More Improvement in a Student's Writing via a Two-Minute Discussion Than I Can by Taking Five Minutes to Write Comments on the Paper

Tenet #10: Repeat After Me: "I Am Not Superman. I Am Not Superman. I Am Not . . ."

. . . then two questions immediately come to mind:

1. How are these editing tenets implemented in a real-world classroom?
2. How can craft issues (what good writers do) be taught in concert with editing issues (mistakes writers make)?

I will now describe how I have set up my classroom in a way that answers these two questions. Let me begin by acknowledging that many of the approaches I share in the next section are ideas I have learned directly from Nina Wooldridge, a high school teacher in Long Beach, California and my co-director at the South Basin Writing Project. The following is a typical classroom sequence illustrating the assessment principles discussed in this chapter.

Step 1: Reading First Drafts of Student Papers

The example first-draft assignment I will discuss in detail is a literary analysis of *Romeo and Juliet.* Students work on these drafts for a couple of days before it is time for me to have a look at them. (Often I will take timed writings completed in one class instead of papers they have been drafting for a few days. Either way, their drafts are collected.)

The evening after I collect the drafts, I read each paper quickly, and as I do so, I keep a legal pad at hand so that I can record a generic list of the problems I find. This creates a t-chart master list of the craft and editing issues I find in their papers. Concurrently, when I finish each paper, I write two brief comments inside the essay. After reading Nancy's literary analysis draft, for example, I wrote: "Your transitions are rough" and "Run-on sentences sometimes confuse the reader." I write two comments only—usually one craft comment and one editing comment, and I write them next to where I see the problems in the paper. I complete my commentary by assessing the overall draft and scoring each of the papers by designating it as one of the following levels: exemplary, accomplished, promising, developing, and beginning. Even though they are not finished writing, my students need to know where their drafts stand. Although I do not yet place grades on any of these papers (remember, they are midprocess), my students know that the descriptors align to a traditional grading scale:

A   Exemplary
B   Accomplished
C   Promising
D   Developing
F   Beginning

Step 2: Creating the Rubric with the Students

Before passing back the first drafts (in this case, their *Romeo and Juliet* drafts), I show the students the list of problems I generated from reading their papers. Some of the problems, I point out, can be fixed right now. For example, I might say, "Not everyone italicized the title of the play in their essay," or "I noticed some of you did not include TAG in your introductions (title, author, genre). Please take a moment and fix this right now." Other problems cannot be fixed on the spot; they require a mini-lesson. I ask students which one problem they would like to see addressed that day ("What can I do today to help you make your paper better?"). After some negotiation, they decide on an issue and then take out the grammar books they are creating as part of their writer's notebooks, and the mini-lesson starts. (See Tenet #3 earlier in this chapter.) I have mini-lessons on file for most of the basic requests. If the request requires more preparation from me, I put it on hold by writing it on the board and telling the students that I will require one night to put that lesson together and that we'll get to it tomorrow.

After the mini-lesson, each student is given a blank Essay Scoring Rubric (see Appendix 12). Rather than simply handing them a rubric that I have already written in its entirety and that they will not comprehend, I create most of the rubric with them. The first column, Scoring Criteria, has five tiers below it. The first tier under Scoring Criteria is always reserved for assessing something organizational about the paper. For example, with my ninth graders' *Romeo and Juliet* essays, I notice a wide variance in the strength of their introductions. I place "effective introduction" in the first tier under Scoring Criteria before handing out the otherwise blank rubrics.

Scoring Criteria	Exceeds the Standard	Meets the Standard	Does Not Yet Meet the Standard
Effective Introductions			

In creating the rubric with my students, I have one key goal: that they understand the differences among writing that exceeds the standards, writing that meets the standards, and writing that fails to meet the standards.

To understand the differences between these levels of writing, students need to be shown examples. I must show them models of writing that meet the standards and models that exceed the standards. I do not show them models of writing that have not yet met the standards. My colleague, Nina Wooldridge, is correct when she says, "They have already seen plenty of bad writing. They do not need to see any more." Before coming to class, I have quickly scanned the papers to find models I will share with the class (or if it is an essay I have taught before, I pull models I have kept from previous years). The next table shows two introductions used as models. Model A is from a student sample; I wrote Model B one year because I did not have a student model on hand that exceeded the standards.

Model A	Model B
Romeo and Juliet, written by William Shakespeare, is a classic love story that leads to a tragic ending—the death of two lovers. After they die the Prince arrives at the scene and proclaims that some shall be punished and some shall be pardoned. This essay will not only argue who should be blamed, but will also argue who should be pardoned for the death of these two lovers.	As this is being written a jury is deciding how hard Zacarias Moussaoui should be punished for his role in the tragedy of 9/11. The jury is faced with a central question: what punishment fairly meets the crime? This debate is not a new one—people have been arguing about appropriate punishment in criminal cases for hundreds of years. In William Shakespeare's classic tragedy, *Romeo and Juliet*, for example, the Prince must decide who should be punished and who should be pardoned in the wake of the deaths of the two star-crossed lovers. Though still being debated, a closer look at the tragedy leads the reader to clearly see who should be pardoned and who should be punished.

I show these examples to the students without telling them which model exceeds the standards and which one meets the standards—I want them to make the distinction. Once they have done so, the negotiation to build the rubric begins. Here is an excerpt from the discussion in my third-period class (I am KG):

KG: Let's look at example one, which is a decent piece of writing. It meets the standards of what a ninth-grade student should be able to do. Look at it again and tell me, what are the elements of this introduction that moves it into the "meets the standard" area? What are the pieces that make it a good introduction?

Adrian: It is good because it has what you want in it.

KG: What I want? Or who wants?

Adrian: The reader wants.

KG: What does the reader want to know?

Adrian: The TAG.

KG: What does TAG stand for?

Numerous students: Title, author, genre.

KG: All right. It has TAG. Let's write this in the rubric under "meets the standard." Adrian says I want that as the teacher, but I would also say that most readers want that. Why does it help the reader to know TAG?

Elizabeth: To know where the information came from. What the essay is gonna be about.

KG: Good. What else is good about example number one? It does have TAG, but can you have an introduction that has the TAG and is still a bad introduction?

Numerous students: Yes

KG: So what else does this intro have besides the TAG that makes it a good intro?

Jonathan: It tells you what it is going to be doing.

KG: And what is it going to be doing?

Diana: It tells you who should be punished and who should be pardoned.

KG: So does the reader know what this essay is going to be about when you finish the first paragraph?

Numerous students: Yes.

KG: And that is because the essay has a strong . . . what?

Angel: Thesis statement.

KG: Okay, it has a thesis, so we know what its focus is going to be. So let's write, "Thesis statement is clear" in the box.

As the discussion unfolds, I write the students' comments on the blank rubric on the overhead projector for the class to see. When the discussion of the "meets the standard" model is completed, the rubric, which grew from the classroom discussion, has begun to take shape:

Scoring Criteria	Exceeds the Standard	Meets the Standard	Does Not Yet Meet the Standard
Effective Introductions		The essay has TAG. The thesis statement is clear.	

With the "meets the standard" box filled, the discussion turns to introductions that exceed the standard:

KG: Let's now look at the second model. Does it have some of the same things that the first model has?

Brenda: Yes.

KG: What does it have that is the same?

Brenda: The TAG and the thesis.

KG: That's right . . . but look at the thesis on the second model. This is what we would call more "implied." What does that mean? The thesis in the first model is very direct. What's the difference between a direct thesis and an implied thesis?

Class: (*silence*)

KG: Look at example one and tell me the sentence that directly tells you what the essay will be about.

Angel: "This essay will not only argue who should be blamed, but will also argue who should be pardoned for the death of these two lovers."

KG: Right. Because that is a direct thesis the reader knows very clearly what this essay will be about. It comes right out and says it. The intro in the second essay is more implied. Do you see the words, "This essay will . . ." anywhere in this intro?

Numerous students: No.

KG: What does it say? Where is the thesis implied? Where is it hinted? What is the writer going to do?

Jordan: He is going to take a closer look at the event.

KG: A closer look at what?

Jordan: The tragedy.

KG: *Why* is he going to take a closer look?

Jordan: To see who should be punished and who should be pardoned.

KG: Good. This is implied, but it still is a thesis statement. In a way, implied thesis statements are harder to write. It shows a higher level of craft. So this model has the same TAG and it has an implied thesis. What makes the intro better than the first one?

Yamaly: It makes a connection to something that really happens.

KG: I love when writers make connections. Good. Besides making a connection, what else about this intro elevates it into "exceeding expectations"?

Angel: It just gets into it better.

KG: How so?

Angel: It starts with an anecdote.

KG: What is an anecdote?

Angel: A little story.

KG: And when you say it "gets into it better," what do you mean?

Angel: It, like, draws the reader in more. It captures your attention. It makes a connection, like Yamaly said.

KG: So even though this essay starts with a 9/11 anecdote, do you know by the end of the intro what it is about?

Numerous students: Yes.

KG: Why does the writer start with this anecdote? What purpose does it serve?

Adrian: To entertain the audience and make them want to come back for more.

Jonathan: To hook the reader.

Ines: To make it more interesting.

KG: One of things we see in really good introductions is that often they don't sound like anyone else's. The first model is a strong introduction, but it is going to sound a lot like other people's introductions. So . . .

what do we want to call that when yours doesn't sound like everyone else's?

Sandra: Weird.

Citlalli: Special.

Brenda: Unique.

KG: Let's reward the writer. We do not want to call the writer "weird."

Sandra: How about "original."

KG: Good. Let's add "original" to the scoring guide, and in parentheses I will write "does not sound like everyone else's."

By now the "exceeds the standard" box has been filled in by the students:

Scoring Criteria	Exceeds the Standard	Meets the Standard	Does Not Yet Meet the Standard
Effective Introductions	The essay has TAG. The thesis statement is clear (direct or implied). The intro is original (it doesn't sound like everyone's).	The essay has TAG. The thesis statement is clear (usually direct).	

From this discussion students have enough context quickly to come up with the scoring criteria for an introduction that does not yet meet the standard, thus completing the top tier of the rubric:

Scoring Criteria	Exceeds the Standard	Meets the Standard	Does Not Yet Meet the Standard
Effective Introductions	The essay has TAG. The thesis statement is clear (direct or implied). The intro is original (it doesn't sound like everyone's).	The essay has TAG. The thesis statement is clear (usually direct).	TAG is incomplete, missing, or confusing. Thesis statement is incomplete, missing, or confusing.

While the first tier of the rubric is reserved for organizational structure (in this case, "effective introductions"), the second tier of the rubric is reserved for issues dealing with the content of the piece. In a literary analysis essay I determined that "level of analysis" should be on the rubric. Again, I show students two student models—one that meets the standard and one that exceeds the standard (I have put the analysis in each example in italics):

Model A	Model B
Meets the Standard	*Exceeds the Standard*
One person who is to blame but is often overlooked is Romeo. Romeo makes a series of bad decisions. He loses his temper and kills Tybalt. He marries Juliet too quickly. He buys drugs from the apothecary. *But of all the decisions Romeo makes, the dumbest is his decision to commit suicide when he thinks Juliet is dead. Killing himself didn't bring his love back. In fact, just the opposite occurs: it causes Juliet to really die. Suicide never solves problems. It usually creates new ones. Romeo's selfish act created pain for both families, because as a result of his bad decision, both the Montagues and the Capulets lost beloved children. Romeo is at the center of the tragedy.*	Friar Lawrence, a man of God, commits the sin of deception, which has an enormous influence on the actions of Romeo and Juliet. Hoping the rivalry of the families will vanish, he accepts to marry them without the consent of their parents. However, this only makes matters worse when Juliet is forced to marry Paris. Friar Lawrence develops a plan that demands that Juliet fake her own death by drinking a sleeping potion. The Friar later admits, "Then gave I her, so tutor'd by my arts, a sleeping potion; which so took effect as I intended, for it wrought on her the form of death." (Act V, Scene III). *His plan, unfortunately, does not work and becomes the root cause of the tragedy. But this could have been prevented, if only Friar Lawrence had given more careful consideration to the outcome. It is ironic that he tells Romeo and Juliet not to rush into marriage, yet the Friar himself rushes into the decision to come up with the fake death plan. He did not follow his own advice. His unwise actions are to be blamed because he did not take the necessary time to think through his decision.*

Both examples have analysis in them. Though Model B is a bit heavy on summary, it reaches a higher level of analysis by recognizing the irony of the Friar's making a rash decision after cautioning the lovers to take things slowly.

Again, through sharing models and facilitating classroom discussion, the class creates rubric criteria for "level of analysis":

Scoring Criteria	Exceeds the Standard	Meets the Standard	Does Not Yet Meet the Standard
Level of Analysis	The paper analyzes in a way that creates new thinking and understanding.	The paper moves past summary and into analysis.	The paper summarizes instead of analyzes.

Our attention turns to the third tier of the rubric, which is always reserved for issues of craft (see list of craft elements earlier in this chapter). I noticed in my reading of the students' first-draft essays that I was getting a lot of simple sentences. I pull some student examples to show them varying degrees of sentence sophistication. In their revisions, I want the students to get more sentence variety by branching their sentences, so after examining some branching models, this, too, is added to the rubric:

Scoring Criteria	Exceeds the Standard	Meets the Standard	Does Not Yet Meet the Standard
Sentence Branching	The essay exhibits sophisticated use of sentence branching.	The essay exhibits competent use of sentence branching.	The paper is written in mostly simple sentences.

Upon the completion of the third tier, my students and I have constructed the following rubric:

Scoring Criteria	Exceeds the Standard	Meets the Standard	Does Not Yet Meet the Standard
Effective Introductions	The essay has TAG. The thesis statement is clear (direct or implied). The intro is original (it doesn't sound like everyone else's).	The essay has TAG. The thesis statement is clear (usually direct).	TAG is incomplete, missing, or confusing. Thesis statement is incomplete, missing, or confusing.
Level of Analysis	The paper analyzes in a way that creates new thinking and understanding.	The paper moves past summary and into analysis.	The paper summarizes instead of analyzes.
Sentence Branching	The essay exhibits sophisticated use of sentence branching.	The essay exhibits competent use of sentence branching.	The paper is written in mostly simple sentences.

Step 3: Personalizing the Rubric

Notice that the bottom two tiers of the rubric are left blank, and recall that when I read the students' papers for the first time I wrote two comments on each student's paper. These two comments, tailored for each student, now become what will be assessed in the bottom tiers. (Earlier in this chapter, I used the following two examples from Nancy's paper: "Your transitions are rough" and "Run-on sentences sometimes confuse the reader.") This means that each writer will have a rubric that will contain common elements (the first three tiers) as well as elements that are *specific to each writer's needs*. I ask the students to look in their papers and find the two comments I have written in the margins of their papers. Each student writes the two comments on his or her rubric. After Nancy read the two comments in her draft, she added them to the two bottom tiers of her rubric:

Scoring Criteria	Exceeds the Standard	Meets the Standard	Does Not Yet Meet the Standard
Effective Introductions	The essay has TAG. The thesis statement is clear (direct or implied). The intro is original (it doesn't sound like everyone else's).	The essay has TAG. The thesis statement is clear (usually direct).	TAG is incomplete, missing, or confusing. Thesis statement is incomplete, missing, or confusing.
Level of Analysis	The paper analyzes in a way that creates new thinking and understanding.	The paper moves past summary and into analysis.	The paper summarizes instead of analyzes.
Sentence Branching	The essay exhibits sophisticated use of sentence branching.	The essay exhibits competent use of sentence branching.	The paper is written in mostly simple sentences.
Transitions (Added by Nancy after reading the comment in her paper)			
Run-on Sentences (Added by Nancy after reading the comment in her paper)			

All the students in this class have the same top three tiers on their rubrics: the top tier is always reserved for an organizational issue (in our example, introductions); the second tier highlights content (in our example, level of analysis); and the third tier features a craft issue (in our example, sentence branching). The last two tiers are tailored to each student (in Nancy's case, problems with transitions and with run-on sentences). I always make sure that at least one of the two bottom tiers is reserved for an editing issue. These bottom two tiers, added to the rubric by the students after reading my comments, do not yet have descriptors in the horizontal columns (the columns for "exceeds the standard," "meets the standard," "does not meet the standard").

Step 4: Revision in the Classroom

After students get their first drafts back, I begin meeting with them in small groups. For example, Nancy is not the only student having trouble with transitions. While reading the drafts I noticed that five or six other students were having the same problem. I make an announcement to the class: "If I have indicated that you have problems with transitions, please meet me at the conference table. Bring your essays, your rubrics, and your writer's notebooks."

When that group convenes, I conduct a short mini-lesson on writing effective transitions to that group of students. They take notes in their writer's notebooks, copying models and/or writing the rules. During this conference, I also negotiate with the students what the descriptors will be in the remaining blank boxes on their rubrics and have them write them in. More important, the students then go back to their seats with their rubrics and begin revising their transitions *in their own papers*. I have found that simply handing them worksheets does not work. Though they can learn to do the skill required in the worksheets, the learning seldom transfers to their own writing. The acquisition of the skill is more likely to occur when the students work on improving that skill in their own essays.

When the first group leaves, I make a new announcement: "If I have indicated in your paper that you are having comma problems, bring your rubric and essays to the conference table." The process, with a new group of students and with a new focus, is repeated.

When conducting editing conferences with students, I constantly focus on helping them to acquire the "staples" (see the Big Eight on page 150). When I read the *Romeo and Juliet* essays, for example, I made note of the following recurring problems:

1. Wrong verb tenses
2. Run-on sentences
3. Comma splices
4. Fragments
5. Problems citing passages from the play
6. Pronoun vagueness/ over-using "you"

Because so many of my students were having trouble with keeping their analysis in the present tense, I did a whole-class mini-lesson on that topic. For the remaining five problem areas, I met in five conference groups over a two-day period while students were revising their essays. When I finished with the small groups, individual writers had conferences with me on an as-needed basis. When conferencing with individual writers, I am mindful of three rules:

Rules for Writing Conferences

1. The goal is to complete each conference in less than three minutes. Sometimes I use an egg timer to keep me on track.
2. Students must come to the conference with a purpose. They cannot simply hand me their papers and say, "I need help," or "Will you check my paper?" They must have a focus in mind when they approach. For example, a student might say, "I am not sure about my verb tenses in this paragraph," or "Is my thesis statement clear?"
3. If I am busy conferencing with another student, students write their names on the board and I call them in order when I am ready. If there is

a list, students are told to return to their seats and to work on other facets of their papers until I can get to them.

Step 5: Determining the Grade

After students have been given time to revise and edit their papers one more time, they staple their scoring guides to the top of their essays and turn them in.

Before grading an essay, I look at the last two tiers of its scoring guide (the part of the scoring guide that is unique to that particular student). Once I know what I need to focus on, I read the paper quickly with the elements of the rubric in mind. I then highlight the student's performance for each scoring criteria on the rubric. For example, after reading Nancy's *Romeo and Juliet* essay, I marked the rubric as shown in Figure 7.6).

Each level of proficiency translates to the following grades:

Exceeds the Standard	Meets the Standard	Does Not Yet Meet the Standard
A	B–C	D–F

In Nancy's case, her essay met the rubric's expectations in regard to her introduction, her level of analysis, her sentence branching, and her ability to eliminate run-on sentences. Her transitions still did not meet the standard.

Overall, Nancy's essay scored in the "C" range. Using the overall descriptor scale mentioned earlier in this chapter (A=Exemplary; B=Accomplished; C=Promising; D=Developing; F=Beginning), I write "Promising" on Nancy's paper. Before returning the paper, I quickly reread it with two different color highlighters at hand. With one color I highlight six editing errors—errors that Nancy will later address on her Independent Correction Sheet (see Tenet #6 on page 150). I make an effort to highlight any editing error that was established as a Scoring Criteria on the student's personalized rubric. As mentioned earlier in the discussion of Tenet #6, I stop highlighting when I have marked six errors. With the second color highlighter (blue) I mark any spelling errors. These errors will be added to Nancy's Spelling Demons page in her writer's notebook. Finally, I write one or two brief comments on Nancy's paper. I try to restrict my comments to those that will help her become a better writer. Often I will simply write a "see me," and I will make a shorthand notation next to it for reference in a future conference. As stated earlier, I am mindful that there is more bang for the buck in a future two-minute conference than there is in me spending five minutes writing comments on the paper.

Once up to speed, the process of marking the final draft paper in this manner generally only takes three to four minutes. This is less time than I used to take to write numerous comments on a student's paper, but I have found that it drives much better revision. In a perfect world I'd comment extensively on this final draft as well, but I have too many students and not enough time. Besides, I have *already* commented on the paper (midprocess).

Figure 7.6 *A highlighted (graded) student-made rubric*

Name Nancy
Date _____
Period 3

Scoring Guide For Romeo and Juliet Essay

Scoring Criteria	Exceeds Expectations for the Standard	Meets the Standard	Does Not Yet Meet the Standard
Effective Introductions	The essay has TAG. The thesis statement is clear (direct or implied). The intro is original (it doesn't sound like everyone else's).	The essay has TAG. The thesis statement is clear (usually direct.).	TAG is incomplete, missing, or confusing. Thesis statement is incomplete, missing, or confusing.
Level of Analysis	The paper analyzes in a way that creates new thinking and understanding.	The paper moves past summary and into analysis.	The paper summarizes ~~listed o~~ instead of analyzes.
Sentence branching	The essay exhibits sophisticated use of sentence branching.	The essay exhibits competent use of sentence branching.	The paper is written in mostly simple sentences.
Transitions	Transitions between the paragraphs are advanced.	The essay has clear transitions between paragraphs.	Transitions are missing or are rough.
Run-on sentences		Has few, if any, run-on sentences.	Has a number of run-on sentences.

Teacher Notes:

Upon grading the papers, I hand them back to the students. They review their papers to see which of their sentences have been highlighted (indicating error) and begin correcting them on their Independent Correction Sheets. Remember, students must correct their errors correctly to maintain the grade given to the essay; failure to do so results in the paper dropping one grade. Upon completing that task, students review any spelling errors (highlighted in blue) and correctly add those to their Spelling Demons charts. The papers are then resubmitted to me so that I can read them quickly to see if they have fixed their errors correctly. In a day or two, I hand them back to students to place in their writing folders.

If a student receives a mark lower than what was expected, he or she can choose to rewrite the paper. Nancy, for example, does not have to be satisfied with her "C." If she so chooses, she can rewrite her paper. In my classroom, no draft is ever "final" until the student deems it so. Though it is a standing policy in my class that any student may rewrite any graded essay, there is a small prerequisite to rewriting any paper: the student must first have a short conference with me. This increases the odds that the revision will move the paper to a better place. Sometimes a student will rewrite his or her essay three or four times to get to the desired grade. I like that—it reminds me of a line from a famous writer: "Writing is never finished. It's just due." I want my students to know that as long as they maintain the will, they can continually rewrite until they are satisfied with their progress.

An approach to assessing my students' writing that includes both written comments and conferencing while they are still in the middle of the writing process produces a number of advantages over the traditional, end-of-paper grading approach:

Assessing Midprocess	Assessing at the End of the Process
Reading the papers midstream affords the teacher the opportunity to tailor instruction while the students are still working on the paper, thus increasing their chances of revising meaningfully.	Reading the papers at the end of the process tailors instruction after the students haven completed the paper, thus decreasing their chances of revising meaningfully. This type of assessment "sucker punches" students.
Identifying the problems earlier helps both teacher and students to create the scoring rubric, thus generating buy-in.	The rubric, often incomprehensible, is handed down "from above," thus reducing buy-in.
The rubric not only addresses whole-class writing problems, but is also tailored to target the needs of individual students.	The rubric only addresses whole-class issues and is not individualized. Because it is "one-size-fits-all," students see it as "just another rubric."

Final Thoughts on Assessing Student Writing

My students read the novel *Animal Farm,* in which the animals take over the farm and write "The Seven Commandments"—commandments the animals hope will improve their lives as they take ownership of the farm. Inspired, I will close this chapter with "The Seven Commandments of Building Successful Young Writers"—commandments I hope will help teachers to enable their students to take ownership of their writing.

The Seven Commandments of Building Successful Young Writers

Commandment #1: Remember that all writers, especially young writers, are fragile. They break easily. Don't pound them by pouncing on every error. Nurture them by keeping the focus narrow and attainable. In regard to editing, focus on teaching the Big Eight editing skills first, and then branch out.

Commandment #2: Start with the overarching goal that every student in the class will improve as a writer. Focus less on grading and more on improvement. Expect more out of remedial students; expect more out of average students; expect more out of honors students. "Everyone improves" becomes the mission of an effective writing classroom.

Commandment #3: Don't focus solely on editing issues; help students develop their craft as well. The best writer in your class is you. Model how you write by frequently writing in front of them. Show students that effective writing extends far past correctness. Show them excellent models of student craft. Show them models from professional writers. You cannot model enough. Show them how you do it.

Commandment #4: Don't wait until the end of the writing process to provide feedback. Assessment in the middle of the writing process drives better revision than assessment at the end of the process. Don't "sucker punch" grade. Coach the students as their papers are developing.

Commandment #5: Conference, conference, conference. Remember that you can achieve more in a two-minute conference than you can by spending five to seven minutes writing comments on a paper. Developing writers need face time with the most experienced writer in the class (again, that's you).

Commandment #6: Students should have voice in developing the rubric. A rubric can drive better writing if students understand its language. This understanding of what is expected from the task should come *before* they have finished the paper. Buy-in will occur when the students take part in creating the rubric and when they see that each rubric is personalized to some degree to their needs. When it comes to rubrics, one size does not fit all.

Commandment #7: If you worry too much about the first six commandments, you'll become nuttier than Barry Bonds at a Slim-Fast Convention. Do your best. Rome was not built in a day. Accept the notion that you will come up short at times. When the task of teaching writing to adolescents seems insurmountable, take a deep breath. Walk your dog. Get lost in a trashy novel. An occasional margarita, on the rocks, is helpful.

A Closing Thought: The Stampede Is Upon Us

There is a literacy stampede bearing down on our students, yet the skill of writing—a cornerstone of literacy—is being badly shortchanged in our schools. To make matters worse, this neglect of writing is coming at a time when the writing demands required in the real world are intensifying. Students are writing less at a time when they desperately need to be writing more. A lot more.

In Chapter 2, I shared the recent recommendations put forth by the National Commission on Writing. I think they are worth repeating in closing:

- Every state should revisit its education standards to make sure they include a comprehensive writing policy.
- More out-of-school time should be used to encourage writing.
- Districts should insist that writing be taught in all subjects and at all grade levels.
- Every district should require each teacher to successfully complete a course in writing theory and practice as a condition for teacher licensing.

- Schools should aim to double the amount of time most students spend writing.

The last bullet is particularly telling: *our students should be writing twice as much as they are currently writing.*

Because of the multitude of demands that bombard both teachers and administrators, many schools have lost sight of the importance of writing. Our priorities are out of whack. It is my contention that a school that teaches its children the curriculum without concurrently teaching them how to write well is a school that has failed. A school that has a league championship basketball team, yet graduates players from that team who cannot coherently write, is a school that has failed. A school that offers many interesting clubs for students to join yet neglects to teach these same students how to write well is a school that has failed. A school that puts more energy into putting on rousing pep assemblies than it does in teaching its student body to write across the curriculum is a school that has failed. A school that spends its faculty meetings debating the school's tardy policy instead of having its teachers meaningfully discuss how best to teach writing is a school that has failed.

Harsh? Perhaps. But with all the interesting activities going on in our schools we have lost sight of the literacy stampede thundering over the ridge. This stampede is now upon our students, and there is no time to waste. With the six pillars outlined in this book in mind, it is time for our students to get writing. It is time to teach them the writing skills that will enable them to run with the bulls.

Appendixes

Appendix 1: Twenty Books Every Teacher of Writing Should Own

Title	Author	One Reason to Own This Book
A Fresh Look at Writing	Donald Graves	For me, it starts with Graves, and this is my favorite
A Writer Teaches Writing	Donald Murray	Excellent resource for developing a student's writing craft
Because Writing Matters	National Writing Project and Carl Nagin	The state of the state of writing
Bird by Bird	Anne Lamott	Contains many passages to read to students who have trouble getting started
Clearing the Way	Tom Romano	You will read student papers differently after reading this book
How Writing Shapes Thinking	Judith Langer and Arthur Applebee	A classic, but more true today than ever
In the Middle	Nancie Atwell	The seminal book on reading and writing workshop
Inside Out	Dan Kirby, Dawn Latta Kirby, and Tom Liner	Packed full of writing ideas
Learning to Confer (video)	Shelley Harwayne	A framework to guide teachers in responding to student writing
Nikki Giovanni in the Classroom	Carol Jago	Uses a great poet to prompt great poetry writing from students
On Writing	Stephen King	It helps students to know the writing trials and tribulations of one of our most prolific writers
Rethinking Rubrics in Writing Assessment	Maja Wilson	After reading this you'll never look at rubrics the same way
The Art of Teaching Writing	Lucy Calkins	A classic that helps teachers respond to young writers
The Revision Toolbox	Georgia Heard	Great ideas to help students revise their drafts
The Writer's Desk	Jill Krementz	Beautiful photographs of where famous writers sit to write
What a Writer Needs	Ralph Fletcher	Contains many practical writing ideas
Why We Must Run with Scissors	Barry Lane and Gretchen Bernabei	Great ideas for teaching persuasive writing
Writing Essentials	Regie Routman	This book models numerous practical, effective writing lessons
Writing on Demand	Anne Ruggles Gere, Leila Christenbury, and Kelly Sassi	Tips for teaching on-demand writing
Writing with Power	Peter Elbow	Demonstrates the importance of writing with a purpose

Appendix 2:   Reading a Movie

Notes on Scene 1	Notes on Scene 2	Notes on Scene 3

Reflections

Appendix 3:   Author's Purpose

What Was the Author's Purpose in This Piece?	How Does the Author Create This Purpose?	Reflections

Appendix 4:   Twenty-five Prompts for Timed Writing Practice

1. The goal of junior and senior high school is a high school diploma. No matter what interests and skills you have, your focus is earning your diploma.

   Why is a high school diploma important? Write an essay in which you explain your point of view. Use specific examples, reasons, and details to develop and support your point of view.

2. "Every man who rises above the common level has received two educations: the first from his teachers; the second, more personal and important, from himself."—Edward Gibbon

   Which education do you believe is most important; the education you have received inside the school system, or the education you have received outside the school system? Why? Write an essay in which you explain your point of view. Use specific examples, reasons, and details to develop and support your point of view.

3. Trustworthiness, respect, responsibility, fairness, caring, and citizenship have been identified as the pillars of character.

   Identify which of these pillars you believe is most important. Write an essay in which you explain your point of view. Use specific examples, reasons, and details to develop and support your point of view.

4. Students in this school district speak more than seventy-six languages! Many students enroll in classes to learn a second language.

   Do you think students should learn a language in addition to the language they already speak? Write an essay in which you explain your view. Use specific examples, reasons, and details to develop and support your point of view.

5. Taking a good look at ourselves is a useful thing to do. In this essay we want you to look at your strengths. Decide on one of your strengths as the topic for this essay.

   Write an essay in which you explain what you think is one of your most significant strengths. Explain why you think that strength is important by showing how that strength helped you in several instances.

6. All humans make choices or decisions daily. Some are important; some are not so important. We choose what clothes to wear. We decide whether or not to do our homework. We choose certain people for friends. Sometimes the decisions we make change our lives.

   Discuss an important decision you have made in your life. Explain the decision and how it affected you. Tell whether you would make the same decision again.

7. In our lifetime many people, places, and things change from what we remember from our youth. Sometimes the changes are subtle, like the repainting of a house down the street, while other times they are more obvious, like the demolition of a remembered landmark.

In an essay describe a person, place, or thing that has changed in some way. Describe what it was like before the change and what it was like after the change. Tell your reader how you feel about the change.

8. We all dream about meeting a famous person, perhaps a movie star, a singer, or an athlete. We wonder, "What would it be like?" "Where would we go?" "What would we talk about?" If you could spend a day with a famous person, whom would you choose and what would you do?

Identify a famous person with whom you would like to spend an entire day. Give details to explain how you would spend the day, where you would go, and what you would say. Make sure the reader knows why you chose this person.

9. All of us have heard about certain individuals who have become heroes when they were least expecting to. This may account for the fact that heroes are not born but rather are made by circumstances.

What is your definition of a hero? Describe the characteristics of a hero. Cite a specific incident or circumstance where you believe someone acted heroically.

10. In twelve years of school most students spend time in more than fifty different classes and courses. With all that experience, students develop certain ideas about what they like and don't like about school and about the courses they take. Students have definite opinions about what schools "should" and "should not" be like. From your experiences, what ideas do you have for changing or improving schools?

Identify one change you would make in order to improve your school. Explain how this change would make your school better or more effective. Give specific reasons to help the reader understand your position.

11. The environment has become one of the major challenges of the past forty years. Air and water pollution, wildlife conservation, and control of waste materials are major concerns. Many individuals and groups have strong feelings about these issues.

Do we have a responsibility to protect and preserve the environment? Why or why not? Give specific reasons to support your position.

12. Many television shows have characters who are teenagers. Although the people who write and direct these shows are adults, they try to portray the teenagers realistically. Sometimes these portrayals do not seem real to teenagers.

Write about a television show in which you think teenagers are portrayed realistically. Tell your reader what traits or actions make these characters seem real.

13. Another high school has just been built two miles from yours. A younger friend has the choice of attending your school or the new one next year. He has asked you to help him make the decision.

Help your friend make the decision. Write a letter to your friend describing some of the advantages and/or disadvantages of choosing your high school. Try to be convincing.

14. In many novels, plays, and short stories, a character is challenged in some important way. As a result of the challenge, he or she changes for the good or for bad. The kind of change reveals an idea the author wants you to understand. For example, when a character becomes happier at the end of a novel than he was at the beginning, the author may be showing you what goes into making someone happy.

    Select one major character from a novel, play, or short story you have read. Write an essay in which you describe how the character changes and tell what the author wants you to understand about the character as a result of the change. The reader of your essay is familiar with the novel, play, or short story you select.

15. President Kennedy challenged Americans by saying, "Ask not what your country can do for you. Ask what you can do for your country." In some ways this philosophy can be applied to your school. Rather than only receiving benefits from your school, what can you do as a teenager to improve your school?

    Describe a condition at your school that needs improving, such as its appearance or the attitude of the students. Explain what you think you could do to help improve it.

16. During the time you have been in school, you have had many teachers. Each of these teachers was unique. Some of your teachers, such as art or shop teachers, had to have special talents besides teaching. Others, such as coaches and drama teachers, worked with students beyond the classroom. These qualities and teaching techniques made each of them different.

    Describe the qualities that make up an excellent teacher. Consider the good teachers that you have had and what made them good teachers. Use a specific anecdote(s) to support your description of an ideal teacher.

17. "It's not whether you win or lose, it's how you play the game."—Vince Lombardi

    Explain what point the author is making in the quotation. Explain why you agree or disagree with the author. Give specific examples, reasons, and details to develop and support your point of view.

18. Your school newspaper is planning to publish a feature section on the best movies of the year, and you have been invited to write about your favorite movie.

    Choose a favorite movie that you have seen. Write an evaluation of this movie. Support your evaluation with convincing details from the film. Don't just tell what happened. Consider such elements as why the main character and/or the setting was appealing, how you reacted to the central problem, and what feeling the film gave you. Convince other students who read your school newspaper that you favorite movie really is as good as you think it is.

19. "Sometimes we, ourselves, are our own worst enemies."

From a novel, story, or play, select a character who seems to have been his or her own worst enemy. Show how the character was able or unable to overcome these problems. Tell why you think the character was able or unable to do so.

20. A large number of students who begin high school do not graduate. Educators are concerned about this trend.

    Explain the cause of the high dropout rate from your point of view. Consider obvious and not-so-obvious causes. Support your explanation with examples from your own experience and/or from what you have read.

21. In an effort to reduce drug use on its campuses, the school district is paying an outside firm for the use of drug-sniffing dogs. These dogs are randomly brought on each campus to sniff student cars, lockers, and backpacks.

    In a multiparagraph essay, explain your position on this issue. Make sure the reader knows whether you support or oppose this policy. Support your thesis with specific examples and/or details.

22. In some high schools, many teachers and parents have encouraged the school to adopt a dress code that sets guidelines for what students can wear to school. Some teachers and parents support a dress code because they think it will produce an environment that is safer and more conducive to learning. Other teachers and parents do not support a dress code because they think it restricts the individual's freedom of expression.

    Should high schools adopt dress codes? Support your answer with specific reasons and examples to support your position.

23. We are all influenced by creative work found in our world.

    Choose a creative work (e.g. film, music, book, art, or poem) that has had a significant influence on you. Describe the work and tell the reader why the work is important to you. Make sure the reader understands how the work has influenced you.

24. The U.S. Postal Service has honored many individuals, from presidents to singers to cartoon characters, by placing their portraits on postage stamps. Whom would you nominate to honor with a postage stamp?

    Write an essay explaining to the reader whom you would choose to be honored on a postage stamp. Explain why that person should be honored, and support your nomination with specific examples and details.

25. Recent studies show that the amount of homework assigned to students is increasing. Students in kindergarten now are being assigned homework, and homeowork demands are intensifying at each subsequent grade level.

    Is this movement toward increasing homework a positive trend? Does more homework create more learning? Plan and write an essay in which you develop your point of view on this issue. Support your position with reasoning and examples taken from your experience and observations.

Appendix 5:   Vocabulary Used in a Writing Classroom

Term	"Un-dictionary" Definition
Analyzing	Interpreting phenomenon that is difficult to explain
Audience	For whom am I writing this piece?
Context	The circumstances or events that exist around the writing
Craft	Those things good writers do
Development	The "stuff" of the paper
Discourse	The "type" of writing and the language used (rhetoric) specific to that task (e.g., persuasion, literary analysis)
Editing	Fixing mistakes writers make
Evaluating	Focusing on the worth of a person, object, idea, or other phenomenon
Expressive	Reflecting on your own life and experiences, often looking backward in order to look forward
Genre	The form of the piece (e.g., poem, essay, letter)
Heuristic	Type of strategy that encourages learners to discover solutions for themselves
Inform	Presenting information in a surprising way
Inquiring	Wrestling with a question or problem
Invention	A synonym for "prewriting"
Proposing solutions	Describing a problem and possible course of action
Purpose	The reason why we write a piece
Recursive	Moving both backward and forward. Nonlinear. The writing process is recursive and differs from writer to writer. In fact, there is no single writing process.
Revision	Literally, "re-seeing" the paper. In revision we take steps to improve our papers. The chief goal of revision: moving your paper to a better place.
STAR	The four steps of revision: substituting, taking stuff out, adding stuff, rearranging
Scope	The level of attempt the writer made in creating the piece
Seeking common ground	Writing to bring people together; respecting the values of all readers
Sequence	The order of information or topics in the writing
Share and respond	The process of reading each other's papers with the intention of helping to improve the drafts. Different heuristics may be used to achieve this (e.g., highlighting golden lines, question flood).
Subject	The main topic of the piece
Taking a stand	Persuading the audience to accept a particular position on a controversial issue
Thesis	The big idea being put forth in the piece; a proposition advanced by the writer
Tone	The writer's attitude toward the topic in the writing
Unity	The cohesiveness of an essay
Voice	Evidence of the author's personality on the written page
Writing process	The steps writers move through: invention/draft/sharing and responding/revising/editing/publishing
Writing small	Narrowing a topic to find power through small detail

Appendix 6: Yes/No (Author's Argument)

Central Question the Author Is Exploring:

	What Is the Author's Argument?	How Does the Author Support the Argument?
Yes		

	What Is the Author's Argument?	How Does the Author Support the Argument?
No		

Author's Thesis:

Appendix 7:   Writing Smaller/Funneling

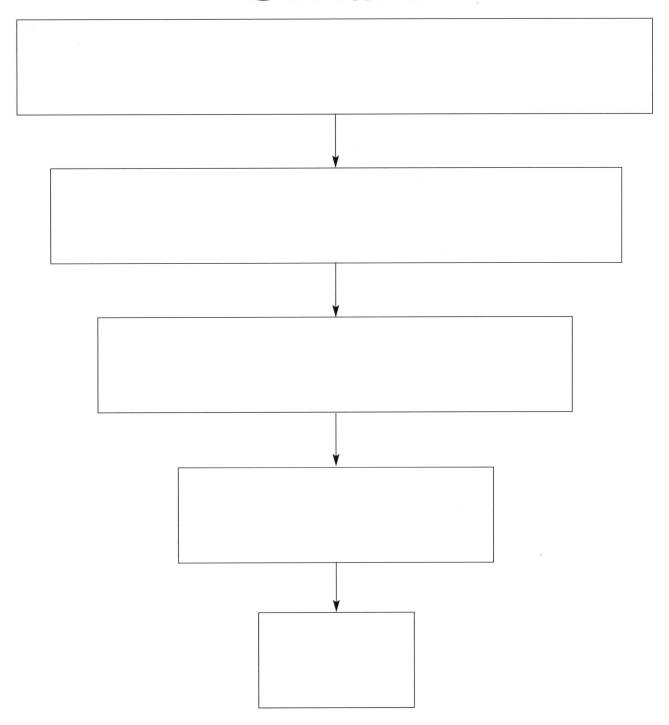

Appendix 8:   Topic Blast

Topic Blast!

Appendix 9:   The Big Eight Purposes for Writing

Purpose	Explanation	Examples
Express and reflect	The writer • expresses or reflects on his or her own life and experiences. • often looks backward in order to look forward.	• Attending my first Lakers game with my dad and what it means to me as I raise my own children • Telling the story of my grandmother's journey to America and what it taught me • Discussing the pain of my parents' divorce • Attending my first concert and reflecting on my musical journey since then
Inquire and explore	The writer • wrestles with a question or problem. • hooks with the problem and lets the reader watch him or her wrestle with it.	• What are the things I need to do if I want to prepare myself to have a chance at making the NBA? • How did my grandmother find the strength to overcome all her obstacles? • What are possible reasons my parents got a divorce? • Why is live music so important to me?
Inform and explain	The writer • states a main point and purpose. • tries to present the information in a surprising way.	• Explain the most important trades the Lakers made to help them win a championship • Discuss my grandmother's philosophy of life • Explore the history of divorce in America • Inform the reader of the history of a rock band
Analyze and interpret	The writer • seeks to analyze and interpret phenomena that are difficult to understand or explain.	• Analyze the reasons why the NBA stars lost in the Olympics • Analyze a choice my grandmother made and reflect whether it was wise or not • List in order the top factors that led to my parents' divorce • Interpret song lyrics from my favorite band
Take a stand	The writer • seeks to persuade audiences to accept a particular position on a controversial issue.	• Instant replay should be allowed in the NBA • My grandmother fits the definition of a hero • Divorce should be illegal • Musical groups should get involved in political campaigns
Evaluate and judge	The writer • focuses on the worth of person, object, idea, or other phenomenon. • usually specifies the criteria for the object to be seen as "good" or "bad."	• How to determine the best player in the NBA • My grandmother received the most effective medical treatment • My parents' divorce was best for all in the long run. Who benefited most? Who suffered most? • The greatest all-time song by this band is?
Propose a solution	The writer • is calling for action. • describes the problem, proposes a solution, and provides justification.	• How the Lakers can improve their defense • How I can make sure my own children understand their great-grandmother's legacy • Suggestions for how the divorce rate can be lowered • How the band could rediscover its artistic integrity
Seek common ground	The writer • aims to calm the intensity. • respects the values of all readers.	• Instead of arguing which one is better, write about the strengths of both college and pro basketball • Discuss why my grandmother's decision to leave her native country was both a good and bad idea • Balance the ill effects divorce has on children with the benefits some children receive via divorce • Compare two great songs from a band and explain why an argument could be made for each one being the best song.

Adapted from Bean, Chappell, and Gillam 2003.

Appendix 10: Independent Correction Sheet

Independent Correction Sheet

Write the Sentence Where the Problem Occurs Here	Write a Corrected Version of the Sentence Here	Identify the Problem(s) Here
		grammar · punctuation · word choice · sentence structure · run-on · verb tense · commas · documentation · clarity · active voice · spelling
		grammar · punctuation · word choice · sentence structure · run-on · verb tense · commas · documentation · clarity · active voice · spelling
		grammar · punctuation · word choice · sentence structure · run-on · verb tense · commas · documentation · clarity · active voice · spelling
		grammar · punctuation · word choice · sentence structure · run-on · verb tense · commas · documentation · clarity · active voice · spelling
		grammar · punctuation · word choice · sentence structure · run-on · verb tense · commas · documentation · clarity · active voice · spelling
		grammar · punctuation · word choice · sentence structure · run-on · verb tense · commas · documentation · clarity · active voice · spelling

Teaching Adolescent Writers

Appendix 11:   Spelling Demons

My Spelling Demons

Appendix 12:   Essay Scoring Rubric

Scoring Guide for _____

Scoring Criteria	Exceeds the Standard	Meets the Standard	Does Not Yet Meet the Standard

Appendix 13:   Great Quotes About Writing

"To improve the teaching of writing, particularly in the context of academic tasks, is also to improve the quality of thinking of school children." Judith A. Langer and Arthur N. Applebee

"Writing today is not a frill for the few, but an essential skill for the many." National Commission on Writing for America's Families, Schools, and Colleges

"Yes, it's hard to write, but it's harder not to." Carl Van Doren

"Writing is the most complex of all human activities." Hilda Taba

"Writing is not simply a way for students to demonstrate what they know. It is to help them understand what they know. At its best, writing is learning." National Commission on Writing for America's Families, Schools, and Colleges

"At the beginning of a project, every writer needs faith." Donald Murray

"The best writing often works by implication." Donald Murray

"The best writing is rewriting." E. B. White

"If you don't have the time to read, you don't have the time or the tools to write." Stephen King

"The scariest moment is always just before you start. After that, things can only get better." Stephen King

"No tears in the writer, no tears in the reader." Robert Frost

"Good writing is supposed to evoke sensation in the reader—not the fact that it is raining, but the feeling of being rained upon." E. L. Doctorow

"I admire anybody who has the guts to write anything at all." E. B. White

"What is written without effort is in generally read without pleasure." Samuel Johnson

"Words are sacred. They deserve respect. If you get the right ones, in the right order, you can nudge the world a little." Tom Stoppard

"A professional writer is an amateur who didn't quit." Richard Bach

"The first draft of anything is sh*t." Ernest Hemingway

Works Cited

Anderman, L. H., and C. Midgley. 1998. *Motivation and Middle School Students, ERIC Digest.* Champaign, IL: ERIC Clearinghouse on Elementary and Early Childhood Education (ERIC No. ED421281).

Atwell, N. 1998. *In the Middle: New Understandings About Writing, Reading, and Learning.* Portsmouth, NH: Heinemann.

Ballenger, B. 2001. *The Curious Researcher: A Guide to Writing Research Papers.* Boston: Allyn and Bacon.

Bamberg. B. 1978. "Composition Instruction Does Make a Difference: A Comparison of the High School Preparation of College Freshmen in Regular and Remedial English Classes." *Research in the Teaching of English* 12: 47–59.

Bash, D. 2006. "Cheney Accidentally Shoots Fellow Hunter." January 12. http://www.cnn.com/2006/POLITICS/02/12/cheney/index.html.

Bean, J. C., V. A. Chappell, and A. M. Gillam. 2003. *Reading Rhetorically.* New York: Longman.

Brown, H. J. 1991. *Life's Little Instruction Book.* Nashville, TN: Rutledge Hill Press.

Buckner, A. 2005. *Notebook Know-How: Strategies for the Writer's Notebook.* Portland, ME: Stenhouse.

California Department of Education. 2002. "California High School Exit Examination (CAHSEE)." Data for essay score breakdown no longer available online. http://www.cde.ca.gov/ta/tg/hs.

———. 2005. "California High School Exit Examination: Demographic Summary, English–Language Arts (March 2005) for (Grade 10)." September 17. http://www.cahsee.cde.ca.gov/ExitProf1.asp?cYear-2004-05&TestType-E&cAdmin-S&tDate-3/15/05&cGrade=10&Pageno-1.

Calkins, L. 1994. *The Art of Teaching Writing.* Portsmouth, NH: Heinemann.

Chen, D. W., A. DePalma, J. Huffman, L. Hollaway, N. Ives, T. Kelley, P. McGeehan, M. O'Donnell, and L. Polgreen. 2003. "Portraits of Grief: A Driver with Size 15 Boots, a Stealth Joker and a Spiritual Diner." *The New York Times.* March 9.

Cisneros, S. 1991. *The House on Mango Street.* New York: Vintage Books.

The College Board. 2006. "University of California: Los Angeles." http://apps. collegeboard.com/search/CollegeDetail.jsp?collegeId=992&profileId=6.

Cowan, G., and E. Cowan. 1980. *Writing.* New York: Wiley.

Crowhurst, M. 1993. *Writing in the Middle Years.* Markham, Ontario: Pippin Publishing.

Denton, P. 2005. *Learning Through Academic Choice.* Turner Falls, MA: Northeast Foundation for Children.

Donaldson, K. 1967. "Variables Distinguishing Between Effective and Ineffective Writers in the Tenth Grade." *Journal of Experimental Education* 4: 37–41.

Ebert, R. "Movie Reviews." http://rogerebert.suntimes.com/apps/pbcs.dll/frontpage.

Elbow, P. 1998. *Writing with Power: Techniques for Mastering the Writing Process.* New York: Oxford University Press.

Encyclopedia Britannica Premium Service. 2006. s.v. "September 11 Attacks." June 27. Subscription encyclopedia article available at www.britannica.com/ebc/ article-9390535?query=attack%20on%20pearl%20harbor&ct=.

Fletcher, R. 1993. *What a Writer Needs.* Portsmouth, NH: Heinemann.

———. 1996. *Writer's Notebook: Unlocking the Writer Within You.* New York: Avon.

Friedman, T. 2006. *The World Is Flat: A Brief History of the Twenty-First Century.* New York: Farrar, Straus and Giroux.

Gallagher, K. 2003. *Reading Reasons: Motivational Mini-Lessons for Middle and High School.* Portland, ME: Stenhouse.

———. 2004. *Deeper Reading: Comprehending Challenging Texts, 4–12.* Portland, ME: Stenhouse.

Gere, A. R., L. Christenbury, and K. Sassi. 2005. *Writing on Demand: Best Practices and Strategies for Success.* Portsmouth, NH: Heinemann.

Gerstenzang, J. 2006. "Bush Calls Spying Inquiry Inevitable." *Los Angeles Times.* January 12.

Graves, D. 1994. *A Fresh Look at Writing.* Portsmouth, NH: Heinemann.

Greene, M. 1995. "Art and Imagination: Overcoming a Desperate Stasis." *Phi Delta Kappan* 76(1): 378–382.

Hall, D. 2005 "Getting Honest About Grad Rates: How States Play the Numbers and Students Lose." Washington, DC: The Education Trust. Available online at http://www2.edtrust.org/NR/rdonlyres/C5A6974D-6C04-4FB1-A9FC-05938CB0744D/0/GettingHonest.pdf.

Hoffman, J. E. 1998. "To Kill a Mockingbird and Lessons from Life." *Classroom Notes Plus.* Urbana, IL: National Council of Teachers of English. (March): 4–5.

Huffington, A. 2006. "From the Dept. of Contrition (Special Victims Unit)." February 17. htpp://www.thehuffingtonpost.com/arianna-huffington/from-the-dept-of-contrit_b_15885.html.

Jago, C. 1999. *Nikki Giovanni in the Classroom.* Urbana, IL: National Council of Teachers of English.

———. 2005. *Papers, Papers, Papers: An English Teacher's Survival Guide.* Portsmouth, NH: Heinemann.

Johnston, P. H. 2004. *Choice Words: How Our Language Affects Children's Learning.* Portland, ME: Stenhouse.

King, S. 2000. *On Writing: A Memoir of the Craft.* New York: Scribner.

Kirby, D., D. L. Kirby, and T. Liner. 1988. *Inside Out: Developmental Strategies for Teaching Writing.* 2nd ed. Portsmouth, NH: Heinemann.

Krashen, S. 1984. *Writing: Research, Theory, and Applications.* New York: Pergamon Institute of English.

Krementz, J. 1996. *The Writer's Desk.* New York: Random House.

Lamott, A. 1995. *Bird by Bird: Some Instructions on Writing and Life.* New York: Anchor Books.

Lane, B., and G. Bernabei. 2001. *Why We Must Run with Scissors: Voice Lessons in Persuasive Writing, 3–12.* Shoreham, VT: Discover Writing.

Langer, J. A. 2002. *Effective Literacy Instruction: Building Successful Reading and Writing Programs.* Urbana, IL: National Council of Teachers of English.

Langer, J. A., and A. N. Applebee. 1978. *How Writing Shapes Thinking: A Study of Teaching and Learning.* Urbana, IL: National Council of Teachers of English.

Lee, H. 2002 [1960]. *To Kill a Mockingbird.* New York: HarperCollins.

Lokke, V., and G. Wykoff. 1948. "'Double Writing' in Freshman Composition—an Experiment." *School and Society* 68: 437–439.

Los Angeles Times. 2006. "8 Hurt After Car Crashes into an El Pollo Loco." *Los Angeles Times.* January 1.

Macrorie, K. 1988. *The I-Search Paper: Revised Edition of Searching Writing.* Portsmouth, NH: Boynton/Cook, Heinemann.

McQueen, R., A. K. Murray, and F. Evans. 1963. "Relationships Between Writing Required in High School and English Proficiency in College." *Journal of Experimental Education* 31: 419–423.

Murray, D. M. 2004. *A Writer Teaches Writing.* 2nd ed. Boston: Thomson-Heinle.

National Association of Manufacturers. 2005. *2005 Skills Gap Report: A Survey of the American Manufacturers Workforce.* Washington, DC: National Association of Manufacturers. Available online at http://www.nam.org/s_nam/sec.asp?CID=202426&DID=235735.

National Center for Education Statistics. 2003. "Percentage of Students, by Writing Achievement Level, Grades 4, 8, and 12: 1998 and 2002." July 10. http://nces.ed.gov/nationsreportcard/writing/results2002/natachieve.asp.

———. 2004. "The NAEP Writing Achievement Levels." April 19. http://nces.ed.gov/nationsreportcard/writing/achieve.asp.

National Commission on Writing for America's Families, Schools, and Colleges. 2003a. "National Commission Calls for a Writing Revolution." April 25. www.writingcommission.org/pr/pr_4_25_2003.html.

———. 2003b. *The Neglected "R": The Need for a Writing Revolution.* New York: The College Board. Available online at http://www.writingcommission.org/prod_downloads/writingcom/neglectedr.pdf.

———. 2004a. *Writing: A Ticket to Work . . . Or a Ticket Out: A Survey of Business Leaders.* New York: The College Board. Available online at http://www.writingcommission.org/prod_downloads/writingcom/writing-ticket-to-work.pdf.

———. 2004b. "Writing Skills Necessary for Employment, Says Big Business." September 14. http://www.writingcommission.org/pr/writing_for_employ.html.

National Writing Project and Carl Nagin. 2003. *Because Writing Matters.* San Francisco: Jossey-Bass.

The New York Times. 2005. "This Call May Be Monitored." *The New York Times.* December 18.

Noden, H. 1999. *Image Grammar: Using Grammatical Structures to Teach Writing.* Portsmouth, NH: Heinemann.

O'Hara, P. 2002. "Charity Means You Don't Pick and Choose." *Newsweek.* December 23: 13.

Piven, J., and D. Borgenicht. 1999. *The Worst-Case Scenario Survival Handbook: Student Edition.* New York: Scholastic.

Puente Project. 2006. "The Puente Project: A Proven Track Record of Academic Success." http://www.puente.net/results_pg.html.

Reeves, D. B. 2006. *The Learning Leader: How to Focus School Improvement for Better Results.* Alexandria, VA: Association for Supervision and Curriculum Development.

Romano, T. 1987. *Clearing the Way: Working with Teenage Writers.* Portsmouth, NH: Heinemann.

Routman, R. 2005. *Writing Essentials: Raising Expectations and Results While Simplifying Teaching.* Portsmouth, NH: Heinemann.

Salzman, M. 2003. *True Notebooks: A Writer's Year at Juvenile Hall.* New York: Alfred A. Knopf.

Sifry, D. 2006. "The State of the Blogosphere, April 2006, Part 1: On Blogosphere Growth." April 17. www.sifry.com/alerts/archives/000432.html.

Smith, D. B. 1991. *Ever Wonder Why?* New York: Ballantine Books.

Stallard, C. 1974. "An Analysis of the Writing Behaviour of Good Student Writers." *Research in the Teaching of English* 8: 206–218.

Stewart, J. *The Daily Show.* 2006. Monologue broadcast in February about Dick Cheney's hunting accident.

Tomlinson, C. A., and J. McTighe. 2006. *Integrating Differentiated Instruction and Understanding by Design: Connecting Content for Kids.* Alexandria, VA: Association for Supervision and Curriculum Development.

U.S. Department of Education, National Center for Education Statistics. 2002. *The Nation's Report Card: Writing Highlights 2002.* Available online at http://nces.ed.gov/pubsearch/pubsinfo.asp?pubid=2003531.

Vygotsky, L. S. 1978. *Mind in Society: The Development of Higher Psychological Processes.* Cambridge, MA: Harvard University Press.

Warschauer, M. 1999. "Millennialism and Media: Language, Literacy, and Technology in the 21st Century." Speech given to the 1999 World Congress of Applied Linguistics (AILA) and published in *AILA Review* 14: 49–59.

Wilson, M. 2006. *Rethinking Rubrics in Writing Assessment.* Portsmouth, NH: Heinemann.

Woodward, J., and A. Phillips. 1967. "Profile of the Poor Writer." *Research in the Teaching of English* 1: 41–53.

Wurman, R. 1989. *Information Anxiety.* New York: Doubleday.

Zeitz, P. S. 2003. "Africans Need More Than Our Sympathy." *Newsweek.* December 1.

Index